THE WORLD OF
ABNORMAL PSYCHOLOGY

A NEW WAY OF TEACHING ABOUT BEHAVIOR

THE WORLD OF

ABNORMAL PSYCHOLOGY

A NEW WAY OF TEACHING ABOUT BEHAVIOR

A 13-PART TELEVISION COURSE

Toby Kleban Levine, *editor*
Patrick J. Gallagher, *publications manager*
Cristina Boccuti, Tracy T. Meyer, Dina R. Wolkoff,
project assistants

Contributors
Henry E. Adams, Ph.D. *(The University of Georgia)*
Maurice J. Elias, Ph.D. *(Rutgers University)*
Edith Gould, C.S.W. *(Postgraduate Center for Mental Health)*
Bonnie Greenberg, Ph.D. *(Clinical psychologist, Bethesda, Maryland)*
Diane Howieson, Ph.D. *(Oregon Health Sciences University)*
Edward S. Katkin, Ph.D. *(University of New York at Stony Brook)*
Judith Rosenberger, C.S.W., Ph.D. *(Hunter College)*
Mary Helen Spear, Ph.D. *(Prince George's Community College)*

From
The Annenberg/CPB Collection

HarperCollins*Publishers*

THE WORLD OF ABNORMAL PSYCHOLOGY
is a production of Alvin H. Perlmutter, Inc. in association with
Toby Levine Communications, Inc.

Cover photo credits:
Jim Anderson, 1981, 1983; David Seymour, Magnum; Leonard
Freed, Magnum, 1970; Susan Meiselas, Magnum; Gilles Peress,
Magnum; Chris Steele Perkins, Magnum

ISBN: 0-673-46548-9

PRINTED IN THE UNITED STATES OF AMERICA

HarperCollins Publishers, Inc.
10 East 53rd Street
New York, New York 10022
212-207-7000

TABLE OF CONTENTS

THE WORLD OF
ABNORMAL PSYCHOLOGY

A NEW WAY OF TEACHING ABOUT BEHAVIOR

PART I: INTRODUCTION

GETTING STARTED

You are about to begin a television course. Whether this is a new type of learning experience or you are a veteran of television courses, this study guide should assist you to be successful in a relatively independent learning environment.

THE WORLD OF ABNORMAL PSYCHOLOGY is the name of the television series that is part of this course. Depending on your college, the course might be called abnormal psychology, abnormal behavior, or psychopathology. Although THE WORLD OF ABNORMAL PSYCHOLOGY is an introductory course, many colleges require an Introduction to Psychology course (or its equivalent) as a prerequisite.

THE WORLD OF ABNORMAL PSYCHOLOGY uses the immediacy and efficiency of television to introduce the study of human behavior.

- It shows behaviors along a continuum from functional to dysfunctional.

- It combines video case studies with commentary from teachers, clinicians, and researchers to highlight, analyze, and interpret what has been seen.

- It will help guide you from observing specific behaviors to understanding concepts.

- It will show you the effects of psychological disorders on families and society.

By the end of the semester you should be able to discuss the difference between psychological well-being and behavioral disorders, and distinguish behaviors along continua from typical to abnormal and functional to dysfunctional. You will learn about the causes of different disorders, meet people with the disorders, and learn what treatments are effective in returning these people to productive lives.

Often you will learn that alternative explanations of causality exist and that clinicians recommend treatment based on the causality model in which they have been trained and in which they believe. This multiplicity of views is typical of mental health professionals.

COURSE OVERVIEW

The course consists of 13 units. Each unit is equivalent to one week of instruction.

■ **1 Looking at Abnormal Behavior** This unit begins with the question: What is abnormal behavior? It then explores the practices and principles of psychological assessment, introducing the variety of professionals who might be involved in the process and the tools they use, and concludes with a discussion of biological, psychological, and sociocultural approaches to understanding human behavior.

■ **2 The Nature of Stress** Stress is present in everyone's life, but the effectiveness with which one copes with stress is based on many factors. This unit considers a range of stress responses, including some that are dysfunctional, and examines treatment approaches that reduce stress. Posttraumatic stress disorder (PTSD) is studied as an extreme form of stress reaction.

■ **3 The Anxiety Disorders** Anxiety is a natural human response, but for over 30 million Americans, it is problematic. This unit describes a range of anxiety responses, discusses causal factors, and shows how anxiety-based disorders are treated. The text considers anxiety, somatoform, and dissociative disorders; the video focuses on two of the most common anxiety disorders: panic with agoraphobia and generalized anxiety disorder.

5

■ **4 Psychological Factors and Physical Illness** How do our thoughts, feelings, and behaviors affect our physical well-being? This unit draws on recent research studies in several disciplines that examine the influence of psychological factors on physical health. It focuses on psychological approaches used in the treatment of three medical problems: headaches, heart disease, and cancer.

■ **5 Personality Disorders** Personality disorders are among the hardest disorders to diagnose, and many are equally difficult to treat. Yet one in every ten people is afflicted. This unit identifies 11 personality disorders and concentrates on four: narcissistic, antisocial, borderline, and obsessive-compulsive.

■ **6 Substance Abuse Disorders** Substance abuse disorders are, perhaps, the country's most pervasive mental health problem. The video portion of this unit focuses on alcohol, cocaine, and nicotine addiction. It considers the effects of substance abuse on both the individual and society and examines causal factors and treatment approaches. The text considers a wider array of addictive behaviors, including overeating and pathological gambling.

■ **7 Sexual Disorders** For most people, sex is a pleasurable experience. Some people, however, find sex to be difficult or even undesirable. And some use sex to harm either others or themselves. This unit discusses a variety of sexual dysfunctions and sexual disorders (focusing on paraphilia, rape, gender dysphoria, and desire and arousal disorders) and addresses potential psychological, sociocultural, and biological causal factors as well as approaches to treatment.

■ **8 Mood Disorders** Moods are universal human experiences. But sometimes moods become inappropriate, long lasting, or interfere with the ability to function. In short, they become mood disorders. This unit introduces mood disorders from mania to depressive stupor. It explores those factors that contribute to their onset, describes how they disrupt people's lives, and examines treatments that seem to work.

■ **9 The Schizophrenias** This unit explores what it feels like to live with schizophrenia, what factors are believed to contribute to its onset, and what is being done to treat it. The unit draws on the results of numerous research studies that have been conducted in the last decade to help explain this most devastating of disorders.

■ **10 Organic Mental Disorders** Organic mental disorders refer to psychological and behavioral problems that follow physical damage to the brain. This unit focuses on organic mental disorders that result from three causes: physical trauma, disease, and exposure to toxic substances. Assessment, treatment, and prognosis are all addressed.

■ **11 Behavior Disorders of Childhood** The classification of childhood disorders as separate from adult disorders is a relatively recent distinction that recognizes the biological and psychosocial factors that affect a child's emotional development. This unit focuses on three types of children's disorders: developmental, primarily autism; disruptive, including attention-deficit hyperactivity disorder and conduct disorder; and emotional, primarily separation anxiety disorder. The text includes the broader topic of mental retardation.

■ **12 Psychotherapies** Clinicians select from a wide range of therapeutic approaches to treat psychological disorders. In the video portion of this unit, clinicians demonstrate various types of psychologically based therapies (psychodynamic, cognitive-behavioral, and experiential) and show their application with both individuals and groups. The text includes a discussion of biologically based therapies.

■ **13 An Ounce of Prevention** Mental disorders can emerge at any point in the life span. Can they be prevented? This unit examines several community-based projects that focus on specific life stages. Each example uses a unique combination of strategies to lessen the effects of known psychological, sociocultural, environmental, and biological risk factors in the hope that the development of psychological disorders can be averted.

■ COURSE TEXT

The course text is *Abnormal Psychology and Modern Life*, Ninth Edition, by Robert C. Carson and James N. Butcher (HarperCollins, 1992).

■ COURSE ASSIGNMENTS

Each unit has three types of assignments:

• a one-hour television program
• one or more textbook chapters
• a study guide chapter

Check with your instructor to be sure these are the assignments you should follow and to identify any other activities that may be assigned.

■ COURSE SCHEDULE

As soon after registration as possible, find out the following:

• what books are required for the course
• if and when an orientation session has been scheduled
• if any additional on-campus meetings have been scheduled
• when examinations are scheduled for the course
• how you can see THE WORLD OF ABNORMAL PSYCHOLOGY

■ VIDEO PROGRAMS

THE WORLD OF ABNORMAL PSYCHOLOGY may be broadcast on one or more local public television stations, on cable, and/or on a closed circuit network run by your college or university. It also may be available on videocassette at the college library, either for viewing there or for borrowing. Your instructor will advise you what options exist. Determine what time you will watch the program and make this an inviolate part of your schedule.

■ THE STUDY GUIDE

Each unit in the study guide has been carefully assembled to help you succeed in the relatively independent learning environment of television courses.

Theme: briefly states what the unit is about and identifies when certain topics are included in either the video or the text but not in both.

Assignments: tells precisely what to read in the text and study guide and which video to view.

Goals and Objectives: identifies what you are expected to learn in each unit.

Overview: an essay that focuses viewing and discusses how to integrate text and video material. Words and phrases in **boldface** are defined in the next section.

Key Terms: identifies and defines important vocabulary in a manner that facilitates learning and review.

Video Notes: lists key concepts covered in the video to facilitate learning and retention.

Video Review Questions: provides a framework for you to review the video material.

Case Study: simulates clinical situations and helps you integrate and apply the material you are studying. Each case study consists of three parts: a vignette that presents an individual's behavior and thinking; a clinical discussion that presents the clinician's thinking; and a series of case questions that encourage you to think about the material you have learned and apply it to new areas.

Self-Test: a series of multiple-choice questions on both video and text topics.

STUDY TIPS

1. Although the print materials may be read in any order, it is recommended that you read the following three sections of the study guide first: **Theme, Goals and Objectives, Overview**. This will give you a good understanding of what the material is about, alert you to portions of the television programs to which you will want to pay particular attention, and advise you what you will need to know by the end of the unit.

2. Whenever possible, next view the television program — at least once. Because many students find it difficult to take notes while watching television, the study guide unit called **Video Notes** is useful both as a viewing guide — you might check off each concept as it is presented in the video — and as a review tool. Also, if you are reviewing the video on cassette, note that in most cases the major headings of the Video Notes correspond to the segment headings in the video itself.

While you are watching the video, pay particular attention to the behavior of the individuals who exhibit the particular disorder. With very few exceptions (and exceptions always are noted in the program), these are real people telling you about how they really feel.

The video review questions in the study guide also will help you recall what is in the video. It is strongly recommended that you write out your answers to these questions, whether or not your faculty member requires you to hand them in.

3. Next read the entire text assignment. Often, the video and text cover different material. Typically, the text covers many more topics than the video; the video, on the other hand, often provides more depth on selected topics and sometimes covers topics not included in the text at all. You are responsible for information in both assignments.

4. This is a good time to read the **Case Study**. Your faculty member may wish you to turn in your answers to case questions.

5. Several study aids are included to help you complete each unit with confidence that you have achieved the appropriate goals and objectives. The **Key Terms** list includes important words used both in the text and in the video. It is designed so that you can cover one side of the page and test yourself to ensure that you know what these terms mean. The **Self-Test** consists of multiple-choice questions. Again, these cover material presented both in the textbook and in the video. Depending on the type of examination your instructor gives, these questions may be similar to those you will find on examinations.

6. As you move from unit to unit, you should begin to get a sense of some unifying themes. Most behavior, for example, falls somewhere along a continuum. On one end is a productive, fully functioning individual. At the other is a person who is considered disordered. Often it is difficult to find the point on the line where someone becomes more one than the other. Also, for many disorders, one may move back and forth along the line throughout life. Second, you will find some common information about each disorder: how prevalent it is in the population, what is thought to cause it, its symptoms, and methods of treatment. Note that several explanations may be given for a single disorder. This is a common part of this discipline. Individual clinicians may subscribe to one or another theoretical model. As you listen to people talk, think about what model they probably subscribe to. Consider how other models might explain the same concept. In many cases, mental health professionals are still trying to determine if a single answer exists.

7. Keep up with course assignments on a weekly basis. Some students have found that entering study activities in a study log helps them to focus on what assignments require extra attention. This also is a good place to note questions for the course instructor and to judge the best order of study and review for you.

8. Keep in touch with your instructor. Know when he or she has call hours and how to reach him or her by mail. Even during periods when no course meetings are scheduled, the instructor would like to hear from you and to know how you are doing or where you need assistance. You do not need to wait until you have a problem, however. Call to discuss the content of the course and to obtain clarification of course content.

9. Take advantage of all course meetings. They will provide opportunities to discuss content with other students and help you understand the perspective of your instructor.

10. If possible, form a study group. Meetings can be conducted via phone or through electronic mail systems. The video review questions and case study questions provide good outlines for student discussions.

A FINAL NOTE

It is not uncommon for students taking their first course in abnormal psychology to feel they are falling prey to the disorders they are studying. Some students may find themselves prone to what is commonly called "medical school student syndrome" in which they seem to experience each of the disorders studied. Others will have genuine problems which can benefit from professional attention. The Appendix to this Study Guide is attached for those individuals. "Guidelines for Seeking Psychological and Emotional Assistance," by Professor Maurice J. Elias of Rutgers University, contains an excellent discussion of reasons to seek psychological assistance, describes how to find help, and suggests what to look for when you interview a mental health professional.

COURSE TEAM

THE WORLD OF ABNORMAL PSYCHOLOGY was produced by Alvin H. Perlmutter, Inc. in association with Toby Levine Communications, Inc. It was developed with funding from the Annenberg/CPB Project. Funding also was provided by HarperCollins Publishers, Inc.

The Annenberg/CPB Project was created in 1981 to enhance the quality and availability of higher education through the use of telecommunications and information technologies. The Project provides funds to develop imaginative, academically rigorous course materials and to explore new applications of the electronic technologies in order to increase opportunities for individuals to acquire college-level education.

Alvin H. Perlmutter, Inc. (AHP) has produced highly acclaimed information programming for over twenty years. Among its productions have been *Moyers: Report From Philadelphia* (90 three-minute visual essays on the day-to-day events, issues, and anecdotes of the Constitutional Convention of 1787), *Joseph Campbell and The Power of Myth with Bill Moyers* (six one-hour conversations between the mythologist Joseph Campbell and Bill Moyers about the sources of spiritual life, examined from a cross- cultural perspective); *Adam Smith's Money World* (the critically acclaimed series of weekly half-hour programs on economic, business, and financial issues); *The Primal Mind* (a documentary of discovery into the differences between American Indian and Western culture); *The Priceless Treasures of Dresden* (an art special produced in cooperation with the National Gallery of Art); and *The Great American Dream Machine* (public television's first magazine series).

Toby Levine Communications, Inc. specializes in curriculum development and in the development of media-related print materials for use in educational settings. It also is involved in research, design, publishing, promotion, marketing, and distribution of media and media-related products for educational use. Among the telecourses it has helped to develop are *From Jumpstreet: A Story of Black Music*; *Congress: We The People*; *The Africans*, and *Eyes on the Prize*.

Executive Producer and Co-Project Director
Alvin H. Perlmutter

Alvin H. Perlmutter has produced many outstanding programs for network, public, and cable television. Before forming his own independent production company, Mr. Perlmutter was Vice President for NBC News where he was responsible for all network documentaries and news magazine programs. These included a nationally acclaimed three-hour special on American foreign policy and a worldwide live special commemorating America's Bicentennial. In addition, Mr. Perlmutter has originated more than 100 documentaries. Mr. Perlmutter conceived, developed, and served as executive producer of *The Great American Dream Machine*, receiving Emmy Awards for the two consecutive seasons the series was broadcast on public television. Prior to his work in public television, Mr. Perlmutter also served as director of public affairs programming and as program manager of WNBC-TV, New York.

Telecourse Director and Co-Project Director
Toby H. Levine

Toby Levine's career in educational broadcasting and publishing spans a period of 20 years. Prior to founding Toby Levine Communications, she spent six years at a major market public television station where she served as director of educational activities, began and managed an educational marketing and distribution service for public television programs, and developed numerous educational projects. She also has worked at Synectics, Inc., the Children's Museum, and Creative Studies, Inc., all in Boston. Ms. Levine has written numerous publications for students, faculty, and administrators at all academic levels and has given lectures and workshops throughout the United States. Ms. Levine has served as telecourse director and print managing editor for two major prime-time telecourses — *The Africans* and *Eyes on the Prize: America's Civil Rights Years* — and has participated in the development of two additional telecourses: *Congress: We The People* and *From Jumpstreet: The World of Black Music*. She also is the author of a handbook for faculty entitled *Teaching Telecourses: Opportunities and Options*, developed for the Annenberg/CPB Project and the PBS Adult Learning Service.

Senior Advisor
Edward S. Katkin, Ph.D.

Edward S. Katkin is professor of psychology and psychiatry at the State University of New York at Stony Brook, where he teaches Foundations of Clinical Psychology. He holds a B.A. from the City College of New York and a Ph.D. in clinical psychology from Duke University. He is a Fellow of the American Psychological Association, a Charter Fellow of the American Psychological Society, and a past president of the Society for Psychophysiological Research. A licensed clinical psychologist, Dr. Katkin's research and clinical interests focus on psychological factors in physical disorders, and he has published extensively in the area of psychophysiology and behavioral medicine.

Senior Producer
Christopher Lukas

Christopher Lukas has been involved in television and film production for 30 years, including ten years at WNET/New York as producer, writer, director, and program director. He also has served as chairman, Department of Communications, Film, and Video at the City College of New York and has written two books: *Directing for Film and Television* and *SILENT GRIEF: Living in the Wake of Suicide*. Mr. Lukas majored in psychology as an undergraduate at Swarthmore College and was enrolled in the graduate program in psychology at the University of California, Berkeley. At Alvin H. Perlmutter, Inc., Mr. Lukas' projects have included *Moyers: Report From Philadelphia* and *Speaking from the Heart* (23 public service spots for the American Heart Association). At public television station KQED/San Francisco, he was head writer and producer for the first 130 half-hour programs in the *Over Easy* series about older people.

Supervising Producer
Lisa Zbar

As a staff producer for Alvin H. Perlmutter, Inc. for ten years, she has created over 200 full-length medical programs for the Hospital Satellite Network, as well as dozens of industrials and "informationals" for major pharmaceutical companies. Her broadcast work includes *The Primal Mind* and *Native Land*, two PBS documentaries that examined the relationship of native cultures to urban ones.

Producers

Megan Cogswell has a bachelor's degree in psychology and a master's degree in journalism. As a producer at WNET, the PBS station in New York City, she worked for the *MacNeil-Lehrer NewsHour* and produced a dozen documentaries in fields ranging from health and science to education, the arts, and the environment. Recently, she was one of the producers of an ABC Network Special for Barbara Walters.

Kevin Dawkins has had major roles in television production since 1977, working for CBS and the Mutual Broadcasting System, as well as Alvin H. Perlmutter, Inc., where he originally led the Medical/Health Unit. For the past five years, he has had his own production company and has produced over 75 programs for broadcast, healthcare, and corporate clients.

Marsha Zeesman has a bachelor's degree in education and a master's degree in liberal studies. She and Lisa Zbar are members of the Medical/Health Unit of Alvin H. Perlmutter, Inc., which has produced hundreds of programs for the Hospital Satellite Network and for individual health and medical corporations. In addition, she has contributed to *Image and Reality in America with Bill Moyers* and *The Truth About Lies*, both produced by AHP, Inc. for PBS.

Researcher
Gail Evra, Ph.D.

Gail Evra earned a Ph.D. in psychology from the City University of New York. After attending a post-doctoral program in behavioral therapy in 1978, she was awarded a New York State license as a psychologist. Over the next ten years, she combined a private practice with teaching positions at Queens College, New York University, and The New York Institute of Technology. In 1990, she was awarded a master's degree from the Columbia University Graduate School of Journalism.

Publications Manager
Patrick J. Gallagher

Prior to joining Toby Levine Communications, Inc., Patrick Gallagher served as managing editor and production editor of numerous magazines at Heldref Publications, and worked in the public relations department of the American Cancer Society. He holds a B.A. in American Studies and has done graduate work in film production and screenwriting.

ADVISORY BOARD

Judith Rosenberger, C.S.W., Ph.D.
Hunter College

Janet Spence, Ph.D.
University of Texas at Austin

Herbert Weingartner, Ph.D.
National Institute on Aging

SENIOR CONTENT DESIGNERS

James N. Butcher, Ph.D.
University of Minnesota
    Looking at Abnormal Behavior
    Psychological Factors and Physical Illness

Robert C. Carson, Ph.D.
Duke University
    Sexual Disorders
    Organic Mental Disorders

Maurice Jesse Elias, Ph.D.
Rutgers University
    An Ounce of Prevention

William George, Ph.D.
State University of New York at Buffalo
    Substance Abuse Disorders

Marvin Goldfried, Ph.D.
State University of New York at Stony Brook
    Psychotherapies

Russell T. Jones, Ph.D.
Virginia Polytechnic Institute and State University
    Behavior Disorders of Childhood

Danielle Knafo, Ph.D.
New School for Social Research
    Personality Disorders
    Mood Disorders

Suzanne Miller, Ph.D.
Program Development Advisor
Temple University
    The Nature of Stress

Dennis Shulman, Ph.D.
Fordham University
    Anxiety Disorders
    The Schizophrenias

PROGRAM CONTENT CONSULTANTS

Arnold R. Bruhn, Ph.D.
Clinical psychologist, Bethesda, Maryland
  Behavior Disorders of Childhood

Robert C. Carson, Ph.D.
Duke University
  Psychological Factors and Physical Illness

Bernard W. Harleston, Ph.D.
The City College of the City University of New York
  Personality Disorders

Muriel D. Lezak, Ph.D.
Oregon Health Sciences University
  Organic Mental Disorders

Joe L. Martinez, Jr., Ph.D.
University of California, Berkeley
  Mood Disorders
  The Schizophrenias
  Substance Abuse Disorders

Suzanne Miller, Ph.D.
Temple University
  The Anxiety Disorders
  Mood Disorders
  Psychological Factors and Physical Illness
  Substance Abuse Disorders

Sharon Nathan, Ph.D.
Cornell University Medical College
  Sexual Disorders

Judith Rosenberger, C.S.W., Ph.D.
Hunter College
  Looking at Abnormal Behavior
  The Anxiety Disorders
  Psychotherapies

Herbert Weingartner, Ph.D.
National Institute on Aging
  The Nature of Stress
  An Ounce of Prevention

PART II: COURSE MATERIALS

Unit 1.
Looking at Abnormal Behavior

Unit 2.
The Nature of Stress

Unit 3.
The Anxiety Disorders

Unit 4.
Psychological Factors and Physical Illness

Unit 5.
Personality Disorders

Unit 6.
Substance Abuse Disorders

Unit 7.
Sexual Disorders

Unit 8.
Mood Disorders

Unit 9.
The Schizophrenias

Unit 10.
Organic Mental Disorders

Unit 11.
Behavior Disorders of Childhood

Unit 12.
Psychotherapies

Unit 13.
An Ounce of Prevention

UNIT 1

LOOKING
AT ABNORMAL
BEHAVIOR

■ UNIT THEME

This unit begins with the question: What is abnormal behavior? It then explores the practices and principles of psychological assessment, introducing the variety of professionals who might be involved in the process and the tools they use, and concludes with a discussion of biological, psychological, and sociocultural approaches to understanding human behavior.

■ UNIT ASSIGNMENTS

Read: "Introduction" and Unit 1. "Looking at Abnormal Behavior" in *The World of Abnormal Psychology Study Guide*, Toby Kleban Levine, editor (HarperCollins, 1992).

View: Program 1. "Looking at Abnormal Behavior" in THE WORLD OF ABNORMAL PSYCHOLOGY.

Read: Chapter 1. "Abnormal Behavior in Our Times," pages 2-16.
Chapter 3. "Biological, Psychosocial and Sociocultural Viewpoints."
Chapter 16. "Clinical Assessment."
Abnormal Psychology and Modern Life, Ninth Edition, by Robert C. Carson and James N. Butcher (HarperCollins, 1992).

■ GOALS AND OBJECTIVES

1. List some popular plays, movies, and books that describe abnormal behavior and discuss what they convey about how a particular society defines abnormal behavior.

2. Give your definition of abnormal behavior and discuss the reasoning behind it.

3. List three aspects of abnormal behavior that must be considered by those who wish to understand it.

4. Summarize the events that led up to the discovery that brain pathology could cause mental disorders. Discuss the degree to which knowledge of brain pathology explains how a disorder occurs and differentiate this from knowledge that is needed to state why a disorder occurs.

5. Summarize some of the findings of behavior geneticists that have increased our understanding of the causes of mental disorders.

6. Explain the difference between clinical assessment and diagnosis.

7. Describe and differentiate among several medical and neuropsychological procedures that can be used for the physical evaluation of abnormal behavior.

8. Identify a variety of professionals who might be involved in clinical assessment and differentiate among them with regard to training and responsibilities.

9. Discuss the major concepts that underlie the following perspectives and identify leading proponents of each point of view: psychodynamic, cognitive-behavioral, behavioral, and humanistic.

10. Define each of the following and explain its importance for abnormal psychology: classical conditioning, operant conditioning, reinforcement, generalization, discrimination, modeling, shaping, and learned drives.

11. Explain the kind of data gathered by psychological tests and tell how these are used in assessment.

12. Discuss the functions of a staff conference in integrating the assessment data and making decisions about an individual's treatment.

18

UNIT OVERVIEW

by Edward S. Katkin, Ph.D.
State University of New York
at Stony Brook

The primary purpose of this course will be to observe and examine a variety of human behaviors classified as abnormal. The textbook focuses on the causes of abnormality, the prevalence of different forms of abnormal behavior, various theories that have been put forth to explain abnormal behavior, and popular forms of treatment. The video portion of the course focuses on the lives of people who suffer from the various disorders and on their families. The videos also introduce scientists and clinicians who are trying to solve the complex mysteries that lie behind abnormal behavior.

The first issue that must be addressed is the definition of abnormal behavior. Just what is normal and what is abnormal? Clearly, a statistical definition will not do. That is, we do not want to call someone abnormal merely for statistically rare behavior that is not demonstrated by others. Such a definition would be too broad to be meaningful, for it would include star athletes, brilliant mathematicians, and those few people in our society who demonstrate unusual capabilities or talents that are shared by few. Certainly such people are abnormal in a sense, but they are not the ones on whom we focus in THE WORLD OF ABNORMAL PSYCHOLOGY. For the purposes of this course, we will define abnormal behavior as behavior that disrupts one's normal functioning, that interferes with work, with family relations, with one's regular routine in society. Such abnormal behavior may take many forms, from severe mental illness to antisocial behavior to minor difficulties in adjusting to life stress.

■ ASSESSMENT

The first task that confronts the practitioner is to assess the nature of an individual's problem. **Assessment** is important for a number of reasons. Perhaps the most important is that it is essential to know the precise nature of the problem before an effective treatment plan can be implemented. Assessment also helps to create firm criteria that apply to specific disorders so that psychologists can conduct research on abnormal behavior.

Clinical assessment is a multidisciplinary task. A typical assessment of abnormal behavior in a hospital or clinic will always include a clinical interview, in which the practitioner tries to gather information about symptoms, background, and problems so that the patient's behavior can be understood in a framework. Such clinical interviews may be conducted by any member of the interdisciplinary team, which usually consists of a psychiatrist, clinical psychologist, social worker, and psychiatric nurse. The interview may be supplemented by formal psychological testing by a clinical psychologist. In some cases a physical or neurological examination will be conducted by a physician in order to be sure that the abnormal behavior is not secondary to some physical problem or biological malfunction of the nervous system.

■ PRACTITIONERS

The members of the multidisciplinary team approach the problems of abnormal behavior from different perspectives shaped by their training and their background. The psychiatrist is a medical specialist who is licensed to practice medicine and has additional training in abnormal behavior. Thus the psychiatrist may conceptualize abnormal behavior as a disease. The psychiatrist's main responsibility is to provide treatment, by prescribing drugs and/or by providing psychological therapy. The clinical psychologist is not trained in medicine but rather in the science of human behavior. This professional has a Ph.D. degree, which is primarily a scientific research degree. The clinical psychologist is more likely, therefore, to view abnormal behavior as a pattern that can be understood in terms of scientific principles of behavior; the psychologist may not see the problem as a disease. Many clinical psychologists also provide psychological therapy privately as well as in hospitals and clinics, but they may not prescribe medicine. Except for prescribing medicine, psychiatrists and psychologists often function almost identically in clinical settings. And, although psychiatrists are not trained to be researchers, many seek additional training and conduct basic and applied research. Social workers generally focus on the social background and history of the patient and often bring important information to the understanding of abnormal behavior. Social workers are trained extensively in interviewing skills, and they often conduct initial clinical interviews with patients. Some social workers also study therapy techniques and practice therapy in the same manner as psychologists and psychiatrists. Finally, psychiatric nurses supplement general nursing skills with additional specialized training in working with disturbed patients so they can provide special care to patients with psychological problems.

■ PSYCHOLOGICAL TESTING

Often the clinician follows the interview process with the administration of standardized psychological tests to the patient. The virtue of standardized tests is that the same test has been given to thousands of people, both those known to have psychological disorders and others; thus the tester has a normative frame of reference against which to compare the individual patient's results. Psychological testing is a direct outgrowth of the scientific field of psychometrics, a discipline that attempts to develop reliable and valid quantitative measures of human performance.

Three types of psychological tests are used: **objective**, **neuropsychological**, and **projective**. Objective tests ask specific questions for which the individual provides specific answers. The answers are then compared to the typical responses of normal as well as abnormal groups. The objective tests may measure intellectual ability, personality characteristics, or the presence of neurological malfunction. Neuropsychological tests are a specific form of objective test that evaluate the level of functioning of the brain. Neuropsychological testing is often of great value in assessing whether — and the degree to which — dysfunctional behavior is associated with brain damage or disease. Projective testing is based upon the theory that a person asked to describe a vague or nondescript object will project onto the object personal perceptions and feelings, often reflecting one's **unconscious.** Typical projective tests consist of "meaningless" inkblots that people look at and make up stories about. The projective tests often are interpreted in the same manner as objective tests — that is, a specific individual's projections are compared to those of other people, and assessment is based on the extent to which this person's responses are consistent with the responses of known patient groups.

■ THEORETICAL MODELS

A great many theories seek to explain the causes of abnormal behavior, the factors that maintain it, and the best methods to treat it. These theories can be grouped into three broad categories: **biological**, **psychodynamic**, and **behavioral**. The biological model suggests that abnormal behavior is a result of disruptions in the nervous system, whether of genetic origin or as a result of disease or injury. The current focus of biological research is on the chemicals that carry information among nerves in the brain; these chemicals are called **neurotransmitters**. Biological theorists are interested in the possibility that abnormal behavior reflects abnormal functioning of the neurotransmitters.

Psychodynamic theories, most of which are derived to some extent from the seminal work of Sigmund Freud, assert that early childhood experiences are retained in an unconscious part of the mind; although the memory of these experiences is outside of awareness, it influences our behavior. Abnormal behavior, according to psychodynamic theory, is the result of conflicts between the conscious and unconscious portions of the mind. Treatment requires bringing the unconscious material into consciousness.

Behavioral theorists are not concerned with the existence of the unconscious. Rather, they are interested in analyzing present-life factors that may contribute to abnormal behavior. The behavioral theorist assumes that no matter how distressing a patient's behavior may be, environmental factors reinforce and maintain it.

In fact, although psychologists often argue about the underlying theory of abnormal behavior, most practitioners are pragmatic. They do not adhere too closely to any one theory, but tend to use aspects of all of them in an attempt to understand the behavior of their patients. The model that attempts to consolidate these theories has come to be known as the **biopsychosocial** model. This course takes a biopsychosocial approach to viewing abnormal behavior.

■ KEY TERMS

The following terms are used in the text and/or the television programs.

Assessment	The process by which a clinician attempts to understand the nature and extent of the problem of a person seeking psychological help.
Attribution theory	An interpersonal relations theory that explains how an individual assigns internal or external causes to events as a means of establishing expectations in relationships with others.
Behavior genetics	A theory that links such characteristics as behavior, temperament, personality, and intelligence to heredity.
Behavioristic perspective	An approach to understanding human behavior organized around the role of learning. Behaviorists define learning as the modification of behavior as a consequence of experience. The basic elements of behaviorism are classical and operant conditioning, reinforcement, generalization and discrimination, and extinction.
Biological perspective	A viewpoint that focuses on biochemical processes in the brain and elsewhere that become imbalanced and disrupt normal behavior. Abnormal biochemistry is seen as due to such factors as genetics.
Biopsychosocial perspective	A viewpoint that understands behavior as the result of an interaction among biological, psychological, and environmental factors.
Classical conditioning	The process through which one is conditioned to respond in a specific way to a specific stimulus.
Cognitive-behavioral approach	A theoretical model that focuses on underlying cognitions as they apply to and influence thinking and behavior; cognitive-behavioral treatments attempt to alter maladaptive cognitions.
Computerized Axial Tomography (CAT scan)	A scanning technique used to obtain images of parts of the brain.
Conditioning	A simple learning process in which one learns to respond in a specific way to a certain stimulus.

Discrimination	A behavioral process in which an individual learns to distinguish between similar stimuli and to respond to them differently.
Dynamic formulation	A clinical picture of a person based on personality traits, behavior patterns, and environmental demands, among other factors; includes hypotheses about the forces behind a person's maladaptive behavior.
Ego	The part of the Freudian personality model that mediates between the instinctual demands of the id and the rules and prohibitions of the external world (the superego).
Ego-defense mechanisms	The irrational protective measures taken by the ego to cope with anxiety by pushing painful ideas out of consciousness.
Electroencephalogram (EEG)	A graphic record of the electrical activity of the brain.
Epidemiology	The study of the incidence and distribution of disorders in a population.
Extinction	A theory that states that when reinforcement is consistently withheld over time, a previously conditioned response is extinguished.
Generalization	A behavioral process in which a response that is conditioned to certain stimuli may be evoked by other, similar stimuli.
Humanistic perspective	An approach that views basic human nature as good and focuses on freeing people from disabling assumptions and attitudes so that they can develop their potential; emphasizes growth and self-actualization rather than the alleviation of disorder.
Id	A part of Freud's theory of personality, the id is the source of instinctual drives of two opposing types: (1) life instincts or constructive drives that are primarily of a sexual, or pleasurable, nature and which constitute the libido, the basic energy of life; and (2) death instincts, or drives that are destructive and aggressive.
Intelligence test	A psychological assessment used to measure an individual's intellectual ability and functioning.
Interpersonal perspective	An approach that analyzes the individual's past and present relationships in order to understand abnormal behavior.
Intrapsychic conflicts	A part of the Freudian model, in which the interplay among the id, ego, and superego — each of which strives for different goals — can cause inner conflict and lead to mental disorder.
Introjection	A part of object-relations theory in which the child symbolically internalizes a person with whom a strong attachment exists; later, these symbols can influence both the way the child behaves and experiences events.
Learning	The modification of behavior as a consequence of experience.
Medical model	A biological view that focuses on mental disorder as a medical disease which has behavioral rather than physiological symptoms and is either inherited or caused by some brain pathology.

Neurological disease	The disruption of brain functioning by physical or chemical means that can result in abnormal behavior.
Neuropsychological assessment	The clinical assessment of alterations in behavioral or psychological functioning suspected to be a consequence of organic brain pathology.
Neuropsychological test	An assessment designed to measure cognitive and intellectual impairment due to organic abnormalities, such as brain damage.
Neurotransmitter	A chemical substance that transmits nerve impulses from one neuron — the brain's nerve cells — to another.
Nuclear magnetic resonance imaging (MRI)	A highly advanced internal scanning technique that allows visualization of the anatomical features of internal organs.
Objective test	A structured questionnaire, such as a personality assessment, in which a set of response choices is offered. Objective test results are quantifiable and can be compared to the results of other test takers.
Operant conditioning	A goal-oriented learning process in which the response typically precedes the desired stimulus.
Personal constructs	A cognitive-behavioral model describing uniquely individual ways of describing and perceiving other people and events in the world.
Positron emission tomography (PET scan)	A scanning technology that assesses organ functioning by measuring metabolic processes.
Projective test	A personality assessment in which individuals interpret ambiguous materials, theoretically by projecting their own problems and motives into the interpretation.
Psychodynamic perspective	An approach to psychopathology based on the theories of Sigmund Freud that explains behavior by focusing on the inner dynamics of the mind as influenced by childhood experience of biological drives.
Psychosocial assessment	A picture of how an individual interacts with the environment based on examinations of personality, current functioning, stressors, and resources.
Psychosocial perspective	A general descriptive label for the orientations that emphasize and take into account the importance of an individual's early experience, social influences, and psychological processes in examining abnormal behavior.
Reinforcement	The process of strengthening a new response through its repeated association with a particular stimulus.
Sociocultural perspective	An approach to psychopathology based on the premise that development of an individual's personality reflects the larger society as well as family and interpersonal relationships, and that a connection exists between these sociocultural factors and maladaptive behavior.
Self-actualizing	The ability to achieve one's full potential by defining a clear sense of identity and discovering what sort of person one wants to be and why; a primary focus within the humanistic perspective.

Self-concept	In Carl Rogers' formulation, each individual's private world of experience is centered in the self, which the individual strives to maintain, enhance, actualize, and defend; a basic focus of the humanistic perspective.
Significant others	In interpersonal theory, parents and others upon whom a child is dependent for physical and psychological needs.
Social roles	In interpersonal theory, role behavior that is defined and prescribed by society.
Social-exchange view	A view of interpersonal relationships that holds that people form relationships for the purpose of satisfying their own needs.
Superego	In Freudian theory, the part of personality that internalizes the taboos and moral values of society and seeks to inhibit the desires of the id.
Unconscious	In Freudian theory, the portion of the mind that contains experiences of which we are unaware or have repressed; the unconscious includes the id.

VIDEO NOTES

■ **WHAT IS ABNORMAL BEHAVIOR?**

• Abnormality and normality are on opposite ends of a continuum.

• Behavior is considered abnormal when it interferes with daily functioning and the enjoyment of life.

■ **WHERE DO PEOPLE WITH EMOTIONAL PROBLEMS SEEK HELP?**

• The settings at which people seek assistance are varied and include community mental health clinics (the most frequently used); private offices of psychiatrists, psychologists, and social workers; and hospital emergency rooms.

■ **WHAT IS ASSESSMENT?**

(Case Illustrations: Jessica, Chris, "Barbara," Clifford, John)

• Assessment is a series of techniques used to determine the nature of an individual's psychological problems.

• Assessment often involves a series of activities. Procedures may include a clinical interview, the administration of standardized tests, and a medical examination.

• During the clinical interview, practitioners use their expertise, experiences, and insight to gather information that can lead to a judgment about the nature and seriousness of the problem.

Among the questions that the clinician will seek to answer are: Why has the individual presented at this time, i.e., what is the chief complaint or principal problem? In what kind of environment does the person live? What is the person's background? What kinds of problems have occurred in the past?

A mental status examination often begins the process. It allows the clinician to observe the person's behavior and physical appearance and to assess, for example, whether the patient is thinking and speaking coherently and whether the person makes eye contact. At this point the clinician also listens for clues to the nature and severity of the problem and establishes the person's potential for either self-directed or externally directed violence.

• Standardized psychological tests compare a particular patient with what is known about the population as a whole and with patients with clearly defined problems. Typically, they have been administered to thousands of people in different populations. Norms have been developed so that an individual's performance can be compared to that of a group. Dr. Eddie Roca describes such tests as a "psychological x-ray" that provides more objective information than might be available through other assessment procedures.

The Minnesota Multiphasic Personality Inventory, or MMPI-2, is among the most widely used standardized personality tests.

The Wechsler Adult Intelligence Scale measures verbal ability and functioning and puts an individual on a continuum from very superior intelligence to profound retardation.

Projective tests, e.g., the Thematic Apperception Test (TAT), use pictures about which the patient is asked to tell a story. Interpreting the story provides the clinician with information about the patient's fantasy life, imaginative processes, and so forth.

• Neuropsychological tests measure the functioning of the brain and the nervous system.

The Bender Gestalt, for example, screens for visual motor organization. Poor results on such a test might indicate frontal lobe brain damage.

The Trail-Making Test measures visual scanning and visual motor speed to assess possible brain damage.

The Lafayette Pegboard Test measures fine motor coordination in the upper extremities, i.e., eye-hand coordination, which helps determine if a weakness or disability exists on one side of the brain or the other.

• Physical examinations rule out medical problems that might be causing the abnormal behavior.

■ THE PRACTITIONERS

• Psychiatric nurses are trained in nursing but have further specialization in the area of treating people with psychological problems.

• Psychiatric, or clinical, social workers are trained to treat individuals experiencing emotional problems. They tend to look at how an individual functions in the social world in which they live and to conduct a very thorough assessment of the person's social history.

• Psychologists conduct psychological evaluations, often using standardized tests, and are usually involved in treatment as well.

• Psychiatrists have graduated from medical school and have completed a residency in psychiatry. The psychiatrist assesses the need for medication and is licensed to prescribe medication. Psychiatrists treat emotionally troubled individuals in nonpharmacological ways as well.

■ THEORETICAL MODELS

• Several models exist for understanding behavior. Currently the three most prominent models are biological, psychodynamic, and cognitive-behavioral.

• The biological model begins with the idea that behavior is the product of the nervous system and brain. Abnormal behavior results from disruptions in normal biological functioning that result from genetic influence, injury, or disease.

> The biological model might explain depression, for example, as the result of chemical imbalances in the brain, possibly because of a genetic predisposition.

• The psychodynamic model, originally developed by Sigmund Freud, focuses on childhood experiences. Freud believed that personality development is governed by biological needs and that a person's childhood is marked by conflicts over pleasure-seeking drives and aggression. As the child grows into adulthood, these conflicts remain outside of awareness, in the so-called unconscious. But they continue to affect daily life and may emerge as psychological symptoms. In the psychodynamic view, abnormal patterns of behavior are an expression of the ways people contort themselves to struggle with the anxiety linked to their conflicts and to satisfy other unconscious needs. Psychodynamic therapy seeks to understand the origins of conflicts.

> In this model, depression comes about because direct awareness of grief or anger poses a threat to people's relationships. They become depressed in order to avoid awareness of those feelings.

• The cognitive-behavioral model focuses on current factors (events, thoughts, feelings, attitudes) that are controlling and maintaining behavior. Adherents of this model believe that disordered thinking and behavior result from faulty learning experiences.

> In this model, depression may begin with a negative event (losing one's job, for example), which leads to a person concluding he or she is bad, which, in turn, leads to giving up, which leads to continued unemployment and reinforces hopelessness and passivity.

• In practice, most psychologists, psychiatrists, and social workers are not dogmatically attached to any particular model. A theoretical model used by many, including this series, is called a biopsychosocial model. It posits that people's behavior is explained by the confluence of biological, psychological, and social forces.

■ VIDEO REVIEW QUESTIONS

1. What are the primary purposes of the initial interview? What questions was Dr. Eisdorfer trying to answer about Barbara in his initial clinical interview?

2. Dr. Eisdorfer says that one of the most important things a clinician can do in the interview is keep quiet and listen. What does he expect to happen when he does this?

3. What did you observe about Jessica's thinking and behavior when she arrived at the emergency room claiming that voices were urging her to kill her baby?

4. At Jackson Memorial Hospital, several professionals come together to discuss Chris' problems. What do they hope to accomplish by working together?

5. Differentiate between the roles of a psychiatrist, social worker, clinical psychologist, and psychiatric nurse with reference to individuals you saw in the video.

6. Identify and differentiate between four different assessment techniques with regard to their principal purpose.

7. What do you know about Chris from the various assessment techniques used at Jackson Memorial Hospital?

8. Why might you conduct a neuropsychological assessment of someone who is depressed?

9. Differentiate between the manner in which a psychologist committed to the biological model and one committed to the psychodynamic model would explain depression. Discuss how you think their adherence to one model or another would affect the treatment they are likely to recommend for the individual.

10. What is the biopsychosocial model? If you were using the model to assess Chris' condition, what primary questions would you try to answer?

CASE STUDY

by Judith Rosenberger, C.S.W., Ph.D. Hunter College and Edith Gould, C.S.W. Postgraduate Center for Mental Health

Margaret

Excerpt of intake interview with a 48-year-old, working class, self-referred woman. Speech is slow and labored; posture is limp; clothing is dull and somewhat sloppy but not inappropriate. She appears dejected and passive.

Louise (intake interviewer): What brings you here?

Margaret: I don't know what to say. Things just haven't been going right lately. My husband tells me I'm getting to be impossible to live with. I mope around all the time. Everything seems to get on my nerves. I cry over nothing. It's all just a big mess. I've had times when I felt like this before, but now it seems like it's all the time. My husband thinks there may be something really wrong with me. I keep forgetting things. It makes me feel stupid. I used to be more efficient. But to my way of thinking, it's as if I just don't care. So I asked my friend, Elaine, what she thought. She said maybe I should try talking to someone like she does. She feels it's helped her and I'd have to agree. Her doctor had her give me your number. So I'm here. That's about it.

Louise: How long have you felt this way "all the time"?

Margaret: Well, since last Christmas maybe. Let's see, that's about six months or so. I can't remember feeling like myself since then. At first I thought I might be coming down with something, like one of those viruses. So I went to my doctor and he said everything was okay. He did ask me about my periods, and I said I'd noticed some changes. I was always a little moody around my period, but lately it's been pretty intense. I overreact to everything. But this has been going on over a year already, and the lab tests

he did showed no changes. So he ruled out hormonal changes as the reason for my moodiness since the holidays.

Louise: *Tell me more about last Christmas.*

Margaret: I put everything into making Christmas really special since it was the last time we were all going to be together. My son is in the Army and he's stationed in Europe so he can't get home. This is the first time he's been away for more than a few weeks. I miss him. When he was born I stopped working and I've been home ever since. I'm not complaining. I really enjoyed being home even though I felt all alone sometimes. My own mother was hardly ever home — she had to work because my father died when I was only three — so I've always been used to being lonely. I guess that's why I married late. My daughter is different. She rushed right into marriage. And she's got a new baby already. So she wants to do everything at her house now.

I was really busy all fall. I like to bake and sew and go all out with decorations. Now that the kids are grown I have the time. My husband says I go too far, but I like it. It keeps my mind occupied. Maybe I'm just bored — that's probably all there is to it.

Louise: *Besides possibly being bored, what other changes have you noticed in yourself since Christmas?*

Margaret: Well, I'm not sleeping very well. I've been drinking more than usual, also — maybe three drinks a night, every night. It dulls my mind, and makes it a little easier to sleep.

Louise: *This is the second time you referred to trying to shut down your thoughts. What kinds of things do you imagine you might want to avoid thinking about?*

Margaret: I don't know. What really puzzles me is what I'm not thinking about, like my grandson. I'm not excited about him the way I thought I'd be. I guess I can tell you this — frankly, I don't have any interest in him at all. Or when my daughter calls and goes on about all the new things he's doing, I just feel like saying "Who cares! What makes you think your baby is so special! You're no different from anyone else!"

Louise: *You sound angry. Perhaps you feel your daughter is so wrapped up in her own life now that she hardly notices you.*

Margaret: (beginning to cry) Now I feel really stupid. Why should your saying that make me cry? I really don't want her to know how I feel, so I just keep away from her and the baby. The last thing they need is a grouchy old lady around. Of course she's busy. I was, too. When I first had my son, he was the world to me. I feel so selfish saying these things, but I can't help how I feel, and I just get angrier at myself for being such a mess. And I'm starting to look like a mess, too. I've gained about twenty pounds. My clothes are sloppy. I don't fix myself up. No wonder my sex life is practically nonexistent. I get upset with my husband for being turned off, but then I look at myself and think, who can blame him? If I'm not careful my daughter's going to get disgusted with me, too, and then where will I be? I've promised myself I'll try harder, but every day I just break down and don't care any more.

Louise: It's clear that there have been a lot of changes in your life, and you're having trouble coping with them. Not only are you dealing with your son being away and your daughter being unavailable because of her new baby, but you're also having to deal with some very strong feelings about these events. I also hear that your role has changed and you're at loose ends. It's understandable that you might feel upset and at a loss. These are things we can talk more about. Why these changes in your life may have hit you especially hard is something we can explore. Also, we need to keep an open mind about what other kinds of factors might be affecting you right now. You mentioned changes around your periods and your forgetfulness. Various things could explain your weight gain and sleep problems. Let's set up another appointment. We'll talk about how things are going with your husband and daughter. At the same time, I want you to keep track of any of those changes in habits and moods you've observed.

CLINICAL DISCUSSION

The number of factors that must be considered, weighed, and interpreted in an assessment process is far greater than any simple discussion could illustrate. Biological, psychological, and social factors all must be examined.

Margaret describes her reasons for coming for the interview. This is the client's presenting problem. In the course of describing this problem she mentions a number of factors that may indicate alternative explanations. Louise must rule out some explanations, while deferring diagnosis until additional information can be gathered. As is usual, the elimination of biological components takes priority. In Margaret's case, given her age and the fact that she reports frequent premenstrual moodiness, it is critical to rule out hormonal imbalances that could be related to menopause. The fact that her physician already has checked this possibility allows Louise to look for other causal factors. By the end of the assessment it appears that Louise is still weighing the possibility of biological contributions to Margaret's problem: she alerts Margaret to the changes in her appetite and sleep patterns as significant issues that need further consideration.

Margaret's reported memory losses could have a number of causes. Margaret attributes them to her general loss of interest in her life. Memory lapse also could indicate neurological problems. While no specific indicators of neurological malfunction have emerged so far, Louise may need to refer Margaret for testing at some point. The examiner might screen Margaret for a variety of possible neurological and psychological factors that could be contributing to her current difficulties.

A psychological basis for Margaret's emotional and physical changes could be her conflict over her strong feelings of anger and loss. But such conflict does not always lead to depression. Many of Margaret's symptoms (sleep disturbance, overeating, drinking, irritability, distractibility shown in memory loss) also could be indicative of pervasive anxiety. In Margaret's case anger and loss seem to be linked to the change in her role as a mother as the centerpiece of her emotional life. Margaret's bursting into tears when Louise suggested she was angry at her daughter can be seen as confirmation that Margaret is struggling with both anger and sadness. In addition, Louise defines the anger as connected to the loss of her role as mother by following Margaret's lead in pinpointing the last family Christmas as the start of "things not going right."

One of the things that might lead Louise to consider depression in Margaret's case is her history. Her father died when she was three, and her mother was unavailable. These conditions could have made Margaret especially vulnerable to depression as a result of separation from her children.

Another dimension of Margaret's psychological assessment is Louise's observations of how Margaret presented herself, not just what she said. This comprises the mental status evaluation. Specifically, Margaret was found to be coherent (her thoughts were logical, she used the correct words, etc.), appropriate in her feelings when talking about anger (crying softly when Louise reflected understanding of the things that were troubling Margaret), and relevant in relating why she was there (she answered the questions raised and expressed ideas about why she was there). No odd, intrusive, overpressured, or apparently disconnected communication occurred. And, Margaret did not dress or appear in any bizarre way. Louise probably could rule out that Margaret had a thought disorder. Margaret was not so disordered in her mood that she could not keep herself together emotionally or express her concerns. She also wanted to feel better, indicating hope for a future, and further expressed a positive attitude about receiving help by alluding to her friend who had gotten better through therapy.

With these observations of the patient, Louise could begin thinking about why this apparently intact woman has been experiencing such a deflated mood. One final important issue addressed in the interview is the basis, or bases, of Margaret's apparent depression. Is her depressed mood and functioning related situationally to changes in her role as a mother? Did such changes serve as a trigger to reactivate, instead of initiate, a long-standing depressive pattern linked to early losses? Does Margaret describe her current decline in mood and functioning in terms of situational changes, when they actually could be expressions of biological change?

CASE QUESTIONS

1. What is the purpose of an assessment such as the one Louise conducted with Margaret?

2. What are some biological, social, and psychological factors that Louise thought might be contributing to Margaret's difficulties?

3. What is the role of psychological testing in the assessment process for Margaret?

4. Why would a physical screening be necessary for Margaret? What kinds of problems could medical testing confirm or rule out?

SELF-TEST

1. **Therapists with which of the following orientations will typically focus on a medical assessment of underlying organic malfunctions?**
    a) behavioral
    b) biological
    c) humanistic
    d) psychoanalytic

2. **Therapists with which of the following orientations will typically use projective assessment techniques such as the Rorschach test to uncover intrapsychic conflicts?**
    a) biological
    b) humanistic
    c) interpersonal
    d) psychoanalytic

3. **Therapists with which of the following orientations will typically use observation and self-report techniques to identify learned maladaptive patterns?**
    a) behavioral
    b) biological
    c) humanistic
    d) psychoanalytic

4. **If an EEG reveals general dysrhythmias, a _____ may be used to reveal images of the parts of the brain that might be diseased.**
    a) CAT scan
    b) Halstead-Reitan battery
    c) Luria-Nebraska battery
    d) PET scan

5. **Clinical interviews can be effective for revealing all of the following EXCEPT**
    a) a global picture of the client's life situation.
    b) an overall impression of the client.
    c) brain pathology underlying maladaptive behavior.
    d) specific crises that may require immediate intervention.

6. **Rating scales commonly used by clinicians help the observer to indicate not only the presence or absence of a trait but also its**
    a) appropriateness.
    b) duration.
    c) pathology.
    d) severity.

7. **Which of the following intelligence tests is most often used with children in clinical situations?**
    a) Henman-Nelson Intelligence Test
    b) Iowa Test of Mental Ability
    c) Otis Quick Scoring Intelligence Scale
    d) Stanford-Binet Intelligence Scale

8. **Which of the following is a projective test that uses pictures as its ambiguous stimuli?**
    a) Rorschach Test
    b) The Bender Gestalt
    c) The Draw-a-Person Test
    d) Thematic Apperception Test

9. **Which of the following is the most widely used personality test for clinical assessment and research in psychopathology in the United States?**
    a) California Test of Mental Maturity
    b) Minnesota Multiphasic Personality Inventory (MMPI)
    c) Sixteen Personality Factor Questionnaire
    d) The Bender Gestalt Inventory

10. **Personnel screening is most important when employee mistakes can**
    a) be dangerous to others.
    b) cost the company money.
    c) delay the completion of a project.
    d) displease the company president.

11. In the case study of Esteban, presented in the textbook, his behavior during the initial interview with the psychotherapist was all of the following EXCEPT
  a) excitable.
  b) immature.
  c) impulsive.
  d) psychotic.

12. In a clinical or hospital setting, assessment data are usually evaluated
  a) by a complex computer program.
  b) by an outside consultant on a retainer.
  c) in a staff conference.
  d) in the office of the chief administrator.

13. The idea that abnormal behavior is caused by a diseased brain or central nervous system is termed the _____ viewpoint.
  a) biological
  b) neurotic
  c) psychosocial
  d) sociocultural

14. Suppose surgical techniques reveal that a brain tumor is responsible for certain abnormal behavior in a patient. This discovery addresses the
  a) how but not the why.
  b) what but not the where.
  c) where but not the how.
  d) why but not the how.

15. Which of the following explains the relationship between genetics and abnormal behavior?
  a) Abnormal behavior is inherited from parents.
  b) Children learn mental disorders from their parents.
  c) Genes affect biochemical processes which alter behavior.
  d) Psychological trauma causes changes in the genes.

16. A major reason why research in drug therapy is so promising is that
  a) biochemical changes can be evaluated against behavioral changes.
  b) drugs cannot cause brain damage like ECT.
  c) many mental patients were on drugs before they became ill.
  d) psychoactive drugs have few side effects.

17. Freud called the principles involved in studying and interpreting what his patients said in their free associations
  a) object-relations differentiation.
  b) primary processes.
  c) psychoanalysis.
  d) secondary processes.

18. According to Freud's psychoanalytic perspective, a synonym for one's "life instincts" is
  a) ego.
  b) id.
  c) libido.
  d) superego.

19. According to Freud's psychoanalytic perspective, which of the following mediates between the demands of the id and the realities of the real world?
    a) ego
    b) id
    c) libido
    d) superego

20. According to Freud's psychoanalytic perspective, which of the following is a near-synonym for "conscience?"
    a) ego
    b) id
    c) libido
    d) superego

21. Janie is 14 months old and she tastes everything including dangerous things like pins. She is in Freud's _____ stage of psychosexual development.
    a) anal
    b) latency
    c) oral
    d) phallic

22. Todd is in second grade. He says he loves reading but hates girls. He is in Freud's _____ stage of psychosexual development.
    a) genital
    b) latency
    c) oral
    d) phallic

23. The behavioristic view of abnormal behavior focuses on the role of _____ in human behavior.
    a) insight
    b) learning
    c) morality
    d) thought

24. Jimmie is afraid of his father's library because he was taken there for spankings over and over again. In the classical conditioning paradigm, the library is now a(n)
    a) conditioned stimulus for fear.
    b) conditioned stimulus for spanking.
    c) unconditioned stimulus for fear.
    d) unconditioned stimulus for spanking.

25. For several weeks, Bob's teacher ignored his attempts to answer questions unless he had his hand up. Now he almost never talks without permission. According to the operant conditioning paradigm, talking without permission has been
    a) extinguished.
    b) generalized.
    c) negatively reinforced.
    d) punished.

26. **Donald was once bitten by a big Doberman. Now he is afraid of all dogs, even tiny terriers. This illustrates**
    a) discrimination.
    b) generalization.
    c) negative reinforcement.
    d) positive reinforcement.

27. **Cognitive-behavioral clinicians have shifted their focus from**
    a) covert cognitions to their overt behaviors.
    b) overt behaviors to their underlying cognitions.
    c) reinforcement of overt behaviors to insight.
    d) thinking to overt behaviors.

28. **Which of the following is NOT a major focus of the humanistic perspective on abnormal behavior?**
    a) alleviation of mental disorders
    b) developing the potentialities of individuals
    c) freeing people from disabling assumptions
    d) providing group therapy

29. **In Chris' complex and inconsistent case, seen in the video, a multidisciplinary team met to assess his problem. Chris' team consisted of**
    a) psychiatrists, neurologists, and medical staff.
    b) crisis center staff, psychologists, and medical staff.
    c) psychiatric nurses, a social worker, a psychiatrist, and psychologists.
    d) the admitting physician and a psychiatrist.

30. **Psychiatric social workers**
    a) conduct a thorough social background history.
    b) have training similar to that of a psychiatrist.
    c) often administer standardized psychological tests.
    d) are rarely found on multidisciplinary assessment teams.

31. **Tests that have been administered to thousands of people and have norms that compare an individual's performance against a group are said to be**
    a) projective.
    b) standardized.
    c) categorized.
    d) interpretive.

32. **As seen in the video, Clifford's performance on the Bender Gestalt, the Trail-Making Test, and the Lafayette Pegboard Test enabled Dr. Weinstein to conclude that Clifford**
    a) had no physical or neurological problems.
    b) exhibited antisocial characteristics.
    c) had a superior intelligence that made it difficult for him to function in a society of less gifted individuals.
    d) might have brain damage that contributed to his behavioral problems.

33. In the video, Dr. Eisdorfer stressed that people's behavior and feelings are the result of the coming together of biological forces, internal psychological and behavioral forces, and social and cultural forces. He called this the _____ model.

a) Eisdorfer
b) dynamic
c) biopsychosocial
d) eclectic

[ANSWERS: 1-b, 2-d, 3-a, 4-a, 5-c, 6-d, 7-d, 8-d, 9-b, 10-a, 11-d, 12-c, 13-a, 14-a, 15-c, 16-a, 17-c, 18-c, 19-a, 20-d, 21-c, 22-b, 23-b, 24-a, 25-a, 26-b, 27-b, 28-a, 29-c, 30-a, 31-b, 32-d, 33-c]

SUGGESTED READINGS

Anastasi, A. (1988). *Psychological testing* (6th ed.). New York: Macmillan. One of the standard texts in this area, this book discusses the concepts and practices of standardization sampling and the philosophy and procedures behind the development of most of the accepted psychological tests used today.

Buxton, C. (Ed.). (1985). *Points of view in the modern history of psychology.* New York: Academic Press. This book traces the history of psychology. Of particular interest are the chapters on behaviorism, the psychoanalytic movement, the cognitive school, gestalt psychology, and the role of biology in psychology.

Fine, R. (1990). *The history of psychoanalysis* New York: Continuum. From Freud to today, this brief history of psychoanalysis looks at developmental stages, instinct theory, the unconscious, and defense mechanisms. It also includes discussions of object-relations theory and interpersonal theories within the psychoanalytic tradition.

Freud, S. (1969). *An outline of psychoanalysis* (J. Strachey, Trans.). New York: W. W. Norton. (Original work published 1940). The father of psychoanalysis discusses its thinking and techniques. Not easy reading, but worth the effort.

Gould, S. J. (1981). *The mismeasure of man.* New York: W. W. Norton. This famed historian of science discusses the problems in the philosophy of psychometrics and the implications of implicit racism in the nature-nurture controversy. This series of essays challenges intelligence testing and the common misunderstandings of evolutionary theory in its application to human behavior.

Marx, M. H., & Cronon-Hillex, W. A. (1987). *Systems and theories in psychology* (4th ed.). New York: McGraw-Hill. A popular textbook for history and systems courses, this contains particularly useful chapters on behaviorist, psychoanalytic, gestalt, and cognitive schools.

Meichenbaum, D. H. (1977). *Cognitive behavior modification: An integrative approach.* New York: Plenum. A classic in the field, this is the basic first text in the integration of cognitive and behavioral approaches.

Skinner, B. F. (1953). *Science and human behavior.* New York: Macmillan. The well-known behaviorist presents in easy language how a behaviorist looks at and begins to explain human behavior. This book is still worth reading as an introduction to this way of thinking.

Sundberg, N. D., Taplin, J. R., & Tyler, L. E. (1983). *Introduction to clinical psychology: Perspectives, issues and contributions to human service.* Englewood Cliffs, NJ: Prentice-Hall. This book presents an overview of the profession of clinical psychology as well as the related fields of social work, psychiatric nursing, and psychiatry. Part I is an introduction to the profession and the philosophy of helping. Part II is an overview of interventions based on results. Part III is an overview of interventions based on biological, psychodynamic, and cognitive-behavioral models.

Szasz, T. (1987). *Insanity: The idea and its consequences.* New York: John Wiley & Son. The controversial author centers this book around his view of psychopathology as a social product. This book discusses psychopathology as a metaphor, the problem of responsibility, the concept of illness and insanity, and the function of therapy.

UNIT 2

THE NATURE
OF
STRESS

| ■ UNIT THEME | Stress is present in everyone's life, but the effectiveness with which one copes with stress is based on many factors. This unit considers a range of stress responses, including some that are dysfunctional, and examines treatment approaches that reduce stress. Posttraumatic stress disorder (PTSD) is studied as an extreme form of stress reaction. |

■ UNIT ASSIGNMENTS

Read: Unit 2. "The Nature of Stress" in *The World of Abnormal Psychology Study Guide*, Toby Kleban Levine, editor (HarperCollins, 1992).

View: Program 2. "The Nature of Stress" in THE WORLD OF ABNORMAL PSYCHOLOGY.

Read: Chapter 5. "Stress and Adjustment Disorders" in *Abnormal Psychology and Modern Life*, Ninth Edition, by Robert C. Carson and James N. Butcher (HarperCollins, 1992).

■ GOALS AND OBJECTIVES

1. Differentiate stress from stress reactions and describe chronic and acute causes of stress.

2. Identify biological and psychological stress reactions and differentiate between those that are adaptive and those that are maladaptive.

3. Compare everyday major and minor stressors with traumatic stressors in terms of severity, duration, predictability, controllability, and meaning for the individual.

4. Identify coping strategies and styles that mediate stress.

5. Discuss why two individuals may react differently to the same stressor.

6. Describe biological, psychological, and social treatment possibilities and assess their effectiveness for different kinds of stress reactions.

7. Discuss what is known about posttraumatic stress disorder and the conditions under which it typically occurs.

■ UNIT OVERVIEW

by Edward S. Katkin, Ph.D.
State University of New York
at Stony Brook

This unit focuses on the nature of **stress** and people's adjustments to it. Although we often think of stress negatively, some stressful experiences can be exhilarating. Think of the thrill that a long-distance runner feels at the end of a race, for example. The body is stressed, perhaps to the point of exhaustion, but the runner feels good. Similarly, people often go to amusement parks or horror movies to seek out stressful but thrilling experiences. The increased number of **stressors** in modern society, however, makes some negative feelings of stress a reality for most people.

The critical difference between stress that feels good and stress that is truly distressing, or bad, is largely determined by the degree to which we feel that we have control over events. When we feel as if events are overwhelming and out of our control, we are more likely to feel distress. How someone experiences stress depends upon that individual's perception, interpretation, and sense of control over events. The events in and of themselves are not the stressors, but they may provoke a stress response if the individual does not have adequate coping skills. Thus, what may be stressful for one person may not be for another.

What happens when a person exhibits a stress response? The autonomic nervous system is activated, pumping hormones throughout the bloodstream, raising blood pressure and heart rate, and preparing the person to deal with the situation at hand. In some cases, as when an individual is threatened with physical harm, these reactions may be highly adaptive. In other cases, such as when an individual persistently reexperiences a trauma psychologically, provoking the same biological reactions, the result may be very distressing feelings and, in some cases, the development of such serious diseases as high blood pressure or heart disease.

In general, the stress process involves three stages — an initiating event, a person's appraisal or evaluation of that event, and a response to that event. The response will depend on the person and the stressor and will include both the physiological changes described above and an emotional feeling. Frequently a noticeable change in the person's behavior pattern also will occur.

In the video portion of this unit, you will meet a number of people who are undergoing stress. Some have learned to cope; others have not. Psychology professionals also discuss the nature of stress, people's reactions to it, and methods of treating stress reactions. In particular, you will see individuals who are experiencing heightened stress resulting from events over which they feel they have no control: unemployment or the death of a loved one. The video also presents people who suffer from **posttraumatic stress disorder** (PTSD), a disorder characterized by recurrent psychological and physical stress reactions caused by an extreme traumatic episode. Vietnam veterans and rape victims who suffer from PTSD describe their experiences.

■ HEIGHTENED STRESS

When a person loses a job or, as in the case of Antoinette Warren, whom you will see in the video, goes on strike for an extended period of time, a number of life stresses ensue. Bills cannot be paid, children cannot be taken care of properly, and a variety of uncontrollable feelings develop, including anger, depression, and fear. Sometimes the stressed person will try to reassert control through prayer. If that does not help, the person may feel helpless and trapped.

A common, and usually more extreme, stress-inducing situation is the death of a loved one. The video introduces the survivors of policemen who were killed in the line of duty. They experience sleeplessness, loss of appetite, loss of ability to relate to others, and a morbid feeling that they may never feel right again. When a death is caused by suicide, often the survivor's stress reaction is quite extreme. In addition to the mourning described above, the survivor of a suicide may feel guilty, isolated, and lonely. Often, the stress reaction can be alleviated by the simple act of talking about it and sharing with others, as we see in the survivors' support group visited in the video. Unfortunately, stress sufferers often feel unable to avail themselves of opportunities to speak with others about their experience.

■ POSTTRAUMATIC STRESS DISORDER

Experts agree that posttraumatic stress disorder (PTSD) involves three important elements: an extraordinarily traumatic experience; a persistent psychological reexperiencing of the trauma; and an associated numbing or denial of memories that would normally be expected after a serious trauma. The Vietnam War was an extraordinarily traumatic experience for many soldiers, and it was the development of PTSD in so many Vietnam War veterans that alerted the mental health community to the nature of the disorder and the widespread need for treatment. In the video, some veterans describe how such relatively minor stresses as the sound of a child screaming or an unpleasant odor can trigger the PTSD reaction. This reaction typically is characterized by intense emotion and flashbacks to the original trauma.

Rape victims who have developed PTSD describe psychological experiences that are similar to those of the veterans. Like the veterans, these women need treatment and need to develop coping skills.

■ COPING WITH STRESS

Many psychology professionals believe that the support group is one of the most effective techniques for the alleviation of stress reactions. Many people who have participated in such groups, such as crime victims, report that the ability to talk about their stress, especially with others who have had similar experiences, provides comfort and therapeutic relief. If the support group is not successful, however, individual forms of psychotherapy may be needed. Among the newer forms of therapy for stress victims is **stress inoculation training**, a form of cognitive-behavioral therapy in which the patient is taught to analyze the totality of the stress experience by breaking it down into component pieces that are manageable, and then dealing with the pieces separately. Often this therapy is accompanied by training in specific relaxation exercises that help to reduce body tension and the physiological components of the stress reaction.

■ SUMMARY

In summary, remember that all people are confronted with stressful situations of varying intensity frequently during a lifetime. Most of us deal well with most stress most of the time, but all of us are capable of feeling overwhelmed and unable to control events. Fortunately, even for those of us who succumb to stress, effective treatments exist. Often just the support of friends and loved ones can be extremely helpful in reestablishing a feeling of being in control.

■ KEY TERMS

The following terms are used in the text and/or the television programs.

Adjustment disorder	A maladaptive response to an identifiable psychosocial stressor, or stressors, occurring within three months after the onset of the stressor and lasting no longer than six months. The person is unable to function as usual occupationally or interpersonally, or the reaction exceeds what one might expect. It is expected that the disorder will disappear when the stressor subsides or when the individual learns to adapt.
Coping strategies	The efforts an individual makes to manage stressful demands.
Crisis intervention	A form of psychological assistance to help an individual cope with or adjust to severe or special stress.
Decompensation	The lowering of an individual's adaptive functioning due to sustained or severe stress. Severe decompensation may result in a breakdown.

Defense-oriented response	A response to a stressor that threatens one's feelings of adequacy in which behavior is directed primarily at protecting the self from hurt and disorganization, rather than at resolving the stressor situation. Such reactions protect the self by denying, distorting, or restricting the individual's experience, reducing emotional or self-involvement, and/or counteracting threat or damage.
Disaster syndrome	The reactions commonly experienced by victims of a catastrophe during and after the traumatic experience.
Distress	Negative stress.
Eustress	Stress that results from a positive situation.
General adaption syndrome	A model introduced by Hans Selye to describe the stages of biological decompensation due to excessive stress: (1) the alarm reaction, which activates the autonomic nervous system; (2) resistance, in which the body uses its maximum resources to adapt to the stressor; and (3) exhaustion, in which the body's resources are depleted and the individual loses the a ability to resist so that further exposure to the stress can lead to illness and death.
Posttraumatic stress disorder (PTSD)	A maladaptive reaction occurring as a response to a severe stressor, a stressor that is outside the range of usual human experience and would be markedly distressing to almost anyone. Three general symptoms are characteristic of the disorder: a psychological reexperiencing of the traumatic event, an avoidance of thoughts and behaviors associated with the trauma or a general numbness, and symptoms of hyperarousal.
Stress	The biological and psychological effects of the adjustive demands placed on an individual.
Stress inoculation training	A cognitive-behavioral treatment that focuses on changing how individuals think about stressors. It involves three stages: cognitive preparation, skill acquisition and rehearsal, and application and practice.
Stress tolerance	One's ability to withstand stress without having functioning seriously impaired.
Stressor	An adjustive demand made on a person.
Task-oriented response	An effective or adaptive way of dealing with a stressor in which an individual objectively appraises the situation, works out alternative solutions, takes appropriate action, and evaluates feedback.

VIDEO NOTES

■ WHAT IS STRESS?

• Dr. Norman Anderson defines stress as a three-stage process: (1) an initiating event in the environment, (2) appraisal of the event (i.e., what do we think about it), and (3) an emotional and physiological response.

• Dr. Andrew Baum defines stress as a demand placed on people that requires them to act in more than routine ways and notes that stress may result from positive events (having a baby) as well as negative events (losing a loved one).

■ BACKGROUND STRESSORS

• Such familiar events as noises and interruptions, which often are of short duration, can threaten our sense of competence, well-being, peace of mind, and concentration. When they occur frequently, they can make us feel out of control.

■ WHO IS MOST SUSCEPTIBLE TO STRESS?

• The predictability of the stressor, our control over the stressor, and the meaning of the stressor to us, i.e., how we interpret the event, all determine how easily we will adapt to the stressor.

• To some degree one's response to stress is constitutional: We are born with greater or lesser resources for coping. The degree to which people are affected by stress also is experiential: People who have dealt successfully with stress in the past typically deal successfully with current stressors.

■ EFFECTS OF STRESS

(Case Illustrations: Theodore Beyda, Lisa Dias)
• Stress responses can be both biological and psychological.

• A New York Hospital–Cornell Medical School study that focused on accountants and architects found that a rise in blood pressure was associated with especially stressful work periods. Lisa Dias lessens her stress level by going to a museum; Theodore Beyda controls when he works and when he does not work.

■ THE CONNECTION BETWEEN STRESSORS AND BODILY RESPONSES

• Essentially, in a stressful situation the body becomes aroused and poised for a fight. Hormones, such as epinephrine and norepinephrine, may increase, in turn increasing blood pressure, heart rate, and muscle tone in the skeletal muscles. The increase in hormones also tends to reduce blood flow and the tone of organs that are not needed at the moment, such as those of the digestive system, although increased stomach acid may suddenly be secreted. The pituitary-adrenal system can cause the release of corticosteroids into the bloodstream.

• Unanswered questions: What is the long-term effect of such bodily changes when they are not followed by the physical activities they were designed to fuel? How does stress affect the nervous system? How do stress and its effect on the nervous system affect the endocrine system? How do the endocrine system and its effect on the brain alter behavior?

• Dr. Norman Anderson is studying the effect of daily chronic stress on African Americans who typically show greater cardiovascular responses to stress than white Americans and are at a greater risk for developing hypertension.

■ HEIGHTENED STRESS

(Case Illustrations: Antoinette Warren, Suzi Sawyer, Ginny, Vivian)
• Events that threaten to interrupt our lives in a major way can cause heightened stress, e.g., a divorce, unemployment, an accident, a burglary.

• The more severe or unpredictable, the longer the stressor lasts, or the more out of our control it is, the more likely we are to have a prolonged stress reaction. This reaction may involve depression, anger, or a feeling of helplessness.

- One of the strongest stressors is the death of someone we love.

    Most people go through a range of emotions in reacting to a death, including feelings normally associated with depression.

    Some people find prayer and religion helpful in situations that are basically out of their control.

    Some find support in groups such as COPS and the Samaritans (the suicide survivors group), in which they can discuss their feelings and experiences with individuals who have undergone similar experiences. Such groups help people feel that they are not alone and help them learn from the experiences of others.

    Eventually, most move on with their lives.

■ ADJUSTMENT DISORDER

- Psychologists say people have an adjustment disorder when they continue to show signs that stress is undermining their ability to function for a period of up to six months after the stressor.

■ POSTTRAUMATIC STRESS DISORDER (PTSD)

(Case Illustrations: veterans, rape victims)

- Dr. Mardi Horowitz describes PTSD in terms of three major elements: (1) the occurrence of a major trauma, usually an extraordinary and frequently a terrifying experience; (2) repetitive intrusive experiences, e.g., a pang of intense emotion, recurrent visual images, intrusive memories, etc.; and (3) a kind of numbing or denial of memories.

- Traumas caused by people, e.g., war and rape, tend to create more PTSD victims that natural disasters, e.g., floods.

- Dr. Andrew Baum, who is studying PTSD in veterans, is looking at whether the extreme stress responses of PTSD that occur over long periods of time cause deleterious changes in the body, and if so, what can be done to prevent the responses from occurring. One of Dr. Baum's findings is that the determining factor in whether veterans experience PTSD is not how much combat they have experienced but whether they have intrusive or uncontrollable thoughts. His research focuses on the fact that each time the event is reexperienced in memory, the body is aroused with the same kind of biological stress reaction experienced during the original event.

- Dr. Dean Kilpatrick's research finds similar recurrent memories among rape victims.

■ COPING WITH STRESS

- Getting emotional support and assistance in meeting basic needs from family, friends, and neighbors is very helpful.

- Self-help groups have proven very effective for many. People need to be allowed to show their emotions, including crying, and to talk about their problems.

- When talking is no longer helpful because it has become repetitive and does not lead to change or relief, psychotherapy often helps resolve feelings about stressful situations. Psychotherapy might address such questions as: What does the loss represent to the person? and Why is it so difficult to get over?

• Stress inoculation therapy, a cognitive-behavioral technique, is used by Dr. Dean Kilpatrick and Dr. Connie Best to help rape victims. It provides them with a variety of coping tools to help them gain some control over their emotions. These include deep breathing and such other relaxation exercises as deep muscle relaxation and guided self-dialogue, in which people essentially talk back to themselves to gain control over some of their intrusive thoughts and to replace negative self-statements with positive ones.

■ VIDEO REVIEW QUESTIONS

1. Note five stressors that you experienced in the last week. Note which were brief and which were sustained and indicate your reaction to each.

2. Differentiate between stress and a stressor.

3. Differentiate between reactions to stress that are adaptive and those that are maladaptive. Give examples.

4. Give examples of stress reactions at the biological level, the personal level, and the social level.

5. Differentiate between heightened distress and adjustment disorder.

6. What symptoms are typical of heightened distress? Classify each as biological or psychological.

7. Differentiate between the symptoms of adjustment disorder and those of posttraumatic stress disorder.

8. Using case examples from the video, list the three characteristic components of PTSD and mention some symptoms associated with the disorder.

9. Identify the elements involved in stress inoculation training and tell what roles each plays in reducing stress.

10. List several factors that influence how a person will react to a stressor.

11. Identify several examples of background stressors and discuss their potential effects on us.

■ CASE STUDY

by Judith Rosenberger, C.S.W., Ph.D. Hunter College and Edith Gould, C.S.W. Postgraduate Center for Mental Health

Veronica

I was coming home for the weekend and looking forward to spending time with my parents and my sister, who also was coming home from college. We were going to go to Easter services and have a big family dinner. I felt relieved. My mom had seemed upset lately — she had been fighting a lot with my dad about stuff I really didn't understand — but the excitement of the holiday and the anticipation of having everyone home seemed to have lifted her spirits.

When I got off the bus and turned into the block I saw all the red lights near our house. To tell you the truth, looking back, maybe everything was totally clear for me right then. But the next moment, it was like my whole body and mind kicked in and I switched it all around. I thought, "Maybe there's a fire next door." Nothing looked wrong with my house. So I figured it must be the neighbor's house. But then I noticed all our neighbors milling around in front of my house. Everyone was there but my family. You could tell by the expressions on everyone's face that something terrible had happened. Panic rose up in my throat. I felt cold, and my chest felt like it was being crushed from all sides. My mind started to race. Contradictory thoughts rushed in. "It's nothing. It's something terrible at my house. No, it couldn't be. What could it be? I have to get there fast. No, I don't ever want to go any closer." It was like I was wrestling with another person. I was trying to get through, and at the same time I was trying to hold back. Ignorance would protect me from whatever it was.

I felt like a walking robot, and I guess I acted like one, too, because nobody noticed me coming up behind the crowd. Just then policemen carried out this body covered in a sheet. Blood stains were leaking through. For some reason my mother's arm was hanging off the side of the stretcher. I studied that arm like a scientist, with an attitude of detachment. "Yes, that is in fact the ring that my mother wears. That does look like her wrist with her usual watch." I was gathering data and ignoring the facts at the same time. I became confused. How could this obviously dead person be wearing my mother's rings? Isn't it odd that this dead person has her wrist?

The ambulance doors slammed, and it drove off. Then people noticed me. They all seemed to move toward me at once, saying things like "We're so sorry." and "Are you all right?" I felt very detached and distant, as though I were watching all this in a movie. I had to act as if I was there, but I didn't really feel anything. I was very cool, very composed. I just acknowledged their comments in my most polite way and went inside. My dad looked stunned. But, I didn't even ask what had happened. I just started to console him. It was as if I already knew, without knowing how I found out.

I heard people discussing the facts, but I didn't react. I just nodded to whatever anyone said. Oh yes, I see; my mother shot herself in the head with the big gun Dad kept to protect us from burglars. Yes, it is quite a surprise. It seems especially strange that she shot herself from the front because she was always so concerned about how her face looked.

My sister was hysterical when we met her at the train station. Dad and I took care of her. We made all the funeral and burial arrangements. I walked through it all doing whatever I was supposed to do, but doing it like a zombie. After a week I went back to school, thinking I could put it behind me.

But it wasn't over. It was when I finally got away from the awfulness of the actual circumstances that I started to fall apart. I could hardly sleep, and if I did, I had hideous nightmares about people being mutilated. Blood and dismembered bodies were all over my dreams. I didn't think of my mother at all, but I was haunted by that image of her arm. It came into my mind over and over again. I felt more and more agitated and unable to sit still when I was awake. My own body felt dead and alien, like it belonged to somebody else, and then suddenly I would have these attacks of breathlessness and sweating. I'd be back home, walking up the street, feeling the panic and fighting it just like I did that day. It felt like if I lost control for one minute, I would be launched into an endless voyage to insanity. People around me acted concerned, but to me they looked just like those neighbors who tried to speak to me that day. I withdrew further and had to stay away from anyone coming near me.

Of course, I couldn't study. I couldn't even go to class after the second week. Every minute felt like a battle to maintain my equilibrium, just to live through whatever was happening to me. I could fake it part of the time, and sometimes I even had days when I could go through the motions of going to the library, eating meals, changing clothes. But inside I was on very thin ice, and I could feel the cracks opening up at the tiniest thing that reminded me of the moment I realized my mother had blown her face off and never even said why.

My father just accepted it when I told him I was okay. I was angry that he was so willing to be fooled. That made me feel even more like I had to keep myself wrapped up tight, keep everything inside. Let's face it. People don't really want to hear this stuff for more than about a minute.

I wasn't on top of things at all. I tried to drink myself into sleeping more and feeling less. I started to think maybe I would be better off putting an end to my misery. And I missed my mother so much. I really wanted to be with her. I went home when my dad was out, got some of the things she especially loved to wear, and wore them myself. The aroma of her perfume, still lingering on her clothing, helped me to feel closer to her. And then I started to dream about being with her, and it felt like a place I'd like to be, one that would be a lot better than constantly being thrown into these horrifying replays of the scenes and feelings of that walk down the block. I guess that was when whatever was left of my rational mind kicked in and said, "This is dangerous."

CLINICAL DISCUSSION

Veronica displayed the numbing of feeling and the sense of detachment at the moment of discovering her mother's suicide that is characteristic of individuals experiencing a traumatic event. Some individuals never deal effectively with the trauma. In Veronica's case, for example, this initial denial may be linked to her later development of posttraumatic stress disorder. She also used a dissociative kind of unconscious defensive strategy, automatically disconnecting from the impact of the moment without becoming inwardly disorganized or observably distressed. The massive shut-down in the crisis prevented her from expressing her powerful feelings or sorting out her confused thoughts about what had taken place. It may have saved her from an acute stress reaction, but it contributed to her delayed reaction.

This kind of sudden and shocking event fits the PTSD definition of a stressor that anyone would find traumatic. Veronica did not react with grief or anger at the time of the event. Yet later, she could not stop reliving the events of that day. In these flashbacks she feels the dread she felt walking home and realizing, almost in slow motion, that something terrible was taking place. The feelings of derealization (the concerned neighbors on the street seemed like they were in a movie) and depersonalization (her body felt "dead and alien" like it belonged to someone else) made her feel panicky. Very typically, alcohol became a way of trying to blunt and even out her shifting feeling states. Besides using alcohol to quell her inner turmoil, Veronica found it necessary to avoid any kind of stimuli that might evoke a feeling or thought connected to the chain of events surrounding the discovery of her mother's violent death.

In PTSD, life becomes a constant struggle to avoid exposure to anything that will set off retraumatization. And yet, the PTSD sufferer is continuously besieged from within by memories of the original event. Not surprisingly, work and relationships collapse as energy and attention are concentrated on defensive maneuvers. As Veronica became increasingly exhausted with this failing effort, her despair grew. She is quite right that her fantasy of rejoining her mother is dangerous, because it may represent the potential for suicide.

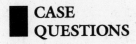

CASE QUESTIONS

1. The first reaction Veronica has to the shock of her mother's suicide is numbness and detachment. How does she try to sustain the state of detachment and prevent herself from reliving the trauma?

2. Flashbacks can combine actual memories of an event with misperceptions of it happening in the present. Cite examples of how here-and-now experiences become linked up with the traumatic memory.

3. What is the role of alcohol in this case?

4. Explain how the sources of Veronica's PTSD might be the same as a posttraumatic stress disorder in a Vietnam War veteran, even though the settings are very different. What are the key features that could be part of both Veronica's experience and a war-related experience?

SELF-TEST

1. **Alma is upset because a book she needs to write a report is not in the library. She is experiencing a(n)**
   a) approach-avoidance conflict.
   b) double-avoidance conflict.
   c) frustration.
   d) pressure.

2. **Carol is faced with either doing a long and boring project or failing her course. She is experiencing a(n) _____ conflict.**
   a) approach-avoidance
   b) double-approach
   c) double-approach-avoidance
   d) double-avoidance

3. Gail is determined to win the local marathon race. Even though her parents are not into such things, she practices several hours after school every day to get ready. Gail is experiencing a(n)
   a) conflict.
   b) external pressure.
   c) frustration.
   d) internal pressure.

4. Iris is a single parent who is trying to hold down a job, take care of her elderly mother, and raise two children. She confided to a friend that she is nearly at her wit's end. Which stressor criterion is probably most responsible for her discomfort?
   a) duration
   b) imminence
   c) importance
   d) multiplicity

5. Which of the following is the most supportive statement a spouse can make when the other partner is worried about passing an examination?
   a) "Don't disappoint me now, get a good grade."
   b) "I know you will get an A."
   c) "I'm not worried, I know you'll pass."
   d) "Just do your best and let the chips fall."

6. Crisis intervention is a way to provide psychological help for people experiencing
   a) acute stress.
   b) chronic stress.
   c) eustress.
   d) self-induced stress.

7. In which of the following levels of reaction to stress are one's learned coping skills?
   a) biological
   b) political
   c) psychological
   d) sociocultural

8. Task-oriented is to meeting the requirements of the stressor as _____ is to protecting the self from psychological harm.
   a) defense-oriented
   b) ego-oriented
   c) self-concept-oriented
   d) self-ideal-oriented

9. Which of the following defense-oriented behaviors is of the damage-repair type?
   a) denying
   b) intellectualizing
   c) mourning
   d) repressing

10. Which of the following defense-oriented behaviors is of the ego-defense type?
    a) crying
    b) mourning
    c) repetitive talking
    d) repressing

11. Which of the following is the proper sequence of Selye's general adaptation syndrome?
    a) alarm, collapse, resistance
    b) alarm, resistance, collapse
    c) collapse, alarm, resistance
    d) resistance, alarm, collapse

12. The imposition of martial law in a country that has just experienced an earthquake probably indicates that it is in the _____ stage of sociocultural decompensation.
    a) alarm
    b) exhaustion
    c) mobilization
    d) resistance

13. The key differences between adjustment disorders and posttraumatic stress disorders include all of the following EXCEPT the
    a) nature of the stressor.
    b) severity of the disturbance.
    c) time frame during which the disorder occurs.
    d) type of coping device used.

14. Tom's wife has been dead for several weeks, but he often thinks of her as being alive and sometimes expects to see her sitting in her favorite chair. Tom's behavior is
    a) a prelude to hallucinations.
    b) delusional in nature.
    c) indicative of abnormal denial.
    d) part of a normal bereavement process.

15. Ulla was found several hours after the plane crash wandering aimlessly through the woods. She did not remember anything that had happened. Which stage of the initial disaster syndrome was she probably in?
    a) posttraumatic stress
    b) recovery
    c) shock
    d) suggestible

16. During which stage of the initial disaster syndrome may posttraumatic stress disorder develop?
    a) postrecovery
    b) recovery
    c) shock
    d) suggestible

17. Which of the following is part of the first stage of a stress-inoculation training program used by cognitive-behavioral therapists?
    a) introducing dead bacteria into the bloodstream
    b) practicing adaptive self-statements while being exposed to threatening stressors
    c) providing information about the stressful situation
    d) rehearsing self-statements that promote adaptation

18. **Everyday stressors of short duration, such as ambulance sirens, traffic jams, loud rock music, and flashing lights, are termed**
   a) irritants.
   b) acute stress.
   c) eustress.
   d) background stressors.

19. **Which of the following is not a factor in determining how stressful a situation is?**
   a) age
   b) the predictability of the stressor
   c) one's control over the stressor
   d) the meaning of the stressor to the person

20. **The family members and friends of people who commit suicide frequently**
   a) are able to cope with the suicide sooner than if the death had been accidental.
   b) feel guilty about how they treated the person.
   c) are better able to cope with the suicide if it was accomplished nonviolently.
   d) will attempt suicide in the same manner.

21. **When people react with persistent anxiety, long-term nightmares, or a numbing loss of any feelings after a natural or man-made disaster, they may be experiencing**
   a) clinical depression.
   b) stress adjustment disorder.
   c) shock syndrome.
   d) posttraumatic stress disorder.

22. **The three key elements in posttraumatic stress disorder are:**
   a) trauma, intrusive experiences, and psychosomatic illnesses.
   b) trauma, intrusive experiences, and a numbing or denial of memories.
   c) expectation of disaster, the disaster, and numbing of memories.
   d) trauma, shock, and intrusive experiences.

23. **One of the major successes of the COPS program is**
   a) convincing law enforcement agencies to create environments in which it is acceptable for officers to show emotion.
   b) insisting that psychologists be available following major traumatic events.
   c) setting up a fund to pay for psychotherapy for officers suffering from posttraumatic stress disorder.
   d) reducing the number of police officers who are killed in the line of duty.

24. **All of the following are strategies for coping with major stress EXCEPT**
   a) letting emotions show.
   b) recreating the experience over and over again.
   c) getting social support.
   d) talking about the situation.

25. **All of the following techniques are used in stress inoculation therapy EXCEPT**
   a) deep breathing.
   b) deep muscle relaxation.
   c) determining why a situation is so stressful.
   d) guided self-dialogue.

26. **Breaking a frightening experience down into its component parts and using positive self-statements to deal with each of the components is the technique of**
  a) role-playing.
  b) psychodrama.
  c) guided self-dialogue.
  d) cognitive restructuring.

[ANSWERS: 1-c, 2-d, 3-d, 4-d, 5-d, 6-a, 7-c, 8-a, 9-c, 10-d, 11-b, 12-d, 13-d, 14-d, 15-c, 16-b, 17-c, 18-d, 19-a, 20-b, 21-d, 22-b, 23-a, 24-b, 25-c, 26-c]

SUGGESTED READINGS

Charlesworth, E. A. (1984). *Stress management: A comprehensive guide to wellness* (rev.ed.). Houston: Biobehavioral Press. The guide considers how to understand and deal with stress in everyday life.

Goldberger, L., & Breznitz, S. (Eds.). (1982). *Handbook of stress: Theoretical and clinical aspects.* New York: Free Press. This collection of articles considers both the physiological and psychological causes and effects of stress and discusses treatments and coping mechanisms.

Kulka, R.A., Schlenger, W.E., Fairbank, J.A., Hough, R.L., Jordon, B.K., Marmar, C.R., & Weiss, D.S. (1990). *Trauma and the Vietnam war generation: Report of findings from a national Vietnam veterans' readjustment study.* New York: Bruner/Mazel. The report documents PTSD in the veteran population discussing who gets it and why and covers other disorders among Vietnam War veterans.

Lukas, C., & Seiden, H. M. (1987). *Silent grief: Living in the wake of suicide.* New York: Charles Scribner's Sons. A survivor and a psychologist investigate the experience of life after the suicide of a loved one. This book skillfully combines the intimate stories of many survivors with practical advice for making the passage more manageable.

Metsakis, A. (1988). *Vietnam wives: Women and children surviving life with veterans suffering from posttraumatic stress disorder.* Kensington, MD: Woodbine House. Families of Vietnam War veterans describe the effects on them of dealing with someone with posttraumatic stress disorder.

Schiff, H. S. (1986). *Living through mourning.* New York: Viking/Penguin. This is a well-written exposition on the process and stages of mourning.

Selye, H. (1956). *The stress of life.* New York: McGraw-Hill. This ground-breaking book led to Selye's theory of the general adaptation syndrome.

Silverman, P. R. (1986). *Widow-to-widow.* New York: Springer Publishing. This book reports on mutual help programs for widowed women as well as peer support in general. It provides a good discussion of the model and process of bereavement and grief, presenting both theory and findings from widow-to-widow groups.

Slaby, A. E. (1989). *Aftershock: Identifying, understanding, curing and preventing posttraumatic stress in your everyday life.* New York: Villard Books. This book describes the pervasive character of this disorder and updates the research on it.

51

UNIT 3

THE ANXIETY
DISORDERS

■ UNIT THEME

Anxiety is a natural human response, but for over 30 million Americans, it is problematic. This unit describes a range of anxiety responses, discusses causal factors, and shows how anxiety-based disorders are treated. The text considers anxiety, somatoform, and dissociative disorders, and the video focuses on two of the most common anxiety disorders: panic with agoraphobia and generalized anxiety disorder.

■ UNIT ASSIGNMENTS

Read: Unit 3. "The Anxiety Disorders" in *The World of Abnormal Psychology Study Guide*, Toby Kleban Levine, editor (HarperCollins, 1992).

View: Program 3. "The Anxiety Disorders" in THE WORLD OF ABNORMAL PSYCHOLOGY.

Read: Chapter 6. "Anxiety-based Disorders" in *Abnormal Psychology and Modern Life*, Ninth Edition, by Robert C. Carson and James N. Butcher (HarperCollins, 1992).

■ GOALS AND OBJECTIVES

1. Describe the principal manifestation of anxiety disorders and summarize the relative occurrence of these disorders among men and women.

2. Describe the symptoms of panic disorders and agoraphobia and explain why they are considered together.

3. List and define several simple phobias and describe the major manifestations of phobias as a class.

4. Summarize the major manifestations of obsessive-compulsive disorder and explain why this disorder is considered maladaptive.

5. Compare and contrast the symptoms of generalized anxiety disorder with those of panic disorder.

6. Differentiate somatization disorder from hypochondriasis and explain why hypochondriasis may be viewed as a type of interpersonal communication.

7. Describe the major manifestations of a conversion disorder and identify some sensory, motor, and visceral symptoms that often appear.

8. Describe the symptoms of multiple personality disorder and summarize what is understood about its causes.

9. Describe the symptoms of a depersonalization disorder and distinguish it from feelings of depersonalization that sometimes occur with personality deterioration.

10. Define neurotic style and discuss the potential consequences of neurotic styles on interpersonal relationships.

11. Explain and illustrate how biological, psychosocial, and sociocultural factors cause and maintain anxiety-based disorders.

12. Describe some biological and psychological therapeutic approaches that have been successful in treating anxiety-based disorders.

UNIT OVERVIEW

by Edward S. Katkin, Ph.D.
State University of New York
at Stony Brook

Of all the psychological disorders that we will discuss, none are more common than the **anxiety disorders,** which will affect over 30 million Americans during their lifetime. Nearly everyone has experienced severe fear at some point in life, and indeed it is quite normal to feel some degree of fear or anxiety when confronted with a threatening situation. Psychologists use the word fear to describe the reaction of a person to a situation that is a clear and present threat; for example, you might experience fear while taking an examination for which you have not prepared. For some people, however, fear becomes anxiety, an unreasonable fear that has little or no objective basis. Anxiety disorders thus represent extreme and debilitating forms of irrational fear. They come in many different varieties, ranging from very discrete irrational fears of such specific things as dogs or heights (called **simple phobias**), to more generalized feelings of dread for which no obvious reason is known, to episodes of outright and overwhelming panic.

Your textbook describes a wide variety of anxiety-based disorders, but the video portion of this unit focuses on two broad categories: **panic disorder with agoraphobia** and **generalized anxiety disorder**. In addition, the video introduces patients who have such associated anxiety disorders as **obsessive-compulsive disorder** and **hypochondriasis**.

■ PANIC DISORDER WITH AGORAPHOBIA

Panic disorder can be an extremely debilitating disorder in which an individual experiences a sudden episode of terrifying fear and dread. Such physical symptoms as a rapidly racing heart, sweating, palpitations, and muscle spasms may be present. The panic comes on quickly, may last for minutes or hours before passing, and is totally overwhelming. An insidious aspect of panic attacks is that people who experience them often develop a fear of having more of them; thus the panic attacks create a secondary anxiety disorder, the fear of having panic attacks.

Sometimes people who have had panic attacks become afraid to leave the security of their home for fear of having a panic attack in an unfamiliar (hence unsafe) setting. These patients are said to be agoraphobic, from the Greek *agora* (the marketplace) and *phobia* (fear). In modern psychology the term **agoraphobia** refers to any unreasonable fear of activities or situations in which the patient would feel insecure or from which escape would be difficult, and in which help would be unavailable. In its extreme form agoraphobia may prevent people from leaving their own homes. In less extreme forms, agoraphobia may be expressed as a fear of crowds, a fear of elevators, or a fear of driving alone.

The video focuses on several individuals who manifest various aspects of panic and agoraphobia. These people are acutely aware of their sense of distress and are eager to change their behavior. This is a key component of anxiety disorders. Mary, for example, has suffered from panic attacks and now is afraid to use her automobile for fear that she will panic while driving. Roger is particularly fearful of crossing bridges; his fear prevents him from carrying out necessary business travel and also compromises his ability to plan any travel beyond a limited distance.

■ GENERALIZED ANXIETY DISORDER

Whereas panic disorders are discrete and episodic, generalized anxiety disorder is characterized by a chronic, recurring sense of fear and severe worrying. The patient with generalized anxiety disorder (GAD) feels worried and frightened most of the time. Typically, the feelings are most extreme in the morning. In the video you will meet Laverne and Donna, two women with this disorder. Laverne describes the intensity of her feelings of dread, and explains how it affects her physically, causing dizziness, muscle tension, and uncontrollable crying. Donna describes how her fear was so irrational that she thought she was going crazy. In an attempt to make sense of her anxiety she sought to create something of which to be afraid. She became afraid of knives, and then focused all her energy and her anxiety on worrying about knives and how they might hurt someone she loved.

■ OBSESSIVE-COMPULSIVE DISORDER

Unit 5 discusses obsessive-compulsive personality disorder. This unit introduces the concept of an obsessive-compulsive anxiety disorder. The difference is important. The video describes Phil, who has an obsessive-compulsive anxiety disorder. His compulsive behavior — he checks the stove 28 times every morning to be sure the gas is off — is his characteristic way of controlling his intense feelings of anxiety and anger that are derived from his father's early death in a fire. Phil is uncomfortable with his behavior and recognizes that it is not normal. His recognition, plus the fact that his behavior is driven by fear and anger and is designed to reduce his anxiety distinguish Phil from someone with an obsessive-compulsive personality disorder.

■ HYPOCHONDRIASIS

Often, people with anxiety disorders attempt to rationalize their anxiety by focusing on imaginary illnesses or bodily disorders. This preoccupation with somatic problems, *in the absence of any real physical problem*, is known as hypochondriasis, an anxiety-related disorder. In the video, you will hear about Maria, a young woman who worries constantly about her health and often interprets the slightest symptoms as evidence of her imminent death. A stomachache induced by an early morning pizza binge, for instance, was interpreted by Maria as a certain sign of stomach cancer. Her therapist believes that Maria's hypochondriasis is a manifestation of intense anxiety about her marriage and about her love relationships in general. In fact, many competing theories of the actual causes of hypochondriasis exist, but psychologists generally agree that the basic underlying cause is intense anxiety.

■ CAUSES OF ANXIETY DISORDERS

As with so many psychological disorders, no single cause for anxiety disorders has been found. Most theorists believe that early childhood history is an important contributing factor. In the video, Roger, for instance, discusses his belief that his panic disorder results from a childhood in which his mother taught him to be insecure and to believe that he could not cope. Scientific evidence to support such a view is weak, however. Some researchers believe that constitutional, or genetic, factors also may predispose certain people to develop anxiety disorders, but scientific support for this view also is quite weak. Basic research on the origins of anxiety disorders is a high priority. The current state of knowledge suggests, however, that biological predispositions of unknown origin interact with childhood and later experiences to contribute to the development of anxiety disorders.

■ TREATMENT

We do know a great deal about effective treatment of anxiety disorders. These are categorized broadly into two types: pharmacological and psychological. Among the pharmacological treatments most commonly used are the so-called antianxiety drugs technically known as benzodiazepines and sold under the names of Valium, Librium, and Xanax. In addition, two common antidepressant drugs, tricyclics and monoamine oxidase (MAO) inhibitors, have been found to alleviate panic disorder. The indiscriminate use of the antianxiety drugs can be quite dangerous, however; the benzodiazepines, in particular, tend to be addictive and can cause unwanted side effects. Most therapists, therefore, prefer to use medications for a short period only and to use psychological treatment for long-term benefit.

Among the psychological therapies that have been used to treat anxiety are cognitive therapies, behavioral therapies, and psychodynamically based insight therapies. Each has a different goal. The cognitive therapies deal with the automatic thoughts that sustain or trigger anxiety; the behavioral therapies focus on learning new behaviors or eliminating habitual behaviors that increase the anxiety. (In the video, for example you will see a thorough exploration of the use of behavior therapy at an intensive treatment center directed by Dr. Alan Goldstein.) The psychodynamic therapies are focused on presumed unconscious conflicts that underlie the anxiety. These therapies assume that unconscious conflicts must be brought to consciousness through a patient's insight and that with insight the conflict will be resolved and the anxiety symptoms will lessen.

Most therapists use a combination of methods. Sometimes pharmacological and psychological treatments are combined; other times behavioral and insight techniques are used together. Regardless of approach, most people with anxiety disorders can be helped significantly with the proper treatment.

■ KEY TERMS

The following terms are used in the text and/or the television programs.

Aggression/assertion inhibition	A neurotic style in which the person is uncomfortable in situations that call for aggressive, self-assertive actions, and instead behaves agreeably to avoid aggressive behavior.
Agoraphobia	The specific fear of being in places or situations from which escape would be difficult, or in which help would be unavailable in the event of a panic attack.
Amnesia	The partial or total inability to recall or identify past experience.
Anxiety	An unreasonable fear that has little or no objective basis.
Anxiety disorders	A group of disorders that feature unrealistic, irrational fear of disabling intensity and avoidance behavior.
Anxiety-response pattern	Barlow's (1988) model for the development of anxiety in which biological, psychological, and environmental events interact, conditioning a system for generating anxiety.
Aphonia	A speech disorder in which the individual is able to talk only in a whisper.
Astasia-abasia	A walking disturbance in which an individual usually can control leg movements when sitting or lying down, but can hardly stand and has a very grotesque, disorganized walk.
Behavioral therapy	A therapy which focuses on removing specific symptoms or maladaptive behaviors, developing needed competencies and adaptive behaviors, and modifying environmental conditions that may be reinforcing and maintaining the maladaptive behaviors.
Cognitive mediation	An attempt by the therapist to change behavior by changing the individual's inner thoughts or beliefs that may be causing, or reinforcing, the neurotic behavior.
Compliance/ submission inhibition	A neurotic style exhibited by those who are fearful of tendencies to comply or submit to rules or solutions offered by authority figures.

Compulsion	A repetitive behavior performed in response to an obsession and irrationally designed to neutralize discomfort.
Conversion disorder	A physical malfunction or loss of bodily control involving no underlying pathology but apparently related to psychological conflict or need (formerly called hysteria).
Depersonalization disorder	A dissociative disorder involving an alteration in one's perception or experience of the self.
Dissociative disorders	A group of disorders involving a disturbance in the experience of one's personal identity.
Fugue	A reaction in which the person not only is amnesic, but also wanders away from home, often assuming a partially or completely new identity.
Generalized anxiety disorder	A disorder characterized by chronic (at least six months' duration), unrealistic, or excessive worry about two or more elements in one's life; traditionally described as free-floating anxiety.
Hypochondriasis	A somatoform disorder characterized by fears of having a serious disease where no evidence of illness can be found.
Intimacy/trust inhibition	A neurotic style exhibited by those who feel unusually strong anxiety over establishing close personal attachments with others.
Malingering	The act of faking the symptoms of a physical or mental disorder in order to realize some gain, such as avoiding unpleasant work.
Mass hysteria	A conversion disorder afflicting a group of people; a rarity in modern times.
Multimodal therapy	A combination of more than one approach in the treatment of an individual.
Multiple personality disorder	A dissociative disorder involving the existence of two or more distinct personalities.
Neurosis	A nonpsychotic emotional disturbance characterized by exaggerated use of avoidance behavior and defense mechanisms against anxiety.
Neurotic style	A general way of behaving that interferes with one's effectiveness and personal satisfaction; symptomless in the sense that such an individual would not be diagnosed with an anxiety-based disorder, but still exhibits maladaptive behavior.
Obsession	An intrusive, persistent thought or image, frequently involving unpleasant or irrational content.
Obsessive-compulsive disorder	An anxiety disorder in which individuals feel obsessed with something that they do not want to think about and/or compelled to carry out some action, often pointlessly ritualistic.
Panic disorder	A disorder defined and characterized by the occurrence of one or more unexpected panic attacks not triggered by the person's being the focus of others' attention.
Panic disorder with agoraphobia	A diagnosis in which agoraphobia accompanies panic disorder; occurs in the majority of cases of panic disorder.

Psychogenic amnesia	A dissociative disorder in which an individual is unable to recall information. The forgotten information is not lost, it is merely beneath the level of consciousness. Psychogenic amnesia is a fairly common initial reaction to extremely traumatic experiences.
Responsibility/ independence inhibition	An aversion to exercising personal independence or legitimate authority over others.
Simple phobia	A persistent fear of some specific object or situation that presents no actual danger or the perception of the danger is exaggerated.
Social phobia	The fear of being watched by other people or of doing something embarrassing in public.
Somatization disorder	A somatoform disorder, beginning before age 30, that is characterized by multiple complaints of physical ailments over a long period that are inadequately explained by independent findings of physical illness or injury.
Somatoform disorders	A group of disorders involving complaints of a physical problem, for which no organic basis can be found.
Somatoform pain disorder	A somatoform disorder characterized by the report of severe and lasting pain in the absence of an organic cause.

■ VIDEO NOTES

■ WHAT IS ANXIETY?
• Anxiety is a normal response that helps people decide whether or not a situation is dangerous.

> Normal anxiety differs from abnormal anxiety on the basis of its intensity and duration in relationship to the actual situation, and on the ability of the individual to function effectively.

• The anxiety disorders are the most common of the mental disorders with the possible exception of substance abuse and affect one in every six Americans at some point in their life.

■ PANIC DISORDER AND AGORAPHOBIA
(Case Illustrations: Paula, Mary, Roger, Patrick)
• These separate disorders often occur together.

• Panic attacks are discrete episodes with a very rapid onset characterized by such responses as racing heart, faintness, muscle weakness, dry mouth, trembling, sweatiness, disorientation, and a feeling of being out of control.

• People who have panic disorder not only experience panic attacks, but live in fear of the next one. Sometimes this leads to a second, but related, disorder called agoraphobia, in which activities and situations are avoided if they make people feel vulnerable to having panic attacks. In its most extreme form, agoraphobia may prevent people from leaving their homes, or even a particular room.

• Intensive treatment programs that use cognitive and behavioral techniques are effective because they provide daily opportunities to practice coping in a small and supportive atmosphere. They also reduce the rate of attrition, setbacks, and loss of motivation that are common in long-term treatment. Individuals attending intensive programs get support from the group and are able to build new habits without interference from the daily triggers of life.

> The treatment program seen in the video uses no medications because of a belief that while drugs may dampen symptoms, they don't cure.

> Clients also are taught how diet may contribute to the disorder and how caffeine, a stimulant, causes physiological reactions that mimic anxiety.

• The role of the brain in anxiety disorders is not well understood. A complex array of imbalances in areas of the brain that control various aspects of the alarm system may exist. We know that various groups of neurotransmitters somehow interact with one another and either cause or inhibit anxiety.

■ GENERALIZED ANXIETY DISORDER
(Case Illustrations: Donna, Laverne)
• Generalized anxiety disorder, once called free-floating anxiety, is characterized by chronic, diffuse, excessive worry.

> In panic disorders, people worry about having a panic attack. With generalized anxiety disorder, they worry about things other than their anxiety.

> The person with chronic anxiety may have difficulty falling asleep, suffer from lots of aches and pains, drink excessively, and depend on tranquilizers and sleeping pills.

> In more extreme cases, panic attack-like episodes may occur.

• About four percent of Americans suffer from generalized anxiety disorder, with women outnumbering men two to one. Patients with chronic anxiety often see a primary care physician rather than a psychologist or psychiatrist, because so many of the symptoms are physiological.

■ ANXIETY DISORDERS: CAUSAL FACTORS
• Most experts feel that no single factor explains anxiety disorders. Among the multiple factors that probably are involved are constitutional vulnerability, including a low tolerance level for anxiety, childhood history, issues of personality development, and current life stressors.

> People who develop agoraphobia often had childhood environments in which they did not feel safe. Parents might have been overprotective, overcritical, or have instilled doubt about the child's competency.

■ ANXIETY DISORDERS: TREATMENT
• Three basic methods are used to treat anxiety disorders: medication, psychodynamically based psychotherapy, and cognitive-behavioral psychotherapies. A combination almost always is used.

> Medication sometimes is used to stabilize the condition of an individual whose disorder is interfering with daily life, for patients with whom psychological treatment has failed, or to right the biological wrongs in a person and prepare them for

psychological treatment. Medication must be taken on an ongoing basis to prevent relapse.

The most commonly prescribed antianxiety drugs are the benzodiazepines (e.g., Valium, Librium, Xanax), which suppress the anxiety symptoms. These are not recommended for pregnant woman, however. Further, some are addictive and require difficult withdrawals. In addition, sedation and cognitive impairment sometimes occur.

Psychodynamically based psychotherapy uses insight to uncover unconscious conflicts.

Cognitive therapy uses relearning techniques to challenge automatic thought processes and replace them with alternative ways of coping.

Behavioral therapy helps people learn new behaviors to use in anxiety-producing situations.

VIDEO REVIEW QUESTIONS

1. What is the difference between normal anxiety and abnormal anxiety?

2. Write a vignette in which a person is having a panic attack. Describe how the person feels in his or her own words.

3. Mary and Donna suffer from different anxiety disorders. Discuss how their symptoms differ.

4. In the video, Dr. Shulman describes the case of Paula, a patient with panic disorder, and you meet Mary, Roger, and Patrick, who suffer from panic disorder with agoraphobia. Using these cases, describe how the two disorders differ.

5. Why do you think Donna is afraid of knives rather than, for example, driving across bridges?

6. Dr. Shulman identifies four areas that he believes contribute to the development of anxiety disorders. What are they and how do they relate to the cases of Paula, Phil, and Maria?

7. In the scene in which Dr. Goldstein talks with Mary, identify which parts of the conversation deal with cognitive strategies and which use behavioral strategies.

8. Discuss the controversy over the use of medication in the treatment of anxiety disorders. What side effects are of concern?

9. Describe the various treatment techniques used at Dr. Alan Goldstein's clinic and tell why he thinks it is important that patients leave their regular environment for treatment.

10. Dr. Goldstein says, "It's really important for people who have these problems to eat well." What does he mean and how would you change your diet to reduce your vulnerability to anxiety symptoms?

CASE STUDY

by Judith Rosenberger,
C.S.W., Ph.D.
Hunter College
and
Edith Gould, C.S.W.
Postgraduate Center
for Mental Health

Preston

Preston is a 30-year-old writer who sought psychotherapy because of recurrent episodes of panic and depersonalization. The episodes began when Preston started travelling regularly to conduct his research. Weeks before a flight, Preston would become apprehensive. By the time he was due to leave he would be feeling overwhelmingly anxious over the prospect of flying. He particularly feared "losing it" on the plane and managed to endure these flights only by taking large doses of tranquilizers. A few times when Preston was alone in his hotel room in a foreign city, he gazed at himself in the mirror and suddenly was overcome by a frighteningly eerie sensation of estrangement from his own face and body. During these depersonalization episodes, Preston's voice seemed as if it were emanating from outside himself. His limbs seemed disconnected from his body. The overall sensation was one of fragmentation, as if he were not in one piece. Preston was concerned he was losing his mind. He dealt with these terrifying episodes by taking tranquilizers and going to sleep. He hoped that upon awakening, he would regain a sense of himself as intact.

Explorations of Preston's childhood revealed a history of separation anxiety, which originated in the loss of his mother when he was three years of age and the subsequent emotional unavailability of his father, who went into a severe depression after his wife's death. Preston recalled his determined efforts not to place any further strains on his father by being needy or seeming scared himself. Over the years he even had felt proud and often had been commended for his show of strength and independence as a child.

As the therapeutic process deepened and Preston made more and more connections between his childhood experiences of loss and his present fears, his panic episodes subsided. After two years of treatment, just as Preston was writing the final chapter of his book, he suffered a relapse of his panic disorder. This time the panic episodes sprang forth full-blown in the middle of the night. Preston would awaken suddenly, trembling. His heart would be palpitating and he felt faint. Convinced he was losing his mind, he would call his therapist and listen to the recording of her voice over the answering machine. Sometimes this would temporarily calm him.

During this two-month period of renewed panic attacks, Preston needed to know that he could reach his therapist by telephone at any time. Since panic disorder in many aspects is a reliving, and not only a mental recollection, of an extremely frightening experience, the therapist allowed Preston to reach her as needed. Asking him once more to cope alone beyond his real limits could have instilled another pseudo-solution of premature independence. In fact, Preston responded to the offer of availability by asking for forwarding phone numbers and extra sessions only two or three times. Therapeutic work revealed that the precipitating factor in Preston's relapse was the imminent publication of his book, which symbolized his having achieved maturity and independence. Preston associated maturity and independence with the termination of his therapy and the loss of his therapist. He was fearful of growing up because, in his mind, it signified not needing his therapist any longer. Preston's relapse might be seen as a regression to the position of the helpless child, who could not survive without the protective presence of the parental caregiver.

As these early conflicts around separation and independence were reworked in the therapy sessions, Preston's panic attacks once again subsided. Except for moments where Preston would feel "weird around the edges," as if a panic attack was about to occur, he went into full remission and was able to initiate the termination of his therapy after the fourth year.

CLINICAL DISCUSSION

The outstanding feature of Preston's condition is his fearful feeling that escalates rapidly into terror out of all proportion to the circumstances that trigger it. While excessive fearfulness could indicate any one of several anxiety disorders, it is the intensity, inescapability, and accompanying depersonalization (loss of feeling intact with his body) in Preston's case that point to panic disorder. In phobias, a person can and does avoid such specific phobic objects or situations as flying, enclosed spaces, or social exposure. Preston's anxiety contains elements of all these fears associated with "losing it" on a plane where no escape from fear and humiliation is possible. Preston, however, continues to fly. He also is relieved to learn through therapy that his current anxiety reactions are displaced from their actual source, and that they made sense in their original circumstances. The ritual thoughts and acts of obsessive-compulsive disorder are not present for Preston, nor is he subject to the global vigilance and worrying of generalized anxiety disorder. Preston's life, therefore, is not restricted by the avoidance strategies that characterize these other anxiety disorders; his panic disorder is based on the prospect of being exposed and alone in the face of catastrophic anxiety itself.

Preston's bond with his therapist brings diminished anxiety even before he fully understands its origins. This is common in panic disorder, where the hidden source often is an early and profound loss of important relationships. Also common is the lack of verbalization by and to the child about those early losses when they occurred, leaving the whole experience unarticulated in the child's memory. Not talking about things like a mother's death also conveys the sense that the surrounding feelings are too awful to face. His father's depression after his wife's death and Preston's resolve to help out by being adult beyond his years indicate his lack of a safe haven in which to struggle with his own feelings and thoughts. Very often the person experiencing losses like Preston's may develop a workable coping system for many years, and then in adulthood be overcome with anxious feelings for no apparent reason. The pattern is similar to the person who copes amazingly well in a crisis only to fall apart afterwards. Being on the brink of success and freedom as an adult, in terms of finishing his book, may have activated the unresolved panic Preston felt at a time when he was trapped and powerless as a child. Psychotherapy helped Preston find the connections in memory that made his current anxiety less weird and inexplicable, and also provided safe companionship on the voyage through reexperiencing and articulating fears and vulnerabilities in the present and past alike. With understanding and the working alliance with his therapist, Preston was able to reverse the spiralling fear of fear that becomes the most crippling aspect of panic disorder.

In the most extreme cases, medication may be required early and quickly to arrest the snowball effects of anxiety that seem baseless and therefore without limit. Quelling the anxiety attack itself may be necessary before understanding and psychotherapeutic alliance can get under way. The blunting of anxiety with medication may cloud or even submerge the reexperiencing process that helps resolve the concealed anxiety sources surfacing in panic attacks. However, medication is needed when the fear of fear is only destructive and not useable for insight work. Having medication available as an option can give many people a sense of some control that stops the onrush of anxiety short of outright panic. In Preston's case, which is a moderate form of panic disorder, the strong bond with his therapist, including her willingness to let him exercise some control over when and how he could reach her, provided the secure environment Preston needed to face painful memories and feelings he had avoided for years.

CASE QUESTIONS

1. Explain the relationship between what Preston reports feeling now and his early loss of his mother and his father's unavailability.

2. Give an example from your own experience of how anxiety can build on itself and get out of proportion.

3. What makes Preston's anxiety about airplane trips seem less like fear of flying and more like fear of leaving?

4. What does psychotherapy do to help relieve Preston's anxiety symptoms? How does this differ from using medication alone?

SELF-TEST

1. DSM-III-R abandoned the term _____ in favor of descriptions of specific symptom syndromes of anxiety-based disorders.
- a) anxiety
- b) intrapsychic conflict
- c) nervous
- d) neurosis

2. Albert can hardly bring himself to leave the house alone. He is afraid to take the bus and panics when he has to stand in line at the supermarket. His wife says he is becoming afraid of more and more things. Albert is suffering from
- a) agoraphobia.
- b) obsessive-compulsive disorder.
- c) panic disorder.
- d) simple phobia.

3. In which of the following groups do phobic disorders most commonly occur?
- a) adolescent boys
- b) adolescent girls
- c) middle-aged men
- d) middle-aged women

4. All phobic behaviors are reinforced by
    a) increased self-esteem.
    b) reduction in anxiety.
    c) repetition.
    d) sympathy from others.

5. Darlene is continually bothered by intrusive thoughts about burning down her house. She has trouble concentrating on her work because these objectionable thoughts keep coming up at unpredictable times. Darlene is suffering from a(n)
    a) compulsion.
    b) delusion.
    c) hallucination.
    d) obsession.

6. Which of the following is a cognitive symptom of obsessive-compulsive disorder?
    a) being compelled to count every person that passes the front walk
    b) feeling compelled to avoid stepping on the black tiles on a black-and-white floor
    c) feeling required to go through a long series of silent prayers before sleeping
    d) washing one's hands several hundred times daily

7. Somatoform disorders involve an anxiety-based neurotic pattern in which an individual complains of bodily symptoms
    a) for which no organic basis can be found.
    b) in order to obtain some special treatment.
    c) that involve tissue damage caused by stressors.
    d) which resemble those of their sick parents.

8. Typically, people with hypochondriasis
    a) are malingering to obtain special treatment.
    b) are in poor physical condition.
    c) believe they are seriously ill and cannot recover.
    d) show fear and anxiety of their terminal disease.

9. Regardless of the specific causal factors involved, the basic motivation for developing a conversion disorder seems to be
    a) avoiding anxiety-arousing stress by getting sick.
    b) changing intrapsychic conflicts into physical ailments.
    c) directing others' attention away from one's sexual problems.
    d) punishing significant others for their inattention.

10. In a fugue state, the person not only is amnesic, but
    a) develops a second personality.
    b) has bizarre hallucinations.
    c) loses the ability to communicate.
    d) wanders away from home.

11. One example of a depersonalization disorder is a reported
    a) encounter with extraterrestrials.
    b) feeling of alienation from one's peers.
    c) out-of-body experience.
    d) shunning by others who look through you as though you were not there.

12. Helga's mother is afraid Helga will never get married. Just when things seem to be going well with one of her boyfriends, she does something to drive him away. Even when she went steady for a while, she never seemed emotionally involved. Helga's neurotic style is _____ inhibition.
    a) aggression/assertion
    b) compliance/submission
    c) intimacy/trust
    d) responsibility/independence

13. If two neurotics form a relationship on the basis of complementary patterns and one partner experiences effective therapy, the outcome usually is
    a) a reduction in the anxiety of the other partner.
    b) a disruption of the relationship.
    c) a strengthening of the relationship.
    d) the termination of the neurotic patterns of both partners.

14. Conditioning is to the acquisition of an irrational fear as _____ is to the spread of that fear to other similar stimuli.
    a) discrimination
    b) extinction
    c) generalization
    d) reinforcement

15. All of the following are side effects of drug therapy for neurotics EXCEPT
    a) drowsiness.
    b) increased chances of developing depression.
    c) increased dependence on the drug.
    d) increased tolerance for the drug.

16. Behavioral therapists often place neurotic clients symbolically or actually in situations that come increasingly closer to the situations they find most threatening. This is known as
    a) aversive conditioning.
    b) controlled exposure.
    c) shaping.
    d) systematic desensitization.

17. Cognitive-behavioral therapists attempt to change the inner thoughts and beliefs that may be causing or reinforcing neurotic behavior. This approach is called
    a) cognitive mediation.
    b) exposure and response prevention.
    c) intrapsychic conflict extinction.
    d) systematic desensitization.

18. Abnormal anxiety may be differentiated from the normal, natural anxiety we all experience by
    a) its duration.
    b) its intensity.
    c) an inability to adequately respond to a danger.
    d) all of the above.

19. A person is diagnosed as having generalized anxiety disorder. Which of the following is likely to be one of the person's symptoms?
   a) hallucinations
   b) loss of contact with reality
   c) panic attacks
   d) substance abuse

20. A woman cannot stop herself from worrying about chemicals used in paints and other home remodeling projects. As a result she moves her family out of the home every time she has any work done on her house. She will not let anyone use any glue in the house, and nervously checks and rechecks for any other types of chemicals which may have entered her home. She may be suffering from
   a) chemical phobia.
   b) hypochondriasis.
   c) generalized anxiety disorder.
   d) obsessive-compulsive disorder.

21. Dr. Shulman suggests that four factors contribute to the development of an anxiety disorder. These are constitutional vulnerability, childhood history, personality development, and
   a) genetic predisposition.
   b) family history.
   c) current life stress.
   d) age-related changes.

22. The three major treatments for anxiety disorders include
   a) intensive psychotherapy, group therapy, and medication.
   b) medication, psychoanalysis, and family therapy.
   c) psychoanalysis, cognitive-behavioral therapy, and psychodynamically-based therapy.
   d) medication, psychodynamically-based therapy, and cognitive-behavioral psychotherapy.

23. At the Agoraphobia Clinic, Mary, Patrick, and Robert
   a) were given antidepressant drugs.
   b) experienced the situations that made them anxious while practicing newly learned coping techniques.
   c) used hypnosis to eliminate panic attacks.
   d) were confronted with the feared situation with no advance preparation.

24. Some people feel the use of drugs to treat anxiety disorders is controversial because
   a) the drugs are addictive.
   b) the effect of the drugs during pregnancy is unknown.
   c) the drugs result in sedation and cognitive impairment.
   d) all of the above.

[ANSWERS: 1-d, 2-a, 3-b, 4-b, 5-d, 6-c, 7-a, 8-c, 9-a, 10-d, 11-c, 12-c, 13-b, 14-c, 15-b, 16-b, 17-a, 18-d, 19-c, 20-d, 21-c, 22-d, 23-b, 24-d]

SUGGESTED READINGS

Beck, A. T., Emery, G., with Greenberg, R. L. (1985). *Anxiety disorders and phobias*. New York: Basic Books. This book considers the changing concepts of anxiety, its symptoms and their significance, as well as the cognitive model and cognitive therapy.

Fenichel, O. (1945). *The psychoanalytic theory of neurosis*. New York: Norton. This is a classic work discussing the Freudian understanding of the neuroses (anxiety disorders), including case histories of neurotics with psychoanalytic interpretations. The book also covers schizophrenia, depression, mania, and personality disorders. This is not easy reading.

Goldstein, A., & Steinberg, B. (1987). *Overcoming agoraphobia: Conquering fear of the outside world*. New York: Penguin. This book defines and traces the roots of this crippling disorder through the presentation of case studies and investigations of the family. The authors describe their intensive program of behavioral therapy and discuss drug therapy.

Levenkron, S. (1991). *Treating and understanding crippling habits*. New York: Warner. This study of obsessive-compulsive disorder discusses it as a function of general social dysfunction, dissolving families, insatiable materialism, and distorted ideas of love, care, and commitment. Therapy and the relationship between therapist and patient are discussed.

Rappaport, J. L. (1989). *The boy who couldn't stop washing*. New York: New American Library. A case study of obsessive-compulsive disorder.

Schreiber, F. R. (1973). *Sybil*. New York: Warner. *Sybil* is a fictionalized account of the experience of a woman who suffered from multiple personality disorder. This book describes her 16 personalities and the therapeutic experience leading to their integration.

PSYCHOLOGICAL FACTORS AND PHYSICAL ILLNESS

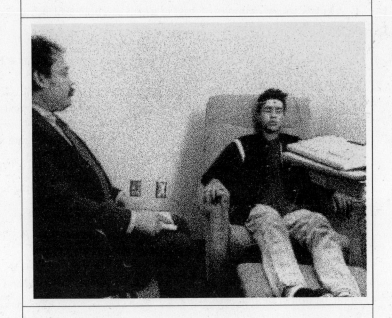

■ UNIT THEME

How do our thoughts, feelings, and behaviors affect our physical well-being? This unit draws on recent research studies in several disciplines that examine the influence of psychological factors on physical health. It focuses on psychological approaches used in the treatment of three medical problems: headaches, heart disease, and cancer.

■ UNIT ASSIGNMENTS

Read: Unit 4. "Psychological Factors and Physical Illness" in *The World of Abnormal Psychology Study Guide*, Toby Kleban Levine, editor (HarperCollins, 1992).

View: Program 4. "Psychological Factors and Physical Illness" in THE WORLD OF ABNORMAL PSYCHOLOGY.

Read: Chapter 7. "Psychological Factors and Physical Illness" in *Abnormal Psychology and Modern Life*, Ninth Edition, by Robert C. Carson and James N. Butcher (HarperCollins, 1992).

■ GOALS AND OBJECTIVES

1. Discuss several examples of ways in which psychological attitudes or lifestyles produce or affect physical problems.

2. Explain how arousal of the autonomic nervous system may cause tissue damage.

3. With reference to the work of Dr. Ronald Glaser and Dr. Janice Kiecolt-Glaser, discuss changes to the immune system that may result from prolonged or extreme stress.

4. Describe the clinical manifestations of coronary heart disease and summarize the evidence linking it to specific personality traits.

5. Identify the symptoms of peptic ulcer and explain how dependency conflicts have been implicated as causal factors.

6. Describe what is thought to be the relationship of the sympathetic nervous system to migraine headaches.

7. Compare the short- and long-term effects of pharmacological and psychological therapy in the treatment of migraines.

8. Discuss the manner in which biofeedback works to treat migraine and other stress-related disorders.

9. Discuss the goals of a psycho-oncologist.

10. Describe anorexia and bulimia, explain some of the psychosocial factors that may contribute to the development of these disorders, and list some of the serious physical conditions that often result.

11. Explain why psychogenic illnesses are typically treated by a combination of medical and psychological measures and describe how such combinations have been used to treat anorexia nervosa.

by Edward S. Katkin, Ph.D.
State University of New York
at Stony Brook

Throughout this course stress will be shown to contribute significantly to the development of a variety of psychological disorders. In this unit we will see how stress also may be involved in the development and maintenance of physical illnesses. In addition, we will consider how behavioral change can alleviate or prevent certain physical disorders.

In psychology and psychiatry the study of the relationship between emotions and disease historically was called psychosomatic medicine. In contemporary usage, however, this term is out of favor, and psychologists refer more generally to the role of psychological factors in physical illness. The most critical point to understand is that the disorders in question are genuine medical syndromes such as ulcers, heart disease, migraine headache, and even cancer; they are not imagined illnesses as in, for example, some of the anxiety-based somatoform disorders.

Currently a great deal of research focuses on the question of whether a person's thoughts, feelings, emotions, or behavior can contribute to physical illness. Most people, indeed, believe that they do, and the weight of scientific evidence is beginning to confirm this idea.

Most current thinking about the relationship between psychological factors and physical illness focuses on the role of the sympathetic nervous system, the part of the **autonomic nervous system** that automatically prepares the body to respond to emergencies. Simply stated, when you are under stress that requires a physical response, such as an athletic competition or the threat of an attack, your sympathetic nervous system will automatically raise your blood pressure, increase your pulse rate, increase the secretion of adrenaline into your bloodstream, and make a number of other biological adjustments that prepare you for the major exertion of energy you need to respond. Psychological states also can arouse the sympathetic nervous system. It is commonly believed that it may be harmful to your health to experience the excessive heart rate and other physical responses to stress without the associated physical exertion that would accompany a genuine emergency.

The video in this unit presents three people who experience serious health complications. In all three, psychological factors may have contributed to the development of their illness. Furthermore, in all three cases you will see how behavioral and psychological treatment is used to alleviate the symptoms of the disease or to help to prevent a relapse.

■ CORONARY HEART DISEASE

Dr. Frank Pink has suffered an apparent attack of angina, a painful feeling in the chest, left arm, and jaw that is usually caused by a spasmodic narrowing of the main arteries that supply blood to the heart. In extreme cases, angina can be fatal, and in many people it is a warning sign of impending **coronary heart disease**. Many factors contribute to heart disease, including genetics, diet, cholesterol level, lack of exercise, smoking, and, importantly, personality factors. People who are characterized as hostile, hard driving, and competitive have been found to be at greater risk for heart disease than others. The precise mechanism by which these personality traits — which are characteristics of the **Type A behavior pattern** — contribute to the development of heart disease is not well known (for that matter, neither is it for the other factors linked to heart disease). Dr. Pink, who admits to being driven, perfectionistic, and prone to hostile outbursts of anger when frustrated, seems to show a hostility pattern characteristic of excess sympathetic nervous system arousal, one effect of which could be the constriction of coronary arteries.

For these reasons, Dr. Pink has entered a stress management program to learn to relax systematically. It is hoped that stress management techniques can prevent overarousal of his sympathetic nervous system. He also is learning to manage his stress responses and to change his lifestyle, in the hope that such changes will prevent the occurrence of a heart attack. Although stress management programs are increasingly popular, as yet no hard scientific evidence proves that they are successful. Much evaluative research is in process to develop a precise understanding of the psychological factors that contribute to heart disease and the most effective techniques to prevent psychologically induced cardiac disorders.

■ MIGRAINE HEADACHE

You also will meet Dillon Vargas, a teenager who has suffered from **migraine** headaches for most of his life. Migraine is a form of headache that usually produces throbbing pains, localized on one side of the head. The pains often are preceded by auras, commonly in the form of scintillating spots in the visual field or a pattern of zig-zag lines. The migraine sufferer usually shows unusual sensitivity to light and sound and may also experience nausea and vomiting. Migraine is not considered a **simple tension headache** and does not respond to aspirin or other standard medications in the way that typical tension headaches do.

Although the actual mechanism of migraine is not well understood, it is generally believed to be the result of a disruption of the regulation of the arteries that provide blood to the brain. Furthermore, it is believed that this disruption is triggered by overarousal of the sympathetic nervous system. Strong evidence in support of the role of sympathetic overarousal is derived from the observation that the most effective medical treatment for the prevention of migraines is propranolol, a drug that blocks the action of the sympathetic nervous system. The use of propranolol for migraine prevention is not always indicated, however, for the drug may have undesirable side effects. Pharmacological treatment also is available to try to reduce the migraine after its onset, but the drugs prescribed for this purpose also have undesirable side effects and are not very effective.

For these reasons, interest in the use of stress management techniques for the prevention of migraine has increased. The logic of using stress management is that the migraine is likely to result from overexcitation of the sympathetic nervous system. Why this overarousal results in migraine for some people is not understood, but migraine affects about 20 million Americans. Migraine runs in families, and it is likely that one must be genetically predisposed to suffer from the disorder. As with all physical disorders that are presumed to have psychological causal factors, an interaction of genetic and environmental stress factors is likely.

In addition to learning relaxation techniques, Dillon also uses **biofeedback** to help manage his stress. Biofeedback is simply an electronically based technique that enables a person to monitor the effects of the sympathetic nervous system on, for example, heart rate, skin temperature, or muscle tension. By getting clear feedback about these functions an individual may gain control over them and learn to relax body functions more efficiently.

■ CANCER

Kathleen Morell has breast cancer, and she believes that severe emotional stress brought it on. She also believes that if she practices relaxation techniques and changes her lifestyle she can prevent the cancer from relapsing.

Is it possible that one's emotions can actually cause cancer? No scientific evidence supports this idea, but some very interesting data suggest that it may be possible. Cancer is linked to a failure of the body's normal immune system, and an increasing body of scientific data indicates that psychological stress can compromise the normal functioning of the immune system. The mechanism appears to involve the effects of hormones that are triggered by sympathetic arousal upon the ability of certain immune cells to proliferate. The branch of psychology that studies the effects of psychological stress on immune functioning is known as **psychoneuroimmunology** (PNI). So far, PNI research has demonstrated that a variety of stress situations can interfere with immune function, but to date no definitive proof supports the conclusion that the degree of this interference is sufficient to cause cancer. Probably, in order to develop cancer, an individual also must have a genetic predisposition.

No effective psychological treatment to prevent or cure cancer is known. Nevertheless, many cancer patients find that their adjustment to the stress of having cancer can be helped by participating in support groups. A recent study found that women with breast cancer who participated in post-surgery group therapy lived longer than a matched group of women who did not participate in such groups. Thus it appears that the emotional support that is derived from psychotherapy may prolong the lives of cancer patients, although it is not understood what the underlying mechanism of such a treatment effect might be.

■ SUMMARY

In summary, stress probably can contribute to the development of heart disease, migraine headache, and other illnesses that are affected by disruption of the sympathetic nervous system, and treatment directed at managing stress response may indirectly contribute to alleviation and prevention of such illnesses. Stress also may disrupt normal immune function, but the implications of that for disease are less clear.

■ KEY TERMS

The following terms are used in the text and/or the television programs.

Anorexia nervosa	An eating disorder that primarily affects women in adolescence and early adulthood. The features include intense abhorrence of obesity and the insistence that one is fat, loss of at least 25 percent of original body weight, and a refusal to maintain weight within the lower limits of what is normal for age and height.
Antigen	A foreign substance that enters the body and is attacked by the immune system.
Autonomic nervous system	The section of the nervous system that regulates the internal organs.
Behavioral medicine	An interdisciplinary approach to the treatment of physical disorders that emphasizes the role of psychological factors in the occurrence, maintenance, and prevention of physical illness.
Biofeedback	A technique that enables a person to influence his or her own physiological processes by monitoring immediate feedback about bodily changes as they occur.
Bulimia nervosa	An eating disorder that primarily affects women in adolescence and early adulthood. The features include a fear of being unable to stop eating voluntarily, preoccupation with weight gain, and attempts to lose weight through binge eating, self-induced vomiting, and overuse of laxatives and diuretics. Although aware of the problem's abnormality, the individual continues the pattern amid secrecy, guilt, and self-deprecation.
Coronary heart disease (CHD)	A potentially lethal blockage of the arteries that supply blood to the heart muscle; clinical manifestations include severe chest pain, myocardial infarction (a blockage of coronary arteries), and disturbance of electrical conduction in the heart muscle.

Essential hypertension	High blood pressure that has no apparent physical cause; assumed to be due to psychological or emotional stress.
Health psychology	A subspecialty within behavioral medicine that deals with psychology's contributions to diagnosis, treatment, and prevention of psychological components of physical illnesses.
Hypertension	Chronic high blood pressure.
Immune system	The blood, thymus, bone marrow, spleen, and lymph nodes that make up the body's defense against such foreign substances as bacteria, viruses, or tumors.
Migraine	An intensely painful, recurring headache; starts with reduced flow of blood to certain parts of the brain followed by a rush of blood to the previously deprived areas, causing rapid expansion of the arteries and stimulation of local nerve endings, which produces the pain; assumed to be related to overarousal of the sympathetic nervous system.
Peptic ulcer	A stomach wound that results when the stomach's acidic digestive juices are produced in excess and eat away the lining of the stomach. Organic factors as well as negative emotional states can lead to peptic ulcers.
Placebo effect	The increased chance of improvement in the condition of someone who believes that treatment will be effective as compared to patients who are pessimistic or neutral.
Psychogenic illness	A physical illness that is psychologically induced or maintained (formerly referred to as psychophysiologic disorders and psychosomatic disorders).
Psychoneuroimmunology (PNI)	The study of the psychological influences on the nervous system's control of immune responsiveness.
Simple tension headache	A headache that occurs when emotional stress seems to lead to contraction of the muscles surrounding the skull which, in turn, results in vascular constrictions, causing head pain.
Type A behavior pattern	A behavior pattern involving excessive competitive drive, impatience or time urgency, and hostility. The Type A pattern — particularly, the hostility element — is thought to be associated with coronary heart disease.
Type B behavior pattern	A behavior pattern that is defined in terms of the absence of Type A characteristics.

VIDEO NOTES

■ INTRODUCTION
• Stress causes bodily changes, e.g., in pulse, heart rate, respiration, blood pressure, and rates of hormone secretion. These changes can be very adaptive in threatening situations but create wear and tear on the blood vessels when they are not accompanied by physical activity. Whether these changes contribute to the onset of disease is unknown.

■ CORONARY HEART DISEASE
(Case Illustration: Dr. Frank Pink)
• Numerous risk factors for coronary heart disease have been identified. Some, like age, gender, and family history, can be assessed but not modified. Others, like blood pressure, cholesterol, weight, lifestyle, and psychological style, can be both assessed and modified.

• Dr. Pink's psychological assessment found that he was anxious, under stress, had had a number of significant changes in his life, and exhibited a Type A behavior pattern. The Type A behavior pattern includes an excessively competitive drive in the absence of well-defined goals, impatience, accelerated speech and motor activities, and hostility. Many psychologists now believe that free-floating and interpersonal hostility are the key elements of the Type A behavior pattern that are linked to heart disease, although research is needed to understand how this behavior interacts with medical history and lifestyle to result in illness.

• Dr. Pink was introduced to stress management to (1) help him understand how to control his environment; (2) teach him how to control how he responds to stressors; and (3) reduce his hostility. Among the techniques he learned in a six-week stress management course are: deep muscle relaxation to attain physiological control and learn to differentiate between tension and relaxation; new methods of goal setting, e.g., allowing for a lack of perfection; finding relaxing activities (in Dr. Pink's case, model plane flying).

■ MIGRAINE HEADACHES
(Case Illustration: Dillon Vargas)

• Migraine headaches can last from minutes to days. They usually affect one side of the head and result in severe pain and throbbing. Exposure to loud noises and bright lights can be excruciating. Some migraine headaches are preceded about 30 minutes before onset by an aura, which might consist of seeing zigzag lines or flashing lights, a tingling or numbness in one's arms and legs, confusion, or restlessness.

• As many as 20 million Americans get migraine headaches every year, with women outnumbering men three to one. Five to seven percent of children get migraines.

• The actual mechanism of migraine is not well understood but is thought to involve uncontrollable constrictions and dilations of the blood vessels in the brain. These are actions of the sympathetic division of the autonomic nervous system that mobilizes when we are in danger. This aroused state seems to trigger migraine headaches in some people.

Other triggers are thought to include physical and emotional stress, changes in altitude or weather, poor sleeping habits, and, in women, hormonal changes . Certain foods, e.g., red wine, aged cheese, and chocolate, also have been implicated. Family history plays a role 70 to 80 percent of the time.

• Treatment of migraine falls into three categories:

Abortive methods treat the headache after it has begun.

Prophylactic methods are regular actions that prevent the onset of the headache. The drug, propanolol, for example, which is widely used to treat heart disease because it prevents the heart from being accelerated, is thought to help prevent migraines by blocking the action of the sympathetic nervous system.

Palliative methods lessen the distress of the headache.

• Most pharmacological interventions have serious side effects.

• Researchers now believe that since stress can be a trigger (perhaps in combination with other factors), stress reduction, including relaxation exercises and biofeedback, can help people keep their arousal states under sufficient control to prevent the onset of the headache.

• Biofeedback provides individuals with immediate information about ongoing physiological processes of which they are not usually conscious, e.g., heart rate, blood pressure, muscular tension, hand temperature (cold hands are a signal that the autonomic nervous system is aroused).

• Recent research indicates that the success of this kind of self-regulatory treatment is virtually identical to that of the most widely prescribed drug for migraine.

■ BREAST CANCER
(Case Illustration: Kathleen Morell)
• The major risk factors in breast cancer are being over 50 years of age, not having had a child, not having a child until after age 30, and having a family history of breast cancer.

• No evidence exists that emotional trauma can directly cause disease, but many studies associate stressful life events with higher levels of disease. Current research is trying to determine how the brain, emotions, and the immune and endocrine systems interact. This field is called psychoneuroimmunology (PNI).

• The immune system functions to distinguish what is self from what is not. If, for example, a virus or bacteria (a not-self) comes in from the outside, the immune system launches two basic kinds of defenses: B cells and T cells.

  B-cells are a type of lymphocyte that produce a product that goes into the bloodstream to neutralize viruses, bacteria, and parasites though the release of antibodies.

  T-cells function in hand-to-hand combat. They fight the actual bad cells.

• The immune system and nervous system communicate with one another through small proteins called neuropeptides. The major site in the brain where neuropeptides are produced is the limbic system, the same part of the brain responsible for emotions. As we experience various emotions, we release corresponding neuropeptides into the bloodstream where they proceed to bind with various cells in the body, including those of the immune system.

• Research studies have shown that the immune system can be modulated by psychological stress. Current studies are exploring how this works and how it relates to long-term and short-term stressors.

• In addition to a full range of medical and surgical treatments, some cancer patients also engage in psychological therapy. Such therapies are concerned with quality of life issues; they provide emotional support and take care of the spiritual needs of people. Both support groups and stress reduction therapies are common.

• Two recent studies suggest that psychological support may have biological consequences.

  Dr. Sandra Levy has found that women who felt they had lots of social support had greater levels of natural killer cell activity than did those who did not.

  A study by Dr. David Spiegel found that patients who participated in group therapy survived an average of 17 months longer from the onset of intervention than women who were not in such a group.

VIDEO REVIEW QUESTIONS

1. Identify several physiological changes that are known to result from stress. Create one scenario in which such changes would be beneficial and another in which they would be detrimental. Explain the different results.

2. Which risk factors for coronary heart disease are controllable and which are not?

3. Describe specific behaviors Dr. Pink exhibited that suggest he has a Type A personality.

4. What were the goals of the stress management program Dr. Pink attended?

5. What alternatives to psychological treatments had been tried with Dillon and with what effect?

6. Describe what is thought to be the connection between action of the sympathetic division of the autonomic nervous system and the onset of migraine headaches.

7. How has biofeedback worked to reduce the frequency with which Dillon has headaches?

8. What is known about stress and the onset of cancer?

9. Describe the relationship between the limbic system and the immune system.

10. Discuss the goals of psychological therapy in the treatment of Kathleen Morrell.

CASE STUDY

by Judith Rosenberger, C.S.W., Ph.D. Hunter College and Edith Gould, C.S.W. Postgraduate Center for Mental Health

John

The first time I remember getting a headache was my first week in school. I was in kindergarten, and the class was getting in a circle for story time. I started to feel queasy and then these little squiggly lines were all around the teacher as I looked at her. I closed my eyes and laid down. The teacher thought I was just tired so she didn't say anything. It hurt so badly that I couldn't even hear the story, and after that we all had a nap anyway. By the time my mom came to get me I was all right enough so nobody knew anything had happened. I didn't have another headache for a long time after that— maybe a year.

The next time, though, it was worse. When the squiggles came and the headache started I tried to just close my eyes and wait it out, but my new teacher yelled at me because she thought I was dozing off in class. I tried to pay attention but then I threw up. It was so embarrassing! They called my mom and she took me home to bed. Everybody figured I had the flu or something. Again, people mainly just let me sleep it off. So it seemed like maybe I did just have the flu.

By the time I got to junior high school, though, there was clearly something wrong and I definitely had headaches. My mom thought I was anxious about starting a new school, and I guess she was afraid to baby me any more, so she insisted I go anyway. I started buying aspirin on my own, but that didn't help. And a couple of times when I saw the school nurse because I was throwing up a lot I tried to tell her I had headaches. But she said stuff like, "You're too young to have headaches. Wait till you grow up. Then you'll have reasons for headaches!" It was confusing.

I noticed the headaches got worse when I got tense, but then I got tense because I was afraid I'd have a headache and be out of it or sick and look like a jerk to my friends. Nobody else seemed to have these things, and they teased me about being a wimp. Things got worse when I played sports or had a big test. The whole thing was a nightmare, and it just got worse the more upset I became. I started making excuses for everything so I wouldn't have to go places or do things where I might get sick. It was so gradual you couldn't say when it really began. Over time I started organizing my life to avoid stuff because if I got into the middle of something and had to leave because I started to feel queasy, the guys would be disgusted with me and the girls would be sort of nice but turned off. I felt lousy about all this and started to feel there was something really wrong with my head.

My mom also got worried. She thought I was depressed. She took me to a counselor, Mrs. Williams. Mrs. Williams started out asking me about my feelings, but pretty soon she was really interested in when my headaches occurred. That was when the patterns started to get clear to me. I saw I was in this cycle of trying to avoid stress so I wouldn't get a headache but then feeling even more stressed out by being different, and that the headaches were the key. And she brought my mom in and we all kept track for a while. Plus, Mrs. Williams was the first one who asked about the squiggles. She called it an aura, and said it was a warning of what was coming. And she also asked about being bothered by light. That was when we put it together that going home and sleeping wasn't just avoiding problems. When I went home to sleep it was quiet and dark and that let my brain relax, too. So it wasn't just people or challenges I was avoiding; it was noise and stimulation. Of course, I was avoiding people and challenges too, because that would often seem to start things off.

Just having an idea about how everything made sense in a way I never had realized seemed to help a lot. I'd say I relaxed some because I didn't feel so weird or unsure if I really was just a wimp. The headaches slacked off, but Mrs. Williams said we had to check out a lot of possible causes. She had me and my mom go for a whole day to a clinic where they did a lot of tests and told me I had migraines. What a relief! First of all, I had something. It wasn't just my imagination or a bad attitude. Plus, I realized that in the back of my mind I'd started to wonder if I had a brain tumor or something really terrible like that. When you don't know anything for sure, you can imagine everything.

I started taking some medicine that definitely gave me some relief, except not all the way. Plus, I started feeling light-headed when I would stand too fast, and sometimes when I was in gym, too. That started to worry me all over again. So we worked back and forth, all of us — Mom, Mrs. Williams, the doctors in the city, and me, too — keeping track and balancing pros and cons.

I've got to say it felt really good to have the support of people who weren't making fun or doubting me. That in itself was a big help. I started to feel more confident that when I felt early signs of a migraine coming on, I could work with it, keep myself calm and try to reduce stress, rather than just feeling like I was about to be ambushed by my brain and laughed at by my friends. Now I'm pretty well on top of the situation. I may get a headache every few months, but less and less. And, I can start to feel them coming on and work with the build-up by training myself to relax. If I can cut out whatever is causing the stress, often I can head them off altogether. If I ever need the medicine again I'll take it, because it helped me regain my confidence even if it didn't do the whole job. There's definitely something about the way my system works that makes me get headaches when other people don't. But when I stop worrying about it or being ashamed, it's not such a big deal.

CLINICAL DISCUSSION

John's experience demonstrates how a physical problem — in this case headaches — can be inextricable from psychological factors — such as John's worry and stress. Many people think of this as the mind/body question: does stress and worry create illness, or does illness create stress and worry? John clearly shows us that the answer is both, but that confusion about the mind/body question can create many obstacles to understanding that can make both stress and physical problems worse, and even can result in misguided treatment. The bodily basis of the symptom had to be ruled out before other sources could be considered in depth.

Before diagnosing, a therapist must listen carefully not only to the symptoms described and the patient's explanation, but also to features surrounding the onset of symptoms and their ebb and flow over time. Mrs. Williams had to decode the symptom by looking for alternate explanations until she could rule out something, rather than assuming from the outset that one explanation would be adequate. Bringing in the mother as well as other experts to discern how body and mind might be interacting is part of diagnosing psychological factors in physical illness, and also a part of treating a problem in which both mind and body are playing a part. As John explained, treating the body alone by way of medication provided some relief, but the fuller recovery depended on his being able to reverse a pattern of stress induction that was psychologically based. Knowledge of his own mind/body interaction was helpful in two ways: it provided a specific technique for calming himself down under stress, and it provided understanding that reduced his mystification and humiliation about having something "wrong with my head."

Tracing the exact starting point of a physical problem with psychological components can be difficult and often is impossible. We don't know if John was upset, as many children are, for instance, by the separation from home that preceded his first headache in kindergarten. We do know from his report that in junior high school, he linked the increase in headaches with his mother's feeling that she had to baby him less. And, we know also from his own words that his headaches were helped when he felt understood and supported by people who were important to him, like his mom, Mrs. Williams, and later the doctors. Yet many children who are upset at leaving home or having family misunderstandings do not get headaches. Perhaps they communicate their feelings more directly or have better resistance to the stress and worry they feel. Looking at it from the other side, a medical problem like a headache can create a greater need for understanding and support rather than being the result of a shortage. So the question of psychological causation or etiology of physical illness result of a shortage. So the question of psychological causation or etiology of physical illness is blurry in John's case, as it is in most cases.

In addition to family relationships, factors in John's physical and social environments had important effects on whether John did or did not have a headache. He mentions the overstimulation of light and noise, and being in groups of people, which seem to be part of the course of the illness. He also describes how the headache lessened if he was allowed to go home and sleep in a quiet, dark room. Besides returning home to mother, the environmental quality may have played a role. His social environment also seems to have had an impact on the course and intensity of John's headaches. The attitudes of his friends were devastating. No doubt this was more the case for John as a teenager than it might be for an adult. Yet the attitudes of important people — friends, bosses, teachers — play vital roles in shaping how the individual may start to explain his problems to himself. John's mother was afraid of babying her adolescent son, and John became self-critical: was he really just a wimp? Had he been a girl, or very young or very old, would there have been less resistance to hearing that he was in pain?

Besides gender and age, cultural and social group differences exist in the way the body expresses psychological distress, and in the degree to which physical distress is permitted expression through complaints. Since boys of John's group apparently were expected to leave home for kindergarten, physical illness became the only available avenue for release. At the same time, had John not been granted exemption on the basis of appearing ill, he might have learned to struggle with incipient headaches spontaneously to the degree that the headaches were psychologically based. Part of the mind/body debate is about removing physical illness through mental effort. This area is as blurry as the area of causation. Still, when a symptom as ambiguous as a headache is suppressed psychologically, and no discernible medical basis like the tumor John feared exists, it is essentially "cured."

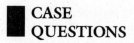

CASE QUESTIONS

1. The term biopsychosocial refers to the manner in which the convergence of factors from the body, mind, and environment can create and/or prolong a symptom. Apply a biopsychosocial framework to John's headaches: What role might each part of this framework play in explaining how his headaches started and continued?

2. Mrs. Williams performed a vital role when she sent John for a diagnostic work-up before she initiated any treatment. This illustrates the importance of ruling out various parts of the biopsychosocial spectrum before settling on an explanation and approach to treating the symptom. What kinds of things are mentioned in the case discussion that would need to be ruled out before selecting a treatment for John's headaches that centered on reducing or managing stressful feelings?

3. The case material contains physical clues that point to a migraine headache pattern for John, as compared to headaches that are linked strictly to tension or muscle strain or the like. What are these clues and what do you know from reading the chapter or seeing the video that explains the biological basis of these clues?

SELF-TEST

1. **Before DSM-III, psychogenic illnesses were called psychophysiologic or _____ disorders.**
   a) pathogenic
   b) psychosomatic
   c) somatopsychic
   d) stress-related

2. **Even when a treatment has no relevant physiological effects, a patient who believes the treatment is going to be effective may show improvement. This is known as**
   a) faith healing.
   b) self-hypnosis.
   c) the Dopler effect.
   d) the placebo effect.

3. **All of the following processes are involved in autonomic nervous system arousal EXCEPT**
   a) decreased blood pressure.
   b) flushing.
   c) increased perspiration.
   d) pupillary dilation.

4. **Which of the following is an example of the body's "adaptiveness" without "intelligence?"**
   a) production of antibodies to fight a cold virus
   b) production of white cells to fight infection
   c) rejection of a transplanted organ
   d) secretion of growth-producing hormones

5. **All of the following are primary components of the immune system EXCEPT**
   a) blood.
   b) bone marrow.
   c) spleen.
   d) thyroid.

6. **All of the following are subpopulations of white blood cells EXCEPT**
   a) B-cells.
   b) erithrocytes.
   c) macrophages.
   d) T-cells.

7. **T-cells are a crucial line of defense against all of the following EXCEPT**
   a) common bacterial infections.
   b) fungal infections.
   c) intracellular bacterial infections.
   d) viral infections.

8. **A relatively new science investigating the psychological influences on the nervous system control of immune responsiveness is**
   a) immunopsychoneurology.
   b) neuroimmunopsychology.
   c) neuropsychoimmunology.
   d) psychoneuroimmunology.

9. All of the following are lifestyle-related patterns that contribute to physical health problems EXCEPT
    a) consuming high fiber foods.
    b) excessive alcohol use.
    c) overeating.
    d) smoking cigarettes.

10. Xavier is known as a go-getter. He seems to thrive on competition no matter what it is. For several months in a row he has been awarded the top salesperson bonus. His coworkers are careful not to stir him up because he is so impatient and angry. His jogging buddies say he talks faster than he runs. According to Friedman and Rosenman, Xavier is probably a _____ personality.
    a) Type A
    b) Type B
    c) Type C
    d) Type D

11. Some consensus seems to be developing that the _____ component of the Type A behavior pattern is the most closely correlated with coronary artery deterioration.
    a) accelerated speech/motor activity
    b) hyperaggression/hostility
    c) impatience/time urgency
    d) introversion/extroversion

12. Stress usually results in higher blood pressure because of the
    a) addition of liquids to the blood.
    b) constriction of blood vessels.
    c) development of atherosclerosis.
    d) increase in the heart rate.

13. Hypertension is a major risk factor for all of the following EXCEPT
    a) amenorrhea.
    b) blindness.
    c) cardiovascular disease.
    d) kidney failure.

14. An ulcer is a small crater-like wound caused by
    a) a buildup of the stomach's mucosa.
    b) a diet excessively high in fiber.
    c) an excessive flow of acidic digestive juices.
    d) stretching of the stomach wall.

15. The second phase of a migraine headache is characterized by a(n)
    a) "aura" that signals the end of pain.
    b) contraction of the muscles surrounding the skull.
    c) reduced flow of blood to the brain.
    d) sudden rush of blood to the brain.

16. **Autonomic responses to various stimuli can be learned by**
    a) classical conditioning.
    b) operant conditioning.
    c) both a and b.
    d) neither a nor b.

17. **All of the following statements about psychosocial measures for treating psychogenic diseases are true EXCEPT**
    a) behavior therapy has been used to cure intractable sneezing.
    b) general relaxation treatment has been successful in alleviating simple tension headaches.
    c) one-to-one verbally oriented psychotherapies have been relatively ineffective.
    d) psychoanalytic therapy has been highly successful in treating psychogenic disorders.

18. **Biofeedback devices monitor an individual's _____ and provide feedback on what they are doing.**
    a) aches and pains
    b) autonomic functions
    c) cognitive structures
    d) immune responses

19. **Some situations threaten a person's physical or psychological well-being and cause the body to fight and stand its ground or flee. The body's reaction is called the**
    a) stress syndrome.
    b) emotion upset.
    c) fight or flight response.
    d) sympathetic response.

20. **In the fight or flight response**
    a) blood circulation decreases.
    b) heart rate increases.
    c) respiration and pulse decrease.
    d) wear and tear on the blood vessels is reduced.

21. **Migraines are**
    a) muscle tension headaches.
    b) a disorder of the cerebral vasculature.
    c) a function of the parasympathetic nervous system.
    d) easily controlled by modern prescription drugs.

22. **Treatments for migraines fall into three categories: abortive, palliative, and**
    a) prophylactic.
    b) intrapsychic.
    c) suppressive.
    d) biophysic.

23. **Relaxation techniques, such as those used by Dillon,**
    a) have been ineffective in controlling migraine headaches.
    b) may indirectly prevent the sympathetic nervous system from becoming overexcited.
    c) are ineffective for someone with a genetic predisposition for migraines.
    d) are always used in conjunction with medication.

24. **The technique that involves providing individuals with immediate information about ongoing physiological processes that they are usually not consciously aware of is**

    a) Transcendental Meditation.

    b) deep muscle relaxation.

    c) biofeedback.

    d) appraisal control.

25. **Neuropeptides are produced in the limbic system, the part of the brain which is the seat of**

    a) emotions.

    b) anger.

    c) the immune system.

    d) personality.

26. **Kathleen Morrell's decision to participate in group therapy with other women who have cancer would seem to be a good idea in view of Dr. Levy's research on social support systems and the immune system. Dr. Levy's research found that women with cancer who felt they had lots of social support**

    a) rarely developed other diseases.

    b) showed a much higher five-year survival rate.

    c) had greater levels of natural killer cell activity than those who did not.

    d) lived three times as long as those who did not.

[ANSWERS: 1-b, 2-d, 3-a, 4-c, 5-d, 6-b, 7-a, 8-d, 9-a, 10-a, 11-b, 12-b, 13-a, 14-c, 15-d, 16-c, 17-d, 18-b, 19-c, 20-b, 21-b, 22-a, 23-b, 24-c, 25-a, 26-c]

SUGGESTED READINGS

Achterberg, J. (1985). *Imagery in healing: Shamanism and modern medicine.* Boston: New Science Library/Shambhala Publications. This book emphasizes experiences, beliefs, motives, and the role of the imagination in health.

Benson, G., with Klipper, M. Z. (1975). *The relaxation response.* New York: Avon Books. This book explains scientific data and philosophical writings from East and West on the innate capability to control our reactions to stress.

Borysenko, J. (1988). *Minding the body, mending the mind.* Reading, MA: Addison-Wesley. Case histories illustrate the power of the mind in healing.

Charlesworth, E. A., & Nathan, R. G. (1984). *Stress management: A comprehensive guide to wellness.* New York: Ballentine Books. This book defines stress and introduces a variety of management techniques for coping with stress.

Cousins, N. (1989). *Head first: The biology of hope and the healing power of the human spirit.* New York: Penguin. The famous positive thinker presents evidence of how an optimistic outlook and a strong relationship with the doctor can decrease pain and increase survival.

Friedman, M., & Ulmer, D. (1984). *Treating type A behavior and your heart.* New York: Fawcett and Crest. Based on the original research into this personality type and its relationship to heart disease, this book contains practical approaches to changing lifestyle.

Kabat-Zinn, J. (1990). *Full catastrophe living: Using the wisdom of your body and mind to face stress, pain and illness.* New York: Delacorte Press. This is a step-by-step guide to the Stress Reduction Clinic at the University of Massachusetts Medical Center directed by the author. The program is based on the use of mindfulness meditation to learn to cope with the stresses of life.

Schwartz, M. S. (Ed.). (1987). *Biofeedback: A practitioner's guide.* New York: The Guilford Press. This history of biofeedback techniques considers their application to various disorders, including hypertension, headache, and elimination disorders as well as various professional and research issues.

UNIT 5

PERSONALITY
DISORDERS

UNIT THEME

Personality disorders are among the hardest disorders to diagnose and many are equally difficult to treat. Yet one in every ten people is afflicted. This unit identifies 11 different personality disorders and concentrates on four: narcissistic, antisocial, borderline, and obsessive-compulsive.

UNIT ASSIGNMENTS

Read: Unit 5. "Personality Disorders" in *The World Of Abnormal Psychology Study Guide*, Toby Kleban Levine, editor (HarperCollins, 1992).

View: Program 5. "Personality Disorders" in THE WORLD OF ABNORMAL PSYCHOLOGY.

Read: Chapter 8. "Personality Disorders" in *Abnormal Psychology and Modern Life*, Ninth Edition, by Robert C. Carson and James N. Butcher (HarperCollins, 1992).

GOALS AND OBJECTIVES

1. Describe features that all personality disorders seem to have in common and explain why such disorders are difficult to diagnose.

2. Describe and differentiate among the following personality disorders: paranoid, schizoid, and schizotypal.

3. Describe and differentiate among the following personality disorders: histrionic, narcissistic, antisocial, and borderline.

4. Describe and differentiate among the following personality disorders: avoidant, dependent, obsessive-compulsive, and passive-aggressive.

5. Describe and differentiate between the following personality disorders: self-defeating and sadistic.

6. Summarize what is known and suspected about biological, psychological, and sociocultural factors that may cause personality disorders.

7. List several reasons why personality disorders are especially resistant to therapy.

8. List and describe five characteristics that are typical of antisocial personalities.

9. List and explain several biological, psychological, and environmental factors that may contribute to the development of an antisocial personality disorder.

10. Evaluate the success of traditional psychotherapy in treating the antisocial personality disorder.

UNIT OVERVIEW

by Edward S. Katkin, Ph.D.
State University of New York
at Stony Brook

This unit looks at a set of abnormal behavior patterns called **personality disorders**. In modern thinking, personality disorders are not considered diseases, but rather aberrations in the development of an individual's personality. This is a critical distinction. In such clinical syndromes as anxiety disorders or mood disorders, patients typically are aware of some aspect of their own behavior that is disturbing or unsatisfying to them that they would like to change or remediate. People with personality disorders typically do not see the disturbed behavior as a problem; they accept the behavior as a normal part of themselves. Such people usually interpret difficulties in their lives as emanating from circumstances or from others, not from themselves.

Psychologists believe that each individual is unique, demonstrates some predictability, and tends to possess characteristic ways of perceiving the world and reacting to others. These personality (or character) traits are developed over a lifetime. Their development is influenced by significant other people, but most especially by parents. Many theorists also believe that certain characteristics of temperaments, such as activity level, gregariousness, and shyness, may be inherited, and that they affect how other people react to the individual. Thus the development both of individual personality traits and of the total personality may be the result of the interaction of genetic, social, and environmental factors.

Personality disorders, therefore, are personalities that have developed as any personality will, but along the way the emerging personality acquired characteristics that interfere with the establishment of normal healthy relationships. Personality disorders have been categorized according to some shared characteristics into three subgroups, or clusters. The first of these includes the **paranoid, schizoid**, and **schizotypal** personality disorders; the second cluster includes the **histrionic, narcissistic, antisocial,** and **borderline** personality disorders; the third cluster includes the **avoidant, dependent, obsessive-compulsive,** and **passive-aggressive** personality disorders.

Although each of these disorders has its own unique characteristics, they all share common features. Most importantly, people with personality disorders frequently experience seriously disrupted interpersonal relationships. These typically create greater distress for others than they do for the individual. In fact, it is frequently due to the other people that the person with the disorder is referred to treatment. The second characteristic is that these patients typically do not appear to be seriously disturbed. In many cases their behavior is an exaggerated form of tendencies that can be found in all of us, making the diagnosis of personality disorders very difficult. For instance, many of us become somewhat anxious when our living space gets excessively disorganized. We do a frenzied bit of cleaning and get relief only when things are in their place. As we will see in the case presented in the video, however, for a person with an obsessive-compulsive personality disorder, this need for order can become all consuming and interfere with daily life and relationships. It also is difficult to estimate the prevalence of personality disorders in society. Because most people with such disorders do not present themselves for treatment (they do not feel or appear to others to be "mentally ill"), they are not easily identified in epidemiological surveys. They come to the attention of psychologists when they get into trouble with authority, e.g., at school, work, or with the law.

Four personality disorders are introduced in the video: narcissistic, antisocial, borderline, and obsessive-compulsive. The text discusses all types of personality disorders and gives special attention to the antisocial personality disorder.

■ OBSESSIVE-COMPULSIVE PERSONALITY DISORDER

John, the obsessive-compulsive patient described by Dr. Knafo in the video, needs to keep his life clean and well-ordered. The term obsessive-compulsive refers to John's obsessive thoughts about cleanliness and order and his compulsive behavior, which goes as far as alphabetizing his refrigerator contents and marking the exact place on his bed sheets where they are to be turned. All of us can identify with people who have a strong tendency to keep their own space neat and clean — most of us have had parents who have tended to be more compulsive about neatness than we were. The distinguishing feature of the obsessive-compulsive disorder, however, is that the individual's behavior interferes with normal relationships as well as with the accomplishment of normal daily routines. Yet it is difficult for people like John to see the problem. They believe if only other people would accommodate to their ways, everything would be all right!

■ NARCISSISTIC PERSONALITY DISORDER

The narcissistic personality is one who is preoccupied with receiving attention, and who seems to have an exaggerated sense of self-importance. These patients find it almost impossible to maintain healthy relationships because they have no ability to see anybody else's perspective or needs, and they have an insatiable desire for attention and nurturance. In the video you will see a professional actress portray a woman with a narcissistic personality disorder arguing with her boyfriend. Her emotional outburst appears to be out of proportion to the problem, and she focuses all of her complaints on her feeling of not being respected enough, loved enough, or attended to enough. The cause of narcissistic disorder is not well understood. Psychodynamic theorists speculate that a disruption in the early relationship with the mother may contribute to the development of narcissism. Other theorists argue that events later in life are equally important. Still other theorists argue that personality disorders may be genetically transmitted, but as yet no serious evidence supports this.

■ ANTISOCIAL PERSONALITY DISORDER

Whereas people with narcissistic disorders are difficult to live with, people with antisocial disorders are potentially dangerous. The cases of Dean and Patrick, presented in the video, are quite typical. Superficially, these patients look normal, possess at least average intelligence, and present themselves with a certain degree of charm and social skill. It is only when you learn about their behavior that you discover their potential for violence. While both Dean and Patrick are convicted murderers, it is not their murderous behavior that defines their disorder. It is the fact that both men indicate an almost total absence of normal emotional and moral concern about their behavior. The essence of their antisocial personality disorder is that they are not guided by normal social values nor inhibited by normal emotions. In less extreme, but nonetheless insidious, forms, signs of antisocial personality disorder can be seen in unscrupulous businesspeople and professionals who cheat, deceive, and defraud their clients with no apparent moral or emotional reservation. In its extreme form, this disorder is manifest by overt criminal behavior, as we see in Dean and Patrick. Criminal and antisocial are not interchangeable terms, however. Not all people with antisocial personality disorder exhibit criminal behavior, and conversely, not all criminals, despite their lawbreaking, would meet the diagnostic criteria for the disorder.

As with the other personality disorders, we have no clear understanding of or firm evidence for the cause of antisocial personality disorder; both biological and psychodynamic bases may exist. Evidence for a biological interpretation is derived from the fact that antisocial disorders definitely run in families, and also from the fact that the prevalence of the disorder is about three times greater for men than women. Of course both the familial tendency and the gender difference could result from social or environmental pressures.

■ BORDERLINE PERSONALITY DISORDER

Whereas antisocial personality disorders are most prevalent in men, about 75 percent of those with borderline personality disorder are female. People diagnosed with this disorder were once thought to exhibit both neurotic and psychotic symptoms, and that is why it has the odd name of "borderline." Its distinctive characteristics are the presence of severe mood swings coupled with unpredictable, impulsive, and angry outbursts that may be injurious to the individual or others.

The critical difference between the borderline and antisocial disorders is that the person with a borderline disorder experiences guilt, remorse, and appropriate emotions, while the one with an antisocial disorder does not. At the behavioral level, the outcome of the borderline's actions may be as destructive as that of the antisocial, but most often it is constrained by a functioning moral compass and a sense of normal emotion. Nevertheless, the person with borderline disorder remains potentially dangerous. As with the other personality disorders, causal factors are unclear, although the borderline patients often report a childhood history of severe physical or sexual abuse and incest. Of course, a great many people who are abused in childhood do not develop borderline personalities, so the early experience hypothesis can explain only part of the story. It is possible, as with so many other disorders, that the borderline patient has a genetic predisposition that is activated by early abusive experience.

■ SUMMARY

In summary, the personality disorders are characterized by behaviors that create more problems for others than for the people with the disorders. Furthermore, these individuals appear to be similar to all of us in most ways — their behavior is just an exaggerated form of behavior that we all show. Finally, these patients are likely to have had poor early childhood experiences, but that is not sufficient to explain fully the development of the disorder.

■ KEY TERMS

The following terms are used in the text and/or the television programs.

Acting-out	An extreme behavior displayed by an individual, often as a way of dealing with stress.
Antisocial personality	An individual who exhibits irresponsible behavior, fails to conform to social norms, has no regard for truth, and who violates the rights of others without remorse or loyalty, among other behaviors. The terms psychopathic personality and sociopathic personality also are commonly used in referring to this disorder.
Avoidant personality	A personality disorder characterized by hypersensitivity to rejection, social discomfort, and low self-esteem.
Borderline personality	A personality disorder characterized by instability, drastic mood shifts, and behavior problems that include self-mutilation; such individuals are impulsive, unpredictable, angry, empty, periodically unstable, and at times may appear psychotic. Relationships are intense but stormy.
Burned-out psychopath	An individual with an antisocial disorder whose behavior improves after the age of 40 even without treatment, possibly because of weaker biological drives, better insight into self-defeating behavior, and/or the cumulative effect of social conditioning.

Change agents	People who model desired behavior during behaviorial therapy for individuals with antisocial personality disorders.
Dependent personality	A personality disorder marked by extreme dependence on other people, lack of self-confidence, inability to make decisions, and acute discomfort at having to be alone.
Histrionic personality	A personality disorder characterized by attention seeking, excitability, emotional instability, and self-dramatization.
Narcissistic personality	A personality disorder characterized by grandiosity, an exaggerated sense of self-importance, arrogance, exploitation of others, a preoccupation with receiving attention, fragile self-esteem, and hypersensitivity to the perceptions of others.
Neurosis	A nonpsychotic emotional disturbance characterized by exaggerated use of avoidance behavior and defense mechanisms against anxiety.
Obsessive-compulsive personality	A personality disorder characterized by perfectionism and inflexibility, excessive concern with rules, order, efficiency, and work; an insistence that everyone do things one's own way; and an inability to express warm feelings.
Paranoid personality	A personality disorder characterized by suspiciousness, envy, extreme jealousy, and a tendency to interpret the actions of others as demeaning or threatening.
Passive-aggressive personality	A personality disorder characterized by passive resistance to demands for adequate performance. Hostility typically is expressed in such indirect and nonviolent ways as procrastinating, pouting, being stubborn, or being intentionally inefficient.
Personality	The unique pattern of traits and behaviors that characterize an individual.
Personality disorders	A group of maladaptive behavioral syndromes that stem largely from the development of immature and distorted personality patterns and that result in persistently maladaptive ways of perceiving, thinking, and relating to the world (sometimes called character disorders).
Psychosis	A severe psychological disorder involving loss of contact with reality and gross personality distortion.
Sadistic personality	A personality disorder marked by the pervasive use of cruel, demeaning, and aggressive behavior toward other people.
Schizoid personality	A personality disorder characterized by a lack of interest in developing social relationships and an inability to express feelings.
Schizotypal personality	A personality disorder in which egocentricity, avoidance of others, and eccentricity of thought and perception are distinguishing traits; individuals with the disorder are oversensitive and frequently see chance events as related to themselves.
Self-defeating personality	A personality disorder characterized by an individual's avoidance of pleasurable experiences and persistent involvement in relationships in which he or she will suffer.
Splitting	A defense mechanism in which one views oneself or others as all good or all bad without integrating positive or negative qualities into the evaluation.

■ WHAT IS PERSONALITY?

• Personality (or character) consists of deeply ingrained, stable behavior patterns, thoughts, and ways of relating.

■ WHAT ARE PERSONALITY DISORDERS?

• All personality disorders are on a continuum with normal behavior. While 11 personality disorders have been identified, and about one in every ten people has a personality disorder, it can be very difficult to differentiate someone with a disorder from someone who has a slight exaggeration in some personality trait.

■ THE NARCISSISTIC PERSONALITY

(Case Illustrations: Randi, actress Melinda Lopez in role)

• Behaving in a narcissistic way does not necessarily indicate a narcissistic personality disorder. People with unhealthy narcissism lack an internal sense of value and are completely dependent on how others perceive them. They need other people to provide the positive self-regard that they lack.

• Freud believed we are governed by biological drives. He theorized that personality develops through a series of psychosexual stages (oral, anal, phallic, genital) that become focal points and organizers of behavior. If children become stuck at any point, their adult personality may reflect the earlier fixation.

• Object-relations theorists believe that behavior is governed by one's earliest relationship and that one's potential must be activated by an empathic, caring, nurturing mother.

• Heinz Kohut, a object-relationist who concentrated on narcissism, theorized that normal maturation of the self can be arrested by the failure of the early nurturing environment between the child and the mother.

• While the Freudians and the object-relations theorists believe that the early years are crucial, some research suggests that personality development is an ongoing process that is affected from birth to adulthood both by biology and social interactions.

■ ANTISOCIAL PERSONALITY DISORDER

(Case Illustrations: Dean, Patrick)

• This label describes people whose behavior is against society. Such behavior ranges from cheating on income tax to criminal violence. The disorder is found in about four percent of the population, with men outnumbering women four to one. People with antisocial personality disorders often are impulsive and reactive. Criminal violence and abuse of alcohol and/or drugs is typical. The disorder is characterized by a lack of ethical or moral development and an inability to feel remorse or guilt.

• Biological causal factors: One theory suggests that some individuals may have an abnormal level of serotonin, a brain metabolite that appears to modulate a variety of drives such as aggression and competitive behavior. A good deal of evidence suggests a hereditary predisposition toward some types of antisocial behavior, particularly property crime. In families in which the father exhibits chronic criminal behavior and the mother is a substance abuser or has a major personality disorder, the likelihood of the child becoming a violent criminal increases threefold.

• Psychological causal factors: Factors include childhood feelings of inadequacy, inferiority, shame, and humiliation that lead to deep-seated doubts about one's own adequacy as a person.

• Environmental causal factors: Factors include childhood trauma and broken families.

■ BORDERLINE PERSONALITY DISORDER

(Case Illustrations: Kelly, Corey, Linda, Georgette, Chris)

• The term, borderline, reflects psychologists' early but now abandoned beliefs that such people fluctuated between neurosis and psychosis.

• Common character traits include extreme instability and unpredictability, a fear of being alone, manipulativeness in relationships, impulsiveness, and a need for release that sometimes results in violent and/or self-destructive behavior. Unlike people with antisocial personality disorder, those with borderline personality disorder experience pain and remorse from their actions. The disorder is found in about four percent of the population, with women outnumbering men three to one.

• Psychological causal factors: Dr. Knafo suggests that borderlines have a defective sense of identity and are ridden with angry feelings. They see the world as all good or all bad (the splitting defense) and constantly shift between feeling great and feeling terrible. Dr. Cowdry describes their state as dysphoric — an overwhelming sense of feeling bad — and suggests the state typically is triggered by a loss or rejection. He explains self-destructive actions as attempts to end the dysphoria.

• Biological causal factors: Dr. Cowdry explains that the limbic system affects drive states (including aggression) and theorizes that this part of the brain may differ among individuals. Research that found that borderline patients are particularly prone to dysphoria when they are given Procaine, a medication that seems to activate areas of the limbic system, supports this view.

• Environmental causal factors: Recent research suggests that probably 70 percent of individuals hospitalized with borderline personality disorder have had severe physical or sexual abuse early on. Dr. Gewacke feels such patients may be born with a genetic predisposition to the disorder that is activated in certain environments.

■ PERSONALITY DISORDERS: TREATMENT

• Since many people with personality disorders do not find their character traits distressful, they do not seek help. When they do, treatment is challenging, but not impossible.

• Dr. Knafo, a psychodynamic psychotherapist, describes how she treated John, a patient with an obsessive-compulsive personality disorder, by creating a very supportive, well-structured environment in which she could bring consistent attention to the incongruities in John's behavior. In this way the maladaptive character traits ultimately could be lifted out of the level of personality so that John could see them as isolated behaviors he could eliminate.

• Some therapists, e.g., Dr. Budman, think group therapy is extremely effective in treating some personality disorders because the disorders most often manifest themselves in terms of interpersonal behavior.

• Many therapists feel individual and group therapy work best together.

■ VIDEO REVIEW QUESTIONS

1. Dr. Knafo says, "We describe a person through their character traits." Describe the character traits of two people: one with a healthy narcissism and one with a narcissistic personality disorder.

2. Dr. Knafo tells about John, a patient with obsessive-compulsive personality disorder. In what ways does John's behavior seem to cross over the line between an exaggerated personality trait and a personality disorder?

3. Summarize the personality traits exhibited by Melinda Lopez, the actress, in her dramatized fight with her boyfriend and tell why these suggest her character has a narcissistic personality disorder.

4. Select either Dean or Patrick and tell which of his behaviors suggest he has an antisocial personality disorder. What do you learn about his upbringing that may have had an impact on the development of the disorder?

5. What is the serotonin theory and how does it relate to borderline personality disorder?

6. What are the major differences between people with antisocial personality disorder and those with borderline personality disorder? Tell how this relates to Dean, one of the people with antisocial personality disorder, and Kelly, one of the people with borderline personality disorder.

7. What factors in Kelly's background do you think might have contributed to her borderline personality disorder?

8. Why are people with personality disorders less likely to seek treatment than people with other psychological disorders?

9. What are the advantages of group therapy in treating individuals with personality disorders? What are the advantages of treating a person with both individual and group therapy?

10. Psychologists consider the narcissistic, antisocial, and borderline disorders to have enough similarities to comprise a subgroup within the larger group of personality disorders. Identify similarities and differences in the cases illustrating these disorders. Obsessive-compulsive personality disorder is considered to be in a different subgroup. How is John, the person with obsessive-compulsive disorder, more different from the people with disorders in the first subgroup than they are from each other?

CASE STUDY

by Judith Rosenberger,
C.S.W., Ph.D.
Hunter College
and
Edith Gould, C.S.W.
Postgraduate Center
for Mental Health

Lillian

Every day I wake up in a rage. Why is it that some idiot always is trying to make my life more difficult? It never fails. Before I even get to work, never mind finish my shift, some moron goes too far. Next thing I know, I'm in a screaming match with some half-wit who just wants to push his weight around and refuses to admit when he's wrong. Like today, I got to the coffee line and this old biddy couldn't get her money out and then she couldn't get the lid on straight. All I said was for her to hurry up, and this sleazy guy at the counter tells me to relax. Like it was his business! People like that lady should know better than to get on line at that hour when working people like myself have to rush.

So I'm a little late for work. It's because of her, and my boss starts in on me right away. Why was I late? And why was I wearing sneakers? "What's bugging you?" I say, "They're white, aren't they?" "They're not part of the uniform," he says. We get into this argument where he's making a big deal about my shoes and my general attitude. I told him I'd take it to the union. Nowhere in the contract does it say "No Sneakers." I told him he's going to have to pay me more if he wants me to wear leather shoes for this crummy job. Anyway, half the people are too out of it to notice if you're wearing any clothes at all. He told me I was on warning for insubordination. He just doesn't like women who talk back. So I'm going to the union rep's office after lunch. He's a really great guy. I'm sure he'll do the right thing and get my boss off my back. I saw him at a meeting once and could tell he's exactly the kind of person who will listen to me and take care of the problem.

I didn't want to go right away though. I felt depressed about my boss hassling me, so I smoked a joint in the bathroom to soothe my nerves. Then I called my boyfriend, who wasn't in. What a creep he is! I do so much for him. Where is he when I need him? I'll show him: I won't answer the phone for a few days. Let's see how he likes that. I'll give him a dose of his own medicine.

By then I was way behind in getting the trays for morning snack around, so I had to skip some of the patients and hide the food in garbage bags. Sometimes I feel a little guilty because these old birds are so bored they practically live for the next meal, but then I figure they're too fat anyway, from sitting around all the time. If they complain I'll just say they must've forgotten that they'd eaten. Between you and me, half the time I eat part of their food anyway or take the packaged snacks home. They don't pay me enough to buy decent meals, so they probably expect this kind of thing anyway.

It's so boring here. It's dull at home, too. How did my life get so boring? I've been gaining weight since I got here. I can't stop eating. Maybe if I were busier. . . . Oh, and I just remembered the final straw! When I was leaving the bathroom I slipped on somebody's spill and banged my elbow into the door frame. I'm thinking of bringing a claim for that. They should be more careful. After the union thing I'm going home. If the boss gets on my case for leaving early, I'll tell him I injured my elbow. I'm just so fed up with the whole thing I hope nobody gets in my way, or I'll punch them out!

■ CLINICAL DISCUSSION

Lillian is a 32-year-old single woman living in a basement apartment in her mother's suburban house. Her occupational functioning has declined despite a college education. She has lost six jobs in ten years, moving from professional entry level down to her current blue-collar job. She now is working as a housekeeper in a nursing home. She has been on this job for six weeks. As usual, hopes for a trouble-free situation quickly changed to conflict.

Social life for Lillian mainly is limited to drinking companions and occasional brief sexual relationships with men she meets in bars. While not a true addict, she uses a variety of drugs like cocaine, marijuana, and amphetamines, generally ending each day in a stupor and resolving to stay clean tomorrow. She justifies her drug patterns as a response to the stress of dealing with others who are a problem. She is 20 pounds overweight, somewhat unkempt although not bizarre, and appears tired and tense. A primary feature is her combative reactions. She is easily angered, and becomes verbally abusive. Her relationship with her mother, from whom she is unable to separate, is intensely conflictual, at times coming to blows. This has been the case since Lillian's puberty. Her father has been dead for 10 years. He seemed to side with Lillian in her conflicts with her mother, even provoking her outbursts at times. He never took a stand when the conflicts started, however. Two younger brothers are married and live out of town, keeping up little contact with her; Lillian feels her mother favors them. Lillian sees her work, social, and family life as troubled, but has no self-awareness about her part in things.

The pervasiveness and chronicity of her seriously disordered functioning, along with the absence of psychotic symptoms, suggest Lillian has a personality disorder. The dominance of anger, quick movement from hope to disappointment in relationships, workplace conflicts, drug use, and lack of self-appraisal suggest the borderline type of personality disorder. Her major functional problems stem from this pattern of anger and impulsiveness which she then attempts to blame on others. This is the defense of splitting. She splits her experience of herself: This preserves an inflated self-estimate from the destruction she would turn on herself if she saw herself as defective. If she can make the other person seem like the bad one, Lillian feels better about herself. Unlike someone with antisocial personality disorder, Lillian often feels guilty. She protects herself from the full force of feeling bad by unconsciously transforming her guilt for what she can't control in herself into an explanation of how she is victimized by the behavior of others. The central treatment focus and problem will be enabling Lillian to take responsibility for herself without her feeling persecuted by the therapist along the way.

It is important to rule out a psychotic process, especially a paranoid one, as underlying Lillian's combative behavior. Her cognitive, or thinking, processes, do not show evidence of an actual thought disorder. Her thoughts follow sequentially. No outright false beliefs (delusions) or misperceptions (such as auditory or visual hallucinations) are exhibited. She is extremely sensitive rather than suspicious and guarded. It also is important to rule out a mood disorder as the primary cause of Lillian's angry manner. Lillian struggles with depression and feelings of emptiness. She does not have especially happy or elated feelings. On the other hand, she is not intensely self-blaming or self-critical or hopeless. She is apt to be disappointed because she often expects too much (as from the union rep). So poor judgment and lack of self-appraisal get Lillian into depressing circumstances rather than the other way around. Lillian is stable at being unstable: This is the hallmark of the borderline personality disorder.

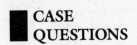

CASE QUESTIONS

1. How do you see the defense of splitting (making herself the good one to avoid feeling like the bad one) work in the example of Lillian in the coffee line? How does this seem necessary from her point of view?

2. Some clinicians think that the anger that is so constant in borderline personality disorder is a natural aggressiveness (a kind of in-born trait or temperament). Other clinicians think it comes from resentment over repeated failures and disappointments, especially in early relationships. How do you see these two possibilities with Lillian?

3. The diagnosis of borderline personality disorder depends in part on ruling out other possibilities. This is called differential diagnosis. How did an anxiety disorder get ruled out for Lillian? How about antisocial personality disorder?

SELF-TEST

1. **Personality disorders typically result in**
    a) defenses against anxiety and guilt.
    b) minimal brain dysfunction.
    c) persistent maladaptive approaches to the world.
    d) stress reactions.

2. **All of the following are special problems that promote misdiagnoses of personality disorders EXCEPT**
    a) categories are not mutually exclusive.
    b) features of these disorders are found in many normal individuals.
    c) no consistent theoretical view on classification exists.
    d) traits must be directly observed.

3. **Alfred is suspicious of everybody and everything. He never takes the blame for his mistakes but ends up blaming somebody else. His office mates "walk on eggs" so he won't accuse them of "setting him up" for some "bum rap." Alfred's personality disorder is**
    a) narcissistic.
    b) paranoid.
    c) schizoid.
    d) schizotypal.

4. **The central problem of the schizoid personality is a(n)**
    a) deep need for love and belonging.
    b) inability to form attachments.
    c) tendency to be occupied with daydreams.
    d) tendency to hallucinate under pressure.

5. **Charles is considered the town's eccentric. He stays by himself in an old house at the end of the lane and almost never talks to anyone. Whenever he does speak he uses Biblical language. He says it makes him feel more religious. Charles' personality disorder is**
    a) narcissistic.
    b) paranoid.
    c) schizoid.
    d) schizotypal.

6. **Dan is always on stage. He will do or say almost anything to get attention. He and his wife are always fighting over their sexual life. Sometimes his coworkers play jokes on him because he will "believe anything you tell him." Dan's personality disorder is**
    a) antisocial.
    b) borderline.
    c) histrionic.
    d) narcissistic.

7. The central element(s) in the narcissistic personality pattern is (are)
    a) dramatic attention-getting devices.
    b) eccentric thinking patterns.
    c) lack of the capacity for empathy.
    d) self-isolation from others.

8. Fred has had a series of stormy relationships with his teachers. He typically finds one that he admires and claims that he worships them. He demands more and more of their time until they finally break off the relationship. Last year, after one of these rebuffs, he stuck a hatpin through both his cheeks and told the teacher he hoped he would bleed to death. Fred's personality disorder is
    a) antisocial.
    b) borderline.
    c) histrionic.
    d) narcissistic.

9. The key predisposing factor to the development of a borderline personality disorder is
    a) eccentric thinking patterns.
    b) insatiable need for attention.
    c) lack of empathy.
    d) lack of self-identity.

10. The keynote of the avoidant personality disorder is
    a) avoiding feelings of guilt at any cost.
    b) lack of empathy.
    c) lack of self-identity.
    d) staying away from potentially embarrassing situations.

11. Herbert's cronies say he is henpecked because he lets his wife make all the decisions in their marriage. He never asks for anything for himself and always goes along with his partner's wishes. Last year his spouse got fed up and threatened to leave him. He went all to pieces, crying, sobbing, and begging her to stay. Herbert's personality disorder is
    a) avoidant.
    b) obsessive-compulsive.
    c) dependent.
    d) passive-aggressive.

12. People say Jim always "drags his feet." He never likes to be told what to do, but he seldom comes right out and says so. He just puts things off or "forgets" to do them. His wife says that when he "helps" with housework, he does a "half-way" job so she won't ask him again. Jim's personality disorder is
    a) avoidant.
    b) obsessive-compulsive.
    c) dependent.
    d) passive-aggressive.

13. All of the following are characteristics typically found in individuals diagnosed as having an antisocial personality disorder EXCEPT

    a) the ability to impress and exploit others.

    b) an exceptional ability to learn from experience.

    c) inadequate conscience development.

    d) irresponsible, impulsive behavior.

14. Which of the following usually is true of individuals diagnosed as having an antisocial personality disorder?

    a) They are normal in both intellectual and conscience development.

    b) They are normal in conscience development but retarded in intellectual development.

    c) They are normal in intellectual development but retarded in conscience development.

    d) They are retarded in both intellectual and conscience development.

15. Buss concluded that two types of parents foster psychopathy. The first includes those who are cold and distant toward the child and the second includes those who are

    a) capricious in supplying affection, rewards, and punishments.

    b) laissez faire in their parenting.

    c) overstrict and sadistic in their punishments.

    d) overzealous in showing affection as a reward for conformity.

16. All of the following are steps in Bandura's behavioral therapy for antisocial personalities EXCEPT

    a) modeling of desired behavior by "change agents."

    b) reduction of material incentives as behavior improves.

    c) use of other psychopaths as negative models.

    d) withdrawal of reinforcements for disapproved antisocial behavior.

17. The individual with a narcissistic personality disorder

    a) has developed an overabundance of healthy narcissism.

    b) does not care how others perceive him/her.

    c) has a shaky sense of self-esteem.

    d) simply is a product of our narcissistic culture.

18. In his work, Kohut focused on

    a) psychosexual stages

    b) the nature of the nurturing environment between mother and child.

    c) peer relationships.

    d) Oedipal conflicts.

19. Abnormal levels of serotonin have been found in

    a) suicidal individuals.

    b) antisocial individuals.

    c) individuals with borderline personality disorder.

    d) all of the above.

20. A sense of self and others that alternates between good and bad is characteristic of
    a) borderline personality disorder.
    b) antisocial personality disorder.
    c) narcissistic personality disorder.
    d) obsessive-compulsive disorder.

21. Individuals with borderline personality disorder who were administered Procaine, which seems to activate areas of the limbic system, were likely to experience
    a) euphoria.
    b) dysphoria.
    c) hypomania.
    d) insomnia.

22. Childhood incest and physical abuse were reported in 70 percent of patients hospitalized with
    a) narcissistic personality disorders.
    b) obsessive-compulsive personality disorders.
    c) antisocial personality disorders.
    d) borderline personality disorders.

23. Group therapy often is helpful to individuals with personality disorders because
    a) their problems manifest themselves interpersonally.
    b) they can get feedback from others.
    c) they gain emotional support.
    d) all of the above.

24. Object-relations theorists posit that a healthy sense of self-esteem is founded on
    a) infants realizing they can care for themselves.
    b) infants receiving emotional validation from their mother.
    c) peer acceptance during adolescence.
    d) healthy resolution of Oedipal conflicts.

25. The absence of feelings of guilt is most closely associated with
    a) narcissistic personality disorder.
    b) borderline personality disorder.
    c) antisocial personality disorder.
    d) obsessive-compulsive personality disorder.

[ANSWERS: 1-c, 2-d, 3-b, 4-b, 5-d, 6-c, 7-c, 8-b, 9-d, 10-d, 11-c, 12-d, 13-b, 14-c, 15-a, 16-c, 17-c, 18-b, 19-d, 20-a, 21-b, 22-d, 23-d, 24-b, 25-c]

■ SUGGESTED READINGS

Cleckley, H. M. (1976). *The mask of sanity: An attempt to clarify some issues about the so-called psychopathic personality* (5th ed.). St. Louis: Mosby. This extraordinarily well-written portrait of what we now call the antisocial personality is well worth reading for the beauty of its observation and the detail of its description.

Kohut, H. (1971). *The analysis of the self: A systematic approach to the psychoanalytic treatment of narcissistic personality disorders.* New York: International Universities Press. This leading theorist presents case histories to illustrate the techniques and support the theoretical interpretation of these disorders.

Masterson, J. F. (1988). *The search for the real self: Unmasking the personality disorders of our age.* New York: The Free Press/Macmillan, Inc. This book takes a wide look at the personality disorders — how and why they develop, what they look like and how to change them. It is interwoven with case histories from the author's practice.

Nelson, M. C. (Ed.). (1977). *The narcissistic condition: A fact of our lives and times.* New York: Human Sciences Press. These essays describe the clinical phenomenon of narcissism, its various expressions on both individual and sociocultural levels, and its treatment within the psychoanalytic tradition.

Shapiro, D. (1965). *Neurotic styles.* New York: Basic Books. This wonderful description of what we now classify as personality disorders includes the obsessive-compulsive personality style, the hysterical personality style, the paranoid, etc. It also presents a psychoanalytic explanation of these disorders.

UNIT 6

SUBSTANCE
ABUSE
DISORDERS

UNIT THEME

Substance abuse disorders are, perhaps, the country's most pervasive mental health problem. The video portion of this unit focuses on alcohol, cocaine, and nicotine addiction. It considers the effects of substance abuse on the individual and society and examines causal factors and treatment approaches. The text considers a wider array of addictive behaviors, including overeating and pathological gambling.

UNIT ASSIGNMENTS

Read: Unit 6. "Substance Abuse Disorders" in *The World of Abnormal Psychology Study Guide*, Toby Kleban Levine, editor (HarperCollins, 1992).

View: Program 6. "Substance Abuse Disorders" in THE WORLD OF ABNORMAL PSYCHOLOGY.

Read: Chapter 9. "Substance-use and Other Addictive Disorders" in *Abnormal Psychology and Modern Life*, Ninth Edition, by Robert C. Carson and James N. Butcher (HarperCollins, 1992).

GOALS AND OBJECTIVES

1. Discuss the prevalence and costs to individuals and society of substance abuse and addictive disorders with particular reference to alcohol, nicotine, and cocaine addiction.

2. List and describe genetic, psychosocial, and sociocultural factors that may be partially responsible for the development of alcohol dependence.

3. Discuss the withdrawal symptoms experienced by alcoholics and describe four different types of alcoholic psychoses.

4. Define treatment matching and discuss its use in reference to substance abusers.

5. Describe and evaluate several biological and psychosocial interventions that have been used to treat alcohol-dependent persons, including some that do not require abstinence.

6. List and explain major causal factors in the development of opiate dependence.

7. Identify some psychosocial and biological treatments for opiate-dependent individuals and evaluate the success of using methadone hydrochloride.

8. Describe some physical and psychological effects of ingesting cocaine and crack and some symptoms that are experienced in withdrawal.

9. List the physical and psychological results of using LSD.

10. Discuss the psychosocial effects and lifestyle changes that can accompany dependence on such drugs as heroin and cocaine.

11. List some biological, psychosocial, and sociocultural factors that may underlie the development of hyperobesity and evaluate several biological and psychosocial interventions that have been used to treat it.

12. Identify some of the medical risks associated with cigarette smoking and discuss its psychological effects.

UNIT OVERVIEW

by Edward S. Katkin, Ph.D.
State University of New York
at Stony Brook

Few issues concerning human behavior have received as much popular attention in recent years as the abusive use of such illegal drugs as **cocaine**, **marijuana**, and **heroin**. Local and national government agencies have focused attention on the issue, and political arguments about how best to deal with this social problem surface in virtually every election campaign. Mental health professionals, however, do not differentiate between legal and illegal substance abuse; they focus on addictive behavior: what causes it and what can be done to treat it.

Technically, substance abuse may be defined as the chronic use of any substance that results in potentially hazardous behavior. Sometimes abuse is referred to as **addiction** or **dependence**. These terms often are used interchangeably; they refer to the use of a substance despite bad consequences, including an inability to reduce or regulate the amount of the substance that is used. In some cases, dependency results in physiological changes in which the body becomes adapted to the substance and undergoes serious disruption if the substance is withdrawn. This **withdrawal** usually is evidence of what is called physical dependence.

Although popular reporting might suggest that substance abuse is a recent development in our culture, actually it is one of the oldest documented behavioral and social problems. Alcoholism has been recorded in history for thousands of years, and substance abuse has been reported throughout history in many cultures. Today, psychologists focus on a variety of addictive and abusive behaviors. Your textbook discusses several, including **narcotic** addiction, **barbiturate** abuse, **amphetamine** abuse, **hyperobesity**, the use of marijuana, and even **pathological gambling**. The video, however, focuses on only three major areas of substance abuse: alcohol, cocaine, and **nicotine**.

■ ALCOHOL ABUSE

It is estimated that about 15 million Americans frequently abuse alcohol. The effects of this behavior are devastating for health. Alcoholics, on average, die more than a decade earlier than nonalcoholics, and about one in ten alcoholics commits suicide. On balance, alcohol abuse results in more death, antisocial behavior, and social disruption than the abuse of heroin, amphetamines, barbiturates, and marijuana combined.

What causes someone to become an alcoholic? There are many competing views on this question, and no certain answer. One popular view is the disease model. It suggests that alcoholism is a progressive disease caused by physiological malfunctioning, perhaps of genetic origin. Other theorists reject the disease model, suggesting that while some biological or genetic predisposition may exist, predisposed people can learn to moderate their drinking behavior and avoid becoming alcoholic.

Another view places a high premium on cultural factors. Incidence of alcoholism among Native Americans is very high, for instance, but little evidence has been found to show that Native Americans are genetically predisposed to be alcohol abusers. Rather, it is likely that Native Americans, who as a group have high levels of unemployment and very little social support, may use alcohol as a (poor) method of coping with social stress. This general model — that alcohol abuse is a learned coping response — has been widely used to explain the cause of alcoholism in the general population as well.

A variety of treatment programs are available to alcoholics. All of them start with detoxification — that is, removing the alcohol from the patient's body and allowing the toxic state to disappear. Detoxification is followed by rehabilitation and aftercare. Another prominent treatment approach is **relapse prevention**. Here, as Dr. Alan Marlatt describes, the recovering alcoholic is trained to become alert to life situations that may cause a relapse of alcohol abuse; these would include stressful or other situations the individual associates with drinking. This treatment approach helps alcoholics to avoid relapse or, alternatively, teaches them how to cope with a temporary relapse in order to prevent it from becoming permanent. The relapse prevention approach is quite different from the approach advocated by Alcoholics Anonymous, which requires its members to practice absolute abstinence.

A different and effective approach is preventive intervention, which aims at preventing the development of the problem. The video presents a group of students at the University of Washington participating in a training program focused on how and why they drink. This program uses a simulated drinking lounge known as the Barlab.

■ COCAINE ABUSE

Not too long ago, many people thought that cocaine was a relatively harmless social drug used mostly by the wealthy. This misperception was laid to rest when an inexpensive variety of cocaine, known as **crack**, became available. Crack provides the user with a pleasant experience that most people find irresistible and consequently addictive. The health and social consequences of crack have been widely publicized. In the video, crack and cocaine abusers describe the extraordinary pleasure they got from the drug. They also developed **tolerance** for it and required more and more of the drug to replicate the experience. Finally, you will hear from cocaine abusers how the drug ultimately left them alienated from friends and loved ones and unable to sustain a normal life.

The causes of cocaine abuse are psychologically similar to those of alcohol abuse: the user believes that the experience is an effective antidote to the pressures and anxieties of everyday life. The chemical action of cocaine in the brain differs from the effects of alcohol, however. Cocaine acts on the brain more quickly and is more potent. It is believed that cocaine prevents the neurotransmitter dopamine from being reabsorbed by nerves. This neurotransmitter, therefore, accumulates in greater concentrations in the synapses between brain cells, and accentuates the impulses that are associated with pleasure. The experience can be so strong that it overshadows all other needs.

Treatment of cocaine abuse also involves detoxification, rehabilitation, and aftercare. As with alcohol abuse, relapse is a major problem, and relapse prevention and aftercare are central features of most treatment programs. A variety of psychotherapeutic programs have been tried for cocaine abuse, but so far no single approach has worked equally well with all patients. For these reasons, after detoxification most therapists attempt to devise individualized treatment programs for the abusers; this practice is known as **treatment matching**. In many of these programs, group support and self-help are critical ingredients.

■ NICOTINE ABUSE

Nicotine is an addictive drug that has become a common feature of daily life for millions of Americans: it is the primary addictive chemical contained in tobacco. Cigarettes are widely available throughout the world, and many smokers are as dependent on them as cocaine abusers are on their drug. Although nicotine addiction does not lead to the same kind of psychological and social malfunctioning as alcohol and cocaine, it does lead to much greater health problems. Cigarette smoking is the leading cause of lung cancer and emphysema, and it is a significant contributor to the incidence of heart disease, high blood pressure, and stroke. Further, nicotine is far more addictive than alcohol. Only about five percent of regular alcohol users become addicted, for instance, compared to about 30 percent of cigarette smokers. Smokers report many of the same feelings that other drug addicts do; when they are tense or upset, the cigarette makes them feel better. When addiction sets in, the absence of nicotine is the primary source of bad feeling, and a cigarette is required for relief.

Treatment of nicotine addiction does not seem to be as pressing a social need as treatment of alcohol and cocaine addiction, because nicotine addiction does not appear to threaten our social fabric in the same way that the other addictions do, although evidence of risk to nonsmokers from second-hand smoke is emerging. Yet, the health hazards of smoking demand both preventive intervention and treatment of nicotine addiction. As with the other addictions, relapse is a major problem. Relapse prevention programs are therefore important sources of effective treatment. In addition, a variety of self-help and professional therapeutic groups have addressed the problem of addictive smoking.

■ SUMMARY

Common themes run through all three types of substance abuse described in the video. A primary risk factor for substance abuse is availability of the drug and exposure to it. In all cases the appeal of the drug is that it is a short-term alleviator of stress and anxiety by virtue of its capacity to alter mood. In all three situations, the absence of the substance leads to a state of distress that is then alleviated only by increasing use of it. And, in all three situations, effective treatment requires detoxification, rehabilitation, and aftercare. Finally, in all three situations, a high rate of relapse after rehabilitation is common, and relapse prevention strategies are critically important.

■ KEY TERMS

The following terms are used in the text and/or the television programs.

Abuse	The pathological use of a substance resulting in potentially hazardous behavior or in continued use despite a persistent social, psychological, occupational, or health problem.
Addiction	See *dependence*.
Alcohol amnestic disorder	An impairment in short- and long-term memory associated with prolonged alcohol abuse; frequently involves confabulation, that is, filling in gaps in memory with imaginary events. (Also known as Korsakoff's syndrome in cases involving thiamine deficiency.)
Alcohol idiosyncratic intoxication	An acute behavioral change after consumption of alcohol by people whose tolerance is chronically or temporarily low, typically followed by amnesia.
Alcohol withdrawal delirium	A reaction that may occur after a recent cessation of or reduction in alcohol consumption. Delirium symptoms include disorientation with respect to time and place, vivid hallucinations, acute fear, extreme suggestibility, marked tremors, and other symptoms. (Formerly known as delirium tremens.)
Alcoholic	Someone whose drinking impairs life adjustment in terms of health, personal relationships, and/or occupational functioning (definition of the 1978 President's Commission on Mental Health).
Amphetamines	A stimulant used to relieve mild feelings of depression and fatigue and to maintain alertness. Amphetamines have a high potential for abuse and are psychologically addictive.
Analgesic	A substance that removes pain without inducing loss of consciousness.

Barbiturates	A group of powerful sedatives that act as depressants by slowing down the action of the central nervous system. Barbiturates are associated with both physiological and psychological dependence and sometimes lethal overdoses.
Caffeine	A chemical compound found in coffee, tea, and cola; it is both a stimulant and a diuretic.
Cocaine	A stimulant that produces a euphoric state during which the user experiences feelings of peace and contentment. Chronically abused, it can promote acute psychotic symptoms in which the user experiences hallucinations.
Crack	A highly addictive and cheaper variety of cocaine that produces an immediate and intense high.
Dependence	A severe substance-use disorder that usually involves a physiological need for the substance, in which the individual shows tolerance for the substance or withdrawal symptoms when it is unavailable.
Endorphins	Opium-like substances produced in the brain and pituitary gland in response to stimulation; believed to be associated with the body's reaction to pain.
Flashback	An involuntary recurrence of perceptual distortions or hallucinations of events that occurred weeks or even months earlier; a potential side effect of LSD use.
Hallucinogens	Drugs whose properties are thought to induce hallucinations by distorting sensory images so that the individual sees or hears things in different and unusual ways; the major hallucinogens include LSD (lysergic acid diethylamide), mescaline, and psilocybin.
Heroin	A powerful analgesic derived from morphine; originally prescribed to replace morphine as a sedative and pain reliever, it acts more rapidly and is more addictive than morphine.
Hyperobesity	Extreme obesity in which the individual is 100 pounds or more above ideal body weight.
LSD (lysergic acid diethylamide)	A potent hallucinogen, LSD is odorless, colorless, and tasteless, and tiny amounts can produce intoxication. LSD affects sensory perception and emotional experiences and induces feelings of depersonalization and detachment; it also increases heart rate, blood pressure, and breathing. LSD use also may involve flashbacks.
Marijuana	A hallucinogen derived from the *cannabis sativa* plant that can be smoked, chewed, or drunk. The effects depend on the quality and dosage, the social setting, and the user's expectations. It usually induces mild euphoria with increased feeling of well-being, heightened perceptual acuity, and pleasant relaxation.
Mescaline	A hallucinogen derived from the peyote cactus; appears to enable the individual to see, hear, and experience events in unaccustomed ways.
Methadone hydrochloride	A synthetic narcotic that is related to heroin and is equally addictive physiologically; used in the treatment of people who are addicted to heroin because it satisfies the addict's craving for heroin without serious psychological impairment.
Morphine	A narcotic derived from opium; used as a powerful sedative and pain reliever, it is both analgesic and addictive.
Narcotic	A drug that dulls the senses, relieves pain, and induces sleep.

Nicotine	A poisonous substance that is the chief active component of tobacco.
Opium	A narcotic that is a mixture of about 18 nitrogen-containing agents known as alkaloids.
Pathological gambling	Gambling that significantly affects the social, psychological, and economic well-being of individuals and/or their family and friends.
Psychoactive drugs	Drugs that affect mental functioning, such as alcohol, barbiturates, minor tranquilizers, amphetamines, heroin, and marijuana.
Relapse prevention	An approach to substance-abuse treatment aimed at maintaining behavior learned to overcome addiction and preventing relapse into previous maladaptive patterns.
Tolerance	The need for increased amounts of a drug in order to achieve the same effect; arises when the body adapts to the presence of the drug.
Toxicity	The poisonous nature of a substance.
Treatment matching	Tailoring a treatment program to meet the needs of a specific individual; includes, for example, taking the cultural context into account when planning treatment.
Withdrawal	Physical symptoms such as sweating, tremors, and tension that accompany abstinence from a drug on which one has become dependent.

VIDEO NOTES

■ USE AND ABUSE
• Psychoactive substances have been used since prehistoric times to modify sensations, thoughts, feelings, and behavior.

> Abuse is the chronic use of a substance that results in potentially hazardous behavior, like driving while intoxicated.

> The terms dependence and addiction refer to a group of behaviors that may include focusing attention on getting the drug, using the drug despite bad consequences, having the drug interfere with normal activity, and being unable to control one's drug use.

> Physical dependence is the state that exists when the body becomes adapted to the presence of the drug and becomes tolerant of it, meaning that the drug does not produce the same effect; when the drug is stopped the body goes into withdrawal syndrome.

■ COCAINE: THE EXPERIENCE
(*Case Illustrations: Greg, David, Patricia*)
• Cocaine can be snorted, injected intravenously, or smoked. The most intense high comes from inhaling the cocaine vapor either by freebasing (distilling cocaine to a purer form, then smoking the result) or using crack (prepackaged rock-like chunks of cocaine freebase).

• Dr. Childress explains that the reason cocaine is so addictive is that it activates the same areas in the brain as normal pleasures and rewards, e.g., food, sex, and water. Normally, after the neurotransmitter dopamine is released, communicating a pleasure message from one neuron to another across a synapse, part of it recycles back to its original neuron to be ready for the next time it is needed. Cocaine prevents the recycling so that more dopamine stays in the synapse between nerve cells and produces an intensified and prolonged pleasure message.

• In addition to the psychological damage, physical consequences range from lung and membrane damage to heart arrhythmias and seizures. Basketball player Len Bias, for example, died after using crack cocaine.

■ ALCOHOL: THE EXPERIENCE
(Case Illustrations: Margaret, Scott)
• An alcohol problem often affects the family as much as the alcoholic.

• A very strong relationship exists between alcohol and violence, although the cause of the relationship is unknown.

■ SUBSTANCE ABUSE: RISK FACTORS
(Case Illustration: Kerry)
• Substance abuse is a complex phenomenon, involving biological, psychological, and environmental factors.

• Biological factors: The disease model suggests that alcoholism is a progressive disease in which heredity plays an important role and physiological malfunctioning predominates.

Many psychologists find it difficult to reconcile this explanation with the fact that people willfully drink. Dr. Marlatt prefers a multifactorial model in which genetics, for example, may create a higher vulnerability but is not sufficient to fully explain the expression of the problem.

• Psychological factors: Individuals with preexisting psychiatric disorders such as anxiety and depression may try to allay their psychological problems by taking drugs.

A traditional Freudian view posits the existence of an addictive personality in which a person's inner conflicts and unresolved issues are motivating forces. Also, many psychologists believe learning theory or conditioning theory plays an important role in whether or not a person becomes an alcoholic, e.g., whether people use alcohol as a coping response.

• Environmental/social factors include peer pressure and exposure. Culture and parental models fit in strongly here.

In the case of cocaine abuse, one factor differentiates it from risk factors for other addictions: exposure alone seems to be enough to get a person started down the path to addiction.

■ A CIGARETTE BREAK
(Case Illustration: Bill)
• The use of nicotine is woven into the fabric of our daily lives. But smoking is the largest cause of both emphysema and lung cancer and is a significant factor in heart disease, high blood pressure, strokes, and bladder cancer.

• As with other drugs, people addicted to nicotine use the drug as a coping device. Even years after quitting, ex-smokers retain the feeling that a cigarette will relieve anxiety or depression.

■ SUBSTANCE ABUSE: TREATMENT AND PREVENTION

(Case Illustration: Meredith)

• Dr. O'Brien believes that substance abuse can be treated successfully, but that it is completely unrealistic to expect abusers to be cured in the same way as a person who has pneumonia. Experts talk about treatment, therefore, rather than cures.

• Treatment programs commonly have three stages: First, the drug must be eliminated from the person's system (detoxification). Next comes a rehabilitation program. Finally the person enters a maintenance period (aftercare) that for some may last a lifetime.

Rehabilitation programs can involve medication, such as disulfiram or Antabuse; psychological treatment, such as psychotherapy or desensitization; and/or sociocultural treatment, such as self-help groups like Alcoholics Anonymous, Narcotics Anonymous, and drug-free halfway houses.

Treatment may take place either in a hospital setting or on an outpatient basis.

• Treatment matching involves tailoring a treatment program to meet an individual's particular needs, style, and beliefs. A person with depression, for example, should be treated for that disorder in addition to drug rehabilitation.

An example of treatment matching is seen at the Seattle Indian Health Board, where clients take part in one-to-one counseling and support groups that build on their shared cultural beliefs. The program combines a 12-step Alcoholics Anonymous philosophy, which stresses complete abstinence and the idea that you must give up control of the disease to a force larger than yourself and accept yourself as you are, with the concept of the Native American medicine wheel, which symbolizes the cycles and changes in life from birth to death and represents understanding of self and harmony with the universe. Alcohol and drug abuse are seen as disrupting the harmony of the circle. According to Dr. Walker, the medicine wheel offers a chance to think about spiritual healing and integrates that belief into the treatment process.

■ RELAPSE AND PREVENTION

(Case Illustration: Barlab)

• Relapse prevention was created to help people anticipate the problems that might arise from the discontinuation of drugs, beginning with withdrawal and continuing with the anticipation of high-risk situations in which various triggers might heighten the possibility of relapse.

• Dr. Marlatt also focuses on prevention, particularly working with students who are of high school and college age, a period during which young people may develop life-long drinking problems.

In a program at the University of Washington, students who are moderate drinkers learn to become more aware of how and why they drink. In the Barlab they monitor their physical reactions to drinking and the power that expectations have on physical and emotional reactions.

• Dr. Childress believes that one of the major reasons cocaine abusers relapse is that cues in the environment trigger strong cravings. The treatment program she directs includes exposing patients to these cues in protected settings and using imagery to recall their worst moments of addiction.

■ FUTURE DIRECTIONS

Some scientists have discovered a reduced amount of activity for a specific enzyme in the bodies of alcoholics that seems to be the product of a single gene. Cocaine researchers also are looking for a genetic marker. Other scientists continue to research and stress the multiple-causes model.

■ VIDEO REVIEW QUESTIONS

1. Define abuse and addiction and differentiate between psychological dependency and physical dependency.

2. Describe the manner in which cocaine is said to stimulate the brain and discuss how this action contributes to the rapid establishment of addiction.

3. What aspects of cocaine make it potentially life-threatening?

4. Identify several biological, psychological, and environmental risk factors for addiction.

5. Describe a situation in which a multiple risk factor model would apply to a particular individual.

6. In what significant way do the risk factors for cocaine addiction differ from those for alcoholism?

7. Describe the ways in which the Seattle Indian Health Board alcoholism treatment program is an example of treatment matching.

8. Discuss the difference between treatment and cure with respect to substance addiction.

9. Discuss the pros and cons of alcoholism treatment programs that require total abstinence and tell how Dr. Marlatt's program differs philosophically.

10. Why did students who participated in the Barlab think they were drunk and behave accordingly? What does this research tell you about environmental factors in alcoholism?

■ CASE STUDY

by Judith Rosenberger, C.S.W., Ph.D. Hunter College and Edith Gould, C.S.W. Postgraduate Center for Mental Health

Jane

I'm 30 years old. I haven't used drugs for five years, and not taking drugs is something I still pay attention to every day of my life. The craving never goes away.

I grew up in a nice, suburban neighborhood, the proverbial lonely rich girl. Images of the Big City glittered in my childhood fantasies. Otherwise, my childhood often was sad. I had few friends because I was shy. Boys never liked me. My father always was away on business, and my mother filled her time with the usual civic and church involvements of a woman of her class and status. I have a vivid memory of lying alone in my bed, maybe when I was in kindergarten, staring at the shadows cast on the wall by the big maple tree

tree outside. I remember that lonely feeling as sharp and painful, like a gnawing emptiness. Looking back, I guess I used food to try to fill up that void. I started getting fat in grade school.

When I was about 14, I became fascinated with photography. My parents immediately bought me a number of expensive cameras and had a fully equipped darkroom built for me. I spent my adolescence hiding out in the darkroom. Sometimes I won prizes for my pictures. The pictures I took in those years were solitary and bleak, and conveyed a sense of being an outsider.

When I was 18, I landed a job through family connections as an assistant in a well-known New York photography studio. Having grown up sheltered, I saw New York as the essence of the glamorous life. But life in New York turned out to be scary and overwhelming. Suddenly I was living the fast-track life of my teenage fantasies. I worked in the studio all day, went out to restaurants and clubs at night, socialized with famous people. But all these people intimidated me. I felt awkward and tongue-tied. I was self-conscious and imagined people thought I didn't fit in. I didn't look sophisticated. Although I had become thin, I still thought of myself as a fat person. I couldn't eat alone in a restaurant because I was convinced people felt sorry for me because I was alone. I couldn't eat in front of friends because I felt ashamed of eating anything in front of anyone. I just couldn't get comfortable in any social situation.

I became more and more exhausted from the pace of my life and the anxiety I felt trying to keep up with it all. Everyone else seemed smarter, prettier, and cooler than me. I still didn't have a boyfriend or many women friends, either. And then the depression set in, like a black cloud settling into my head. I lost my appetite completely and only wanted to sleep. Often I was late for work, and sometimes I didn't show up at all. My boss, who was usually pretty tolerant because he knew my family, sat me down and told me that I had to pull myself together or I would lose my job.

Soon after that, I met someone at a party who gave me some pills and told me how to use them. At first the pills seemed to be the answer to my problems. I could orchestrate my moods. If I was down, I took an upper. If I was up, I took a downer. I felt as if I could handle things. The pills made my life easier, or so it seemed. After about six months I tried to give them up. The crash was horrendous. I couldn't cope with the feelings. For the next year I tried to stop over and over again, but I kept going back to those pills. I felt like a junkie.

Everyone around me was doing cocaine so I figured I'd try that. Cocaine seemed to give me the best lift of all. For the first time in my life I could talk to people without that nervous feeling. I felt fluid, rather than blocked. Words tripped off my tongue. I could flirt. I felt like a somebody. I was using more and more coke, and when I couldn't get it, I used the pills. I stayed high for two or three days at a time. But coming off the coke was worse than the pills. As exhausted as I was, I could not let myself sleep because I was convinced I would never wake up again. My panic got so intense that I had to the pills. As exhausted as I was, I could not let myself sleep because I was convinced I would never wake up again. My panic got so intense that I had to call people I knew to come and sit by my bed while I slept.

So, that was my life, and it went on for years — six or seven, I think. I went into debt. I couldn't keep a job. I had to beg my family for money I claimed was for business investments, and I used it to pay the dealers. My parents told me to come home, but I lied to them and stayed away. I was 25 and burning out fast. I was afraid I was going to end up dead on the street one day. I couldn't take it anymore.

 **CLINICAL DISCUSSION**

Jane's case illustrates the kind of drug use that starts out being socially tolerated or even approved of as a performance-enhancer, and ends up destroying health, relationships, finances, and work life. As it is for many people, Jane's drug use was her way of trying to quell intense feelings of insecurity, low self-esteem, and anxiety.

Her breakdown in functioning occurred when she left home and had to cope on her own. As lonely and shy as Jane might have been at home, her parents nonetheless represented a background of safety and security, upon which Jane depended. The self-consciousness about her physical appearance (feeling fat and unglamorous) that she had hoped to escape by becoming part of the sophisticated scene in the city was only reinforced. Jane was unable to cope on her own but felt she had to conceal her dependence on other people. All these factors made Jane vulnerable to developing a substance abuse problem.

Food was her first abused substance. Taken in excess, it was narcotizing. In childhood, food had become an uncontrollable and increasingly necessary means of gaining comfort. After she rejected food as unfashionable and embarrassing, Jane's anxiety intensified. The pills, and later the cocaine, initially gave her comfort. However, they also set in motion actual physiological changes that accelerated the processes of anxiety and depression that were linked to substance abuse in the first place and intensified the very feelings and sensations she was trying to master. This physiological addiction differs from psychological dependence because the failure to satisfy the cravings for the substance results in acute physiological distress.

Like most substance abusers, Jane started out thinking she was in control and quickly learned she was at the mercy of the drugs. The pleasurable sensations that the drugs created were part of their appeal. The rush of confidence and well-being that Jane felt was a reinforcing aspect of addictive substance use. However, living without the sensations and feelings induced by pills and cocaine was especially difficult for Jane because she had preexisting deficiencies in her capacity to tolerate any kind of psychological distress.

This new dependence on the drugs only increased Jane's anxiety and helpless feeling. She started using one drug (cocaine) to counteract the aftermath of using the other, mood-altering drugs. She concealed the depth of her addiction by spending whatever was required to maintain a constant supply and avoid withdrawal. The relationships she did have, however insufficient in the first place, were destroyed by her need to lie, conceal her needs, and maintain a fictional self-image. This spiral of escalating psychological distress, social dysfunction, and physiological craving is the characteristic picture of the substance abuser. Untangling all these strands would require far more of Jane than simply recovery from physiological dependence.

CASE QUESTIONS

1. What is meant by the idea that drugs may be a way of self-medicating?

2. What psychological factors contributed to making Jane a candidate for substance abuse? How did the social environment in which Jane lived add to her vulnerability?

3. Explain the difference between physiological addiction and psychological dependence.

4. Explain how Jane's case illustrates why addictions are so difficult to break.

SELF-TEST

1. **The life of an average alcoholic is about _____ years shorter than that of a non-alcoholic.**
   a) 3
   b) 6
   c) 12
   d) 18

2. **All of the following are common misconceptions about alcohol and alcoholism EXCEPT**
   a) alcohol can help a person sleep more soundly.
   b) alcohol has strong addictive properties.
   c) alcohol is a stimulant.
   d) one cannot become an alcoholic just by drinking beer.

3. **A person is considered intoxicated when the alcohol content of the bloodstream reaches _____ percent.**
   a) 0.1
   b) 0.5
   c) 1.0
   d) 1.5

4. **Which of the following describes the effects of alcohol on sexuality?**
   a) decreases stimulation and lowers performance
   b) decreases stimulation but raises performance
   c) increases stimulation and raises performance
   d) increases stimulation but lowers performance

5. **Genetic studies of alcoholism show that which of the following groups have the highest rate of alcoholism?**
   a) persons with no alcoholic parents
   b) persons with one alcoholic parent
   c) persons with one alcoholic sibling
   d) persons with two alcoholic parents

6. **For the individual whose personal problems result in a great deal of anxiety, drinking is probably reinforced by**
   a) an increase in anxiety.
   b) a reduction in anxiety.
   c) feelings of alienation.
   d) social interactions.

7. Which of the following treatment approaches appears to be least effective for problem drinking?
   a) behavioral
   b) cognitive-behavioral
   c) Alcoholics Anonymous
   d) psychodynamic

8. Which of the following drugs does not belong in the same classification as the others?
   a) cannabis
   b) librium
   c) mescaline
   d) psilocybin

9. All of the following are true about methadone hydrochloride EXCEPT it
   a) is a synthetic narcotic.
   b) is addictive like heroin.
   c) produces serious psychological impairment.
   d) satisfies the addict's craving for heroin.

10. A well-controlled study by Rounsaville found that when psychotherapy was used in addition to methadone maintenance for heroin addicts,
   a) effectiveness markedly declined.
   b) effectiveness markedly improved.
   c) no difference in the effectiveness emerged.
   d) psychotherapy alone was superior.

11. All of the following are symptoms of withdrawal from barbiturates EXCEPT
   a) anxiety.
   b) convulsions.
   c) narcolepsy.
   d) tremors.

12. Amphetamines are classified as
   a) antianxiety drugs.
   b) narcotics.
   c) sedatives.
   d) stimulants.

13. Amphetamines are
   a) both psychologically and physiologically addictive.
   b) neither physiologically nor psychologically addictive.
   c) physiologically but not psychologically addictive.
   d) psychologically but not physiologically addictive.

14. Individuals who have stopped taking LSD may experience involuntary recurrence of perceptual distortions weeks or months after their last use of the drugs. These recurrences are called
   a) bad trips.
   b) déjà vu.
   c) flashbacks.
   d) regressions.

15. When marijuana is smoked and inhaled, the smoker typically experiences all of the following EXCEPT

    a) a sharpening of short-term memory.

    b) a state of mild euphoria.

    c) feelings of well-being.

    d) heightened perceptual acuity.

16. The most effective psychological treatment for hyperobesity is _____ therapy.

    a) behavioral management

    b) gestalt

    c) psychodynamic

    d) rational-emotive

17. According to a study by Graham, pathological gamblers, alcoholics, and heroin addicts have all of the following common characteristics EXCEPT

    a) impulsivity.

    b) narcissism.

    c) optimism.

    d) self-centeredness.

18. Over half of all fatal car accidents, homicides, and suicides occur under the influence of

    a) marijuana.

    b) alcohol.

    c) cocaine and/or crack.

    d) amphetamines.

19. Cocaine prevents neurons in the brain from recycling dopamine, _____.

    a) producing an intensified, prolonged pleasure message.

    b) blocking the reception of pleasure messages.

    c) reducing anxiety.

    d) depressing the nervous system.

20. In the disease model of alcoholism, _____ plays an important role.

    a) treatment

    b) gender

    c) conditioning

    d) genetics

21. According to Dr. Childress the single risk factor that is sufficient to result in cocaine addiction is

    a) alcohol use.

    b) socioeconomic class.

    c) exposure to the drug.

    d) frequency of other drug use.

22. If a group of people try smoking for several months, about _____ of them will become addicted to nicotine.

    a) 10 percent

    b) 30 percent

    c) 50 percent

    d) 90 percent

23. The three stages of substance abuse treatment are: detoxification, rehabilitation, and
    a) maintenance or aftercare.
    b) group therapy.
    c) long-term individual counseling.
    d) membership in a support group.

24. Tailoring a treatment program to fit the needs of individual patients is called
    a) individualized treatment.
    b) personalized treatment.
    c) substance-person linkage.
    d) treatment matching.

25. In the University of Washington Barlab, students experience
    a) the power of expectations on physical reactions.
    b) the physical effects of small quantities of alcohol.
    c) the physiological effects of social drinking.
    d) alcohol's ability to lower inhibitions.

[ANSWERS: 1-c, 2-b, 3-a, 4-d, 5-d, 6-b, 7-c, 8-b, 9-c, 10-c, 11-c, 12-d, 13-d, 14-c, 15-a, 16-a, 17-c, 18-b, 19-a, 20-d, 21-c, 22-b, 23-a, 24-d, 25-a]

SUGGESTED READINGS

Blum, K., Noble, E. D., Sheridan, P. J., Montgomery, A., Ritchie, T., Jagadeeswaran, P., Nogami, H., Briggs, A. H., & Cohen, J. B. (1990). Allelic association of human dopamine D2 receptor gene in alcoholism. *The Journal of the American Medical Association, 263,* 2094. This article reports on research linking a specific gene to alcoholism. (Read with Gardis, et al., 1990, below.)

Brecker, E. M., & the editors of *Consumer Reports.* (1972). *Licit and illicit drugs.* Boston: Little, Brown. The Consumer's Union report catalogs narcotics, stimulants, depressants, inhalants, hallucinogens, marijuana, caffeine, nicotine, and alcohol. It identifies each drug, discusses its history, reviews its biology, and outlines its uses and abuses. Old but not dated, this work is a good compendium of basic facts.

Cocores, J. (1990). *The 800-COCAINE book of drug and alcohol recovery.* New York: Random House. Written by the medical director of an outpatient recovery center, this book discusses the use of a 12-step drug treatment model in combination with nutritional counseling, exercise, therapy, and medication. It tackles the issues of addiction and recovery in terms of the implications for relationships, sexuality, and reentering society as a person in recovery.

Gardis, E., Tabakoff, B., Goldman, D., & Berg, K. (1990). Finding the gene(s) for alcoholism. *The Journal of the American Medical Association, 263,* 2094. This is an editorial summarizing both the practical and philosophical problems inherent in the search for a genetic basis for alcoholism. It is well reasoned and well written. (Read with Blum et al., 1990, above.)

Gelman, D. (1990, September 24). Some things work. *Newsweek, 116,* 78. This article reviews the state of the cocaine crisis in America and reports on several seemingly successful programs for the treatment of crack addiction.

Holden, C. (1989). Klaber offers expert and blunt opinions on addiction. *Science, 246,* 1381. In an interview, Herbert Kleber, a psychiatrist in the federal government's drug use prevention program, discusses both the behavior of addicted people and how public policy can be used effectively to end substance abuse.

Joseph, A. M., Nichol, K. L., Willenbring, M. L., Korn, J. E., & Lysaght, L. S. (1990, June 13). Beneficial effects of treatment of nicotine dependence during an inpatient substance abuse treatment program. *The Journal of the American Medical Association, 263,* 3043. This encouraging report discusses simultaneous treatment of nicotine addiction with other substance abuse problems.

National Academy of Sciences, Institute of Medicine. (1990). *Broadening the base of treatment for alcohol problems.* Washington, DC: National Academy Press. This extensive report describes the current state of treatment for alcohol problems and discusses changes in the goals of treatment.

Williams, T. (1989). *The cocaine kids: The inside story of a teenage drug ring.* Reading, MA: Addison-Wesley. The author hung out with gang members over a long period of time, gained their trust, and saw firsthand how they lived. The well-written book captures the real lives of teenagers caught between poverty and the allure of the money and power of drug dealing.

UNIT 7

SEXUAL
DISORDERS

■ UNIT THEME

For most people, sex is a pleasurable experience. Some people, however, find sex to be difficult or even undesirable. And some use sex to harm either others or themselves. This unit discusses a variety of sexual dysfunctions and sexual disorders (focusing on paraphilia, rape, gender dysphoria, and desire and arousal disorders) and addresses potential psychological, sociocultural, and biological causal factors as well as approaches to treatment.

■ UNIT ASSIGNMENTS

Read: Unit 7. "Sexual Disorders" in *The World of Abnormal Psychology Study Guide*, Toby Kleban Levine, editor (HarperCollins, 1992).

View: Program 7. "Sexual Disorders" in THE WORLD OF ABNORMAL PSYCHOLOGY.

Read: Chapter 10. "Sexual Disorders and Variants" in *Abnormal Psychology and Modern Life*, Ninth Edition, by Robert C. Carson and James N. Butcher (HarperCollins, 1992).

■ GOALS AND OBJECTIVES

1. List and describe the sexual dysfunctions and differentiate them according to which affect men only, women only, and both sexes.

2. Discuss four factors that may cause sexual dysfunctions.

3. Describe the recent revolution in the treatment of sexual dysfunctions and explain why sexual dysfunctions are not normally considered disorders of individuals but of couples.

4. Differentiate between victimless and nonconsent types of sexual variations and list several examples of each.

5. Summarize the results of research concerning biological and psychosocial causes of gender identity disorder and evaluate sex reassignment surgery as a solution.

6. Define nine paraphilias and summarize what is known about their causes.

7. Define incest and summarize what is known about the psychological effects on its victims.

8. Differentiate between forcible and statutory rape and describe motives that may influence the rapist.

9. Summarize what is known about the successful treatment of sexual variants and deviations.

10. Explain why homosexuality has been removed from the list of officially recognized mental disorders.

UNIT OVERVIEW

by Edward S. Katkin, Ph.D.
State University of New York
at Stony Brook

Few aspects of human behavior elicit more interest, and more controversy, than sexual behavior. This unit focuses on some of the most prevalent forms of sexual disorders and considers their cause and treatment.

Basically, sexual disorders can be divided into two major categories: **paraphilias**, or deviations from normal sexual behavior, and **sexual dysfunctions**, or inabilities to achieve normal sexual function.

Bear in mind that no universally agreed upon definition of normal sexual behavior exists, and attempts to define it are extremely controversial. Even within one society, such as the United States, such definitions vary from community to community, and from subgroup to subgroup. For this reason our legal system has left it to local communities to define the legal boundaries of sexual behavior.

Your textbook describes a great variety of paraphilias and sexual dysfunctions and also includes a section on homosexuality, which is not now considered to be a sexual disorder. The video introduces patients with specific paraphilias and dysfunctions. Specifically, the paraphiliacs include a man with **exhibitionism** and a rapist; the sexually dysfunctional patients include a married woman who has little or no desire for sexual relations and her husband. In addition, you will meet Brad, a man who was born female, and who functioned as a biologically normal female, but who felt psychologically that she was a male. Brad has had surgical, medical, and psychological treatment to become more male and now functions almost entirely as a man. Patients like Brad have a condition known as **gender dysphoria**, meaning that they are psychologically displeased with and unable to accept their biologically defined gender. These gender dysphorias constitute their own category, being neither paraphilias nor dysfunctions.

■ SEXUAL DEVIATIONS (PARAPHILIAS)

Sexual deviations are generally defined as behavior that falls outside broad limits of what is ethically and legally accepted. The video presents Dave, an exhibitionist who periodically would expose himself and masturbate in public. This sexual behavior disturbed Dave and he wished to overcome it, but at times when he felt that his self-esteem was damaged, perhaps by a social rejection, he could not control his impulses to expose himself and masturbate. As with most individuals with paraphilias, Dave is eager to change and has sought treatment.

You also will meet Gene, a convicted rapist serving a long jail sentence. Gene is a repeat offender, and he describes the manner in which he both raped and terrorized his victims. The overlap between rape and general aggression is very well documented. Some theorists believe that the primary motive for rape is not sexual, but rather a need to dominate and humiliate the victim. On the other hand, because the rapist chooses a sexual form of domination and humiliation rather than some other aggressive act, the act must necessarily be considered a sexual deviation.

■ SEXUAL DYSFUNCTION

A great many forms of sexual dysfunction have been identified, and it is estimated that about one-third of the adult population has had a sexual dysfunction at one time or another. Three typical dysfunctions are disorders of desire, disorders of arousal, and disorders of orgasm. The video focuses on two of these, **sexual desire disorders** and **sexual arousal disorders.** Jan has a very low desire for sexual relations with her husband. In many cases of diminished sexual desire the patients report that it is not that their partner is undesirable or unattractive, nor is it that sex activity is unpleasant — they just have a very low level of interest in sexual relations. In Jan's case, interpersonal problems in her relationship with her husband probably contributed to her diminished desire.

Arousal disorders generally refer to cases in which an individual wants to have sex but cannot, for physical or psychological reasons. A common example is a man who cannot have an erection. Frequently, this may be due to medical problems, such as the side effects of medication. The case described in the video refers to people who cannot have sex following the death of a spouse. In such cases, it is assumed that the disorder may be due, at least in part, to a sense of guilt or betrayal the patient may feel for the deceased spouse.

■ CAUSES OF SEXUAL DISORDERS

Although the precise cause of the various sexual disorders is impossible to specify, biological factors seem to play a relatively minor role. In some cases, sexual dysfunction might be partly a result of biological alterations due to either disease or medication. In others, the primary cause of paraphilias and sexual dysfunctions appears to be faulty learning and socialization.

Most theorists agree that sexual attitudes and orientations are learned in childhood, and that at an early age we develop a specific cognitive map that guides our sexual behavior throughout our lives. This cognitive map has been called the **lovemap**. Presumably this map is fairly well defined before we reach adulthood, and it is very difficult to modify. If the map is influenced by distorting early experiences, or goes awry for any reason, the outcome is likely to be deviant sexual behavior or some form of sexual dysfunction. It is common for sexual deviants to have had very abusive parents, for example, and they often report being sexually abused themselves or witnessing sexual abuse in their families.

■ TREATMENT

Most of the successful treatments for sexual disorders have been developed in the past 25 years. Until the 1970s sexual disorders were treated almost exclusively by insight-oriented psychotherapies, and success was limited. Most of what we now know about the therapy of sexual disorders is based upon the pioneering work of Dr. William Masters and Virginia Johnson, the first contemporary research scientists to study normal as well as disordered sexual behavior. As a result of their research, sexual disorders are now treated primarily by cognitive therapies that focus on helping patients to modify thoughts that may interfere with their functioning, and by behavioral therapies that aim to teach patients specific behaviors that will improve their sexual functioning. In addition, Masters and Johnson introduced the couple as the focus of treatment, rather than just the individual. In the video you will meet Dr. Renshaw and see how she deals with arousal and desire disorders.

■ KEY TERMS

The following terms are used in the text and/or the television programs.

Dyspareunia	A sexual dysfunction involving painful sexual intercourse; usually has an organic basis but also may have a psychological basis.
Exhibitionism	A paraphilia in which one intentionally exposes one's genitals to others in inappropriate circumstances and without their consent.
Female sexual arousal disorder	A sexual dysfunction in which a woman has an absence of sexual arousal feelings and is unresponsive to most or all forms of sexual stimulation; its chief physical manifestation is the failure to produce the lubrication-swelling response to sexual stimulation.

Fetishism	A paraphilia in which sexual interest is centered on a particular body part or inanimate object.
Fixated	An arrested psychosexual development at a childhood or adolescent level; within the sexual disorders, sexuality and sexual interest may not have progressed beyond a certain age level.
Gender dysphoria	A feeling of extreme unhappiness about one's biological sex based on a deep confusion between a person's physical sex and his or her sexual identity.
Gender identity disorder	A disorder characterized by confusion or uncertainty between one's biological sex and gender identity, where gender identity is the knowledge of the sex to which one belongs.
Homosexuality	A sexual preference for a member of one's own sex.
Hypoactive sexual desire	A dysfunction in which one shows little or no sexual drive or interest.
Incest	A culturally prohibited sexual relationship between family members, up to and including sexual intercourse.
Inhibited female orgasm	A delay in or absence of orgasm following normal and sufficient stimulation, as determined by a clinician.
Lovemap	The pattern of a person's erotic attachments and preferences and his or her idealized scenario for achieving sexual fulfillment; the basic properties, or template, of a person's lovemap are thought to be largely settled prior to puberty and, once settled, are highly resistant to subsequent alteration. The concept was formulated by John Money, Ph.D.
Male erectile disorder	A sexual dysfunction involving an inability to achieve or maintain an erection for successful sexual intercourse; formerly known as impotence. Primary and secondary erectile insufficiency describe specific forms of the disorder.
Masochism	A paraphilia in which one attains sexual pleasure through self-denial and the infliction of pain on oneself.
Paraphilias	A group of persistent sexual behavior patterns in which unusual objects, rituals, or situations are required for full sexual satisfaction to occur.
Pedophilia	A paraphilia in which the preferred sex object is a child.
Preferential	An individual's preferred sexual partner; for example, a homosexual-preferential pedophile prefers sex with children of the same gender; a heterosexual-preferential pedophile prefers sex with children of the opposite-sex.
Rape	A sexual activity that occurs under actual or threatened coercion of one person by another.
Sadism	A paraphilia in which one achieves sexual stimulation and gratification through the infliction of physical pain or humiliation on a sexual partner.
Sex reassignment	A treatment for gender identity disorder directed toward changing an individual's sexual identity to the preferred one. It can include psychological counseling, to confirm that gender change is the patient's real desire; hormonal therapy to bring about physiological changes; and surgery to remove one's sexual organs and/or replace them with constructed sexual organs of the preferred gender.

125

Sexual arousal disorder	A sexual dysfunction involving a lack of sexual excitement during sexual activity .
Sexual desire disorder	A dysfunction in which a person has little or no sexual drive or interest.
Sexual dysfunctions	A group of disorders that involve an inhibition in sexual response.
Transvestic fetishism	A paraphilia in which sexual arousal and satisfaction are achieved by dressing as a member of the opposite sex.
Vaginismus	A sexual dysfunction, not related to a physical disorder, in which an involuntary spasm of the muscles at the entrance to the vagina prevents penetration and sexual intercourse.
Variant sexual behavior	A behavior in which sexual satisfaction is dependent on something other than a mutually desired sexual experience with a sexually mature member of the opposite sex.
Victimless	A term that refers to acts of variant sexual behavior that do not infringe on the rights of noninvolved others and/or are engaged in by mutually consenting adults who do no physical harm to each other.
Voyeurism	A paraphilia in which one achieves sexual pleasure through secretly watching others; also known as scotophilia and inspectionalism.

■ **VIDEO NOTES**

■ **INTRODUCTION**
• A person's sexual attitudes and behaviors are influenced by a combination of factors.

• Sexual reflexes, like erection and orgasm, are controlled by the medulla, one of the oldest parts of the brain. They are influenced, however, by the more complex, higher regions of the brain where intellect and emotion are processed.

■ **SEXUAL DEVIATIONS**
(Case Illustrations: the football player, Dave)
• Great diversity exists in the way people express their sexuality.

• Behaviors that fall outside ethical and legal limits are considered deviant, although the actual behaviors labelled deviant may differ from culture to culture. Dr. Carson limits the application of the word deviant to those behaviors that are harmful to the individual engaged in them or to others.

• Sexual deviations belong to a category of sexual behavior called paraphilia, which means "beyond love."

• Exhibitionism is an example of a paraphilia.

■ **PARAPHILIA: CAUSAL FACTORS**
• A cycle of behavior generally occurs in which a perceived insult to the masculine self-image is followed by a sense of depression which in turn leads to an urge to expose. The restoration of the exhibitionist's self-esteem is restored by the sexual sensation and the reaction of the victim. This restoration often is temporary and may be followed quickly by renewed feelings of shame and remorse which, in turn, may restart the cycle.

■ PARAPHILIA: TREATMENT

• Treatment typically is provided in both individual and group settings.

• Group therapy helps overcome feelings of aloneness and shame and provides an environment in which others with the same problem can see through one another's defense mechanisms.

• Individual therapy tries to resolve long-standing problems, such as a lack of self-worth or the results of having been raised in a dysfunctional family.

■ THE LOVEMAP

• The lovemap, a concept developed by Dr. John Money, is a template that tells you what you will find sexually arousing.

> It is similar to a native language. You don't have it in your head on the day you are born, but it develops early in childhood, after which it is difficult to change.

> The standard lovemap is heterosexual, although a secondary, homosexual, standard also exists.

• Some lovemaps are defaced or vandalized by life events. Paraphilic behavior is an example of a defaced lovemap.

• More than 90 percent of paraphiliacs are men, possibly because men are exposed to and rewarded for high levels of aggressive behavior. Exhibitionism, voyeurism, and rape all involve elements of power, aggression, and domination.

■ RAPE

(Case Illustration: Gene)

• Rape is a fusion of sexuality and violence.

• As many as one in four women in the United States will be sexually assaulted.

• Individuals commit rape for many reasons, e.g., some people believe that they can have or take whatever they want (antisocial personalities), some become aggressive when their inhibitions are lowered through alcohol or drug use, some need to humiliate another person in order to achieve sexual gratification, some who are aroused by and prefer consensual sex will use force when refused (e.g., date rape).

• To determine a particular individual's motivation to rape requires an analysis of the individual, his family, and the society in which he grew up.

• Like exhibitionists, rapists often go through a clear behavioral cycle. It is not uncommon for some rapists to leave an angry interaction and masturbate to angry thoughts in order to seek relief from their sense of rage. Sometimes this is followed by passive planning in which sexual offenders go to great lengths to plan their offenses to appear impulsive, for example, by drinking to lower their inhibitions.

■ THE RAPIST: TREATMENT

• Breaking the pattern forms the basis of treatment for sexual offenders.

> Cognitive therapy focuses on helping an individual modify faulty beliefs and attitudes that may interfere with functioning.

Victim empathy training, in which the perpetrator must write the details of the crime from the victim's point of view and then engage in role-playing to relive the crime from both persons' points of view, helps the rapist grasp the consequences of his act.

• Some people question whether rapists should be treated or simply jailed. Dr. Becker sees treatment as a means of prevention.

■ GENDER DYSPHORIA
(Case Illustration: Brad)

• A person's genetic sex is determined at conception. At birth, a person's sexual organs almost always match his or her sexual organs. The subsequent development of sexual identity is not well understood, but is clearly influenced by social and biological factors.

• When confusion exists between a person's physical sex and his or her personal sexual identity, the result is gender dysphoria, literally an unhappiness about one's biological sex.

Brad was born female, but always thought of herself as a boy. She has always been sexually attracted to women. To resolve her gender dysphoria, after several years of counseling, Brad began taking male hormones. These changed his body shape, lowered his voice, and led to the growth of facial and body hair. He had a double mastectomy to remove his breasts and a hysterectomy to remove his fallopian tubes and ovaries, but decided not to have a penis constructed. His female genitalia are intact and he is capable of having an orgasm.

• Doctors caution that surgery should not be considered for gender dysphoria until other psychological problems are resolved.

■ SEXUAL DYSFUNCTION

• As many as one in three adults in the United States have experienced some form of sexual dysfunction.

• Sexual dysfunction can occur when one or more physical or emotional elements goes awry.

On a biological level, the nervous system, the circulatory system, and the endocrine system all work to produce the necessary physical components required for sexual arousal and orgasm.

The psychological components of fantasy and desire are equally important in achieving arousal and satisfaction.

• The three basic types of sexual dysfunction are: a loss of desire for sex, the inability to be sexually aroused, and either a lack of orgasm or an inability to control orgasm. These may result from medical problems, be related to medications taken, or be psychological in origin.

■ TREATMENT

• Behavioral techniques that teach the male how to control his ejaculatory response are generally used to treat premature ejaculation.

• Such techniques emerged from the research of William Masters and Virginia Johnson in the 1970s, which changed much of the thinking about sexual dysfunctions. Their methods combine talking in the office with practical assignments that are carried out in the privacy of the home.

• According to Helen Singer Kaplan, many patients also need psychodynamic therapy to work out such related problems as anxiety.

• Masters and Johnson also introduced another important concept in sex therapy: the concept of the couple, rather than the individual, as the focus of treatment.

■ AROUSAL DISORDERS

• A person who wants to participate in intercourse but cannot (because of the inability to have an erection, for example) has an arousal disorder. It was once thought such disorders were totally emotional rather than physical. Dr. Helen Singer Kaplan believes that as many as 50 percent of people over age 50 who have sexual complaints may have some organic or medical condition that contributes to the disorder, e.g., medications that have sexual side-effects, diabetes, arteriosclerosis, or hormone deficiencies. Sometimes the problems are both emotional and physical.

• In treating cases of arousal disorder, Dr. Renshaw focuses both on the relationship and on teaching new sexual techniques that can bring satisfaction without intercourse.

■ DESIRE DISORDERS
(Case Illustration: Jan and Mel)
• Roughly one in three people who seek out sex therapy do so because they feel they do not want sex often enough.

• Dr. Renshaw uses relationship therapy to allow the couple to focus on themselves and on spending time together.

• Dr. Renshaw also uses a technique called sensate focusing as a way to concentrate attention on the pleasures of being touched. Sensate focusing exercises are done at home and emphasize touching without intercourse.

■ VIDEO REVIEW QUESTIONS

1. Discuss what is known and suspected about the relationship between the brain and sexual behavior.

2. What is a sexual deviation? Discuss the reasoning behind your definition.

3. Describe the typical cycle of feelings and behaviors experienced by exhibitionists and discuss how knowledge of this cycle can be used to influence treatment.

4. What is the concept of a lovemap and how does it apply to the case of Brad, the individual with gender dysphoria?

5. Discuss how power, aggression, and domination are related to paraphilia.

6. Find a newspaper article about a rape. Using what you know about the many reasons an individual commits rape, develop a scenario to explain why this particular rape took place.

7. Should rapists be jailed, treated, or both? Explain your point of view.

8. In what way did the work of Masters and Johnson differentiate sex therapy from other types of therapy?

9. Why is it important to treat the couple and not just the individual in sex therapy?

CASE STUDY

by Henry E. Adams, Ph.D.
University of Georgia

Kevin

Doctor, I am so glad to get to talk to someone who might understand. God, I can't believe that I told the police everything. But I was so frightened and they seemed so nice, I blurted out everything I had ever done in my whole life. I should have known that they wouldn't understand.

It's so stupid. I met these people in church. How could they have done this to me? I tried to be nice to them by babysitting their sons. I had to bathe them, didn't I? After all, they were only four and seven. Besides, the little one seemed to get so excited when I took his little clothes off. When I put soap on his little penis, he got an erection. It was as much his fault as mine. He was so seductive and cute, it just turned me on. Yes, I did place my mouth on his penis, but I didn't encourage them to rub my penis; they did it themselves. I put my dick between their legs, but it's not as if I tried anal intercourse with them. I know that might have hurt them. I'm not gay. I love children, particularly boys.

I cannot understand why he told his mother, though. He had agreed that it was our secret because I told him that adults would not understand. I did not threaten him. God, I still love him. It's not just sexual, you know. I really love the company of little boys and love to be around them. Adults are so critical and judgmental, they make me uncomfortable. They play such silly games and have such stupid ideas. They really do not understand or care about children. Anybody who bothered to notice would know that little boys are very sexual creatures. You people just inhibit their natural sexuality. I don't force children against their will. I have never threatened a child to have sex with me. They love me. They want to. Most of them have seduced me.

Oh God, I am so depressed, I want to die. How can I stay in prison? How can I live without my little darling, my sweet boy? I just want to kill myself.

CLINICAL DISCUSSION

Kevin was a very religious young man who had taught Sunday school since he was in college. He did not smoke, drink, or take drugs. While he was a fairly successful professional person, he rarely dated women because he felt that they perceived him as unattractive. He had always had difficulties in knowing how to interact with women on an intimate level.

Kevin was an only child. His parents were both professional people. They rarely socialized, had very few friends, but attended church regularly. His father, an accountant, worked much of the time. He was very strict, religious, and moralistic and was concerned that Kevin know and adhere to the proper rules of conduct and behavior. While he never physically abused his son, his father terrified Kevin. Trivial misconduct often led to punishment and an angry but cold reaction. Kevin's mother, a nurse, was overprotective but rejecting.

In grade school, most of Kevin's friends were younger boys. He was quite shy and timid with girls, as well as with male peers. At around ten years of age, his curiosity about

130

sexuality was piqued by seeing some of his younger, male friends nude, and he began to talk them into games in which they disrobed. This activity eventually developed into mutual masturbation and fondling. He often enticed them into these games either by offering to teach them to masturbate or by exploiting their curiosity about girls and sex.

In high school, Kevin was often the object of teasing or bullying by his peers. He dated only when pressured by his parents or for such special social occasions as the school prom. He viewed these dates as traumatic and had little interest in girls. His sexual and masturbation fantasies were of fondling and fellatio with younger boys, six to eight years of age. Most of his social life centered around the church. He began to assist and later to teach Sunday school classes particularly with six- to eight-year-old children. During this time, he also began to babysit.

Kevin had his sole heterosexual encounter during college when he became intoxicated at a party. An equally inebriated coed decided to initiate him into sexual intercourse. The experience was a disaster because he could not get an erection, and he was embarrassed and traumatized. It reinforced his decision to avoid both alcohol and sexual encounters with females.

After graduation, Kevin returned home and took a job as a C.P.A. He attended church regularly and babysat for his friends. A year later, he was arrested for child molestation. He had babysat two boys, ages four and seven, over a weekend. A few days later, the mother observed the younger boy manipulating his penis while he was bathing. When asked where he had learned this, he said, "It's a secret." On further questioning, he told his mother that he and his brother had bathed with Kevin and that Kevin had taught them a game of making their "weenies" hard by fondling and kissing them. The older boy confirmed his brother's story.

When arrested, Kevin immediately confessed in excruciating detail to sexually abusing 40 to 50 boys over the past ten years. He justified his behavior by stating that parents were too secretive about sex and that he did not feel that he had harmed the children nor was that his intent. On the contrary, he loved children, he felt, more than most people. He further mentioned that he did not know that this activity was against the law. He became quite depressed and withdrawn, and threatened suicide when incarcerated. The community was surprised that such a nice, religious, educated young man could have committed such acts.

Kevin has the rather typical history of a fixated or homosexual-preferential pedophile. His father was a man who intimidated him, and his mother was overprotective yet rejecting. From the beginning of his life, his sense of security and masculinity were undermined. Furthermore, his physical unattractiveness and poor athletic ability led to further rejection by his peers, which aggravated his insecurity. He turned to younger children where he was accepted and respected. These predisposing factors set the stage for the initial sex play with younger boys. This event precipitated his sexual interest in younger boys, which was reinforced and perpetuated by his use of the memory of these sexually exciting occasions to arouse him in his masturbation activities. This behavior pattern, once established, precipitated a number of subsequent elaborations of his disorder. Because he had no sexual interest in girls during adolescence, he was not motivated to learn the heterosocial and heterosexual skills necessary for initiating and maintaining adult sexual and marital behavior. He turned to the church not primarily for religious reasons, but because children are present in the church. He developed a pattern of behavior (i.e., babysitting) that allowed him to have sexual contact with boys much in the same way that males develop patterns of behavior (i.e., "a line") to seduce adult females. He not only was interested in these young boys sexually, he preferred their company socially. He even related to adults as a child in many ways and was perceived by them as "a nice, religious boy." When caught, he reacted in a very childish manner, confessing all, and becoming depressed. His insistence of not being aware of the legal implications of his acts and his belief that children should be exposed to sexual activity are the kinds of cognitive distortions often seen in these cases.

CASE QUESTIONS

1. It is often assumed that homosexuality (preference for sexual activity with mature members of the same sex) is present in homosexual-preferential pedophiles. Does this case contradict that notion? Why?

2. It is often claimed that pedophiles exhibit cognitive distortions (i.e., false beliefs). Can you give some examples of these unusual beliefs in this case? How might these cognitive distortions develop and what purpose do they serve?

3. Kevin was very depressed, even suicidal. What role has depression played in this case and Kevin's activities? Could his behavior warrant another clinical diagnosis? If so, why?

4. Is there a relationship between social behavior (or, loosely, personality) and sexual preference? What aspects of this case support your answer?

SELF-TEST

1. Howard has visited his physician several times to ask what he can do to achieve an erection and maintain it. According to Howard, he has never been able to have successful intercourse. His physician probably diagnosed his trouble as
   - a) organic impotence.
   - b) primary erectile insufficiency.
   - c) psychogenic impotence.
   - d) secondary erectile insufficiency.

2. While Jeanne has a number of male friends, she has never had any sexual feelings. Jeanne's problem would probably be diagnosed as
   - a) functional vaginismus.
   - b) primary orgasmic dysfunction.
   - c) secondary orgasmic dysfunction.
   - d) sexual arousal disorder.

3. Masters and Johnson believe that the primary cause of orgasmic dysfunction in females is
   - a) faulty learning.
   - b) hormonal imbalance.
   - c) intrapsychic conflict.
   - d) organic abnormalities.

4. Transvestism is classified by your authors as a
   - a) nonconsensual sexual deviation.
   - b) organic sexual dysfunction.
   - c) psychosexual dysfunction.
   - d) victimless sexual variant.

5. Research by Money and colleagues has established that the formation of gender identity is mostly determined by
    a) genotype.
    b) hormones.
    c) learning.
    d) physique.

6. The incidence of gender identity disorders in males is estimated to be somewhat LESS than three in _____.
    a) 100
    b) 1,000
    c) 10,000
    d) 100,000

7. All of the following are true about sex-reassignment surgery EXCEPT
    a) men who have become women can often achieve coital orgasm.
    b) men who have become women usually take female sex hormones after the operations.
    c) people who have undergone sex-change operations always are sterile.
    d) women who have become men have normally functioning penises.

8. Persistent sexual arousal patterns in which unusual objects, rituals, or situations are required for full sexual satisfaction are classified as
    a) factitious disorders.
    b) gender identity disorders.
    c) paraphilias.
    d) psychosexual dysfunctions.

9. Jack was arrested for breaking and entering a women's shoe store. When police searched his home they found 100 boxes of women's shoes in his bedroom. Under further questioning, he revealed that they were his only way of gaining sexual satisfaction. Jack's paraphilia was
    a) fetishism.
    b) frotteurism.
    c) pedophilia.
    d) voyeurism.

10. All of the following are synonyms EXCEPT
    a) exhibitionism.
    b) inspectionalism.
    c) scotophilia.
    d) voyeurism.

11. A significant number of cases of exhibitionism are associated with which of the following personality disorders?
    a) antisocial
    b) obsessive-compulsive
    c) narcissistic
    d) passive-aggressive

12. All of the following have been implicated as causal factors in sadism EXCEPT
- a) association with other pathology.
- b) excessive testosterone production.
- c) experiences in which orgasm has been associated with the infliction of pain.
- d) negative attitudes toward sex.

13. Ralph has been arrested several times for sexual abuse of little girls. He becomes sexually aroused when he fondles their genitals, but he has never attempted sexual intercourse. Ralph's paraphilia is
- a) fetishism.
- b) pedophilia.
- c) transvestic fetishism.
- d) voyeurism.

14. Which of the following forms of incest is most common?
- a) brother-sister
- b) father-daughter
- c) father-stepdaughter
- d) mother-son

15. Which of the following is the most frequent type of rape?
- a) anger-excitation
- b) anger-retaliation
- c) power-assertive
- d) power-reassurance

16. When individuals with sexual variant behavior are treated by pairing unpleasant or painful stimuli with their arousal state, _____ has been used.
- a) aversive conditioning
- b) backwards conditioning
- c) deconditioning
- d) discrimination training

17. Oscar can't seem to get full sexual satisfaction from his wife unless he bites her on the shoulder. Since he never actually breaks the skin, she goes along with it and yells as though she really is hurt. This stimulates her husband immensely and they both enjoy great sex. Oscar's paraphilia is
- a) fetishism.
- b) frotteurism.
- c) masochism.
- d) sadism.

18. The lovemap is a
- a) a biological template present from birth.
- b) a psychological template that tells you what your erotic sex and your erotic sexual attraction is going to be.
- c) not affected by life events.
- d) identical for all members of a species.

19. Which of the following types of rape usually is triggered by a blow to the rapist's ego?
- a) anger-excitation
- b) anger-retaliation
- c) power-assertive
- d) power-reassurance

20. When Gene, the rapist in the program, puts himself into his victim's shoes and attempts to describe her thoughts and feelings, Gene is undergoing
- a) thought substitution.
- b) sensate focusing.
- c) cognitive-emotional visualization.
- d) victim empathy training.

21. Unhappiness resulting from a discrepancy between a person's physical sex and his or her sexual identity is called
- a) gender discrepancy.
- b) a discrepant lovemap.
- c) gender dysphoria.
- d) transvestism.

22. Treatment for premature ejaculation
- a) consists of teaching the male how to control his ejaculatory response.
- b) is based on the work of William Masters and Virginia Johnson.
- c) consists of exercises to help the man recognize and control the sensations leading up to orgasm.
- d) all of the above.

23. Jan, the woman in the program who had been married for 20 years, exhibited one of the most common sexual dysfunctions — desire disorder, or
- a) frigidity.
- b) inhibited sex drive.
- c) desire for an unavailable sexual partner.
- d) nymphomania.

[ANSWERS: 1-b, 2-d, 3-a, 4-d, 5-c, 6-d, 7-d, 8-c, 9-a, 10-a, 11-a, 12-b, 13-b, 14-a, 15-c, 16-a, 17-d, 18-b, 19-d, 20-d, 21-c, 22-d, 23-b]

SUGGESTED READINGS

Leiblum, S. R., & Rosen, R. C. (1989). *Principles and practice of sex therapy* (2nd ed.). New York: Guilford Press. An update of this comprehensive treatment handbook, this edition includes discussions of AIDS and of sex therapy in the age of modern sexual mores.

Kaplan, H. S. (1979). *Disorders of sexual desire and other new concepts and techniques in sex therapy.* New York: Simon & Schuster. Dr. Kaplan provides a readable explanation of desire disorders and the ways to treat them.

135

Kaplan, H. S. (1983). *The evaluation of sexual disorders: Psychological and medical aspects.* New York: Brunner/Mazel. This discussion integrates the medical explanations and treatments of sexual disorders with psychological thinking and techniques.

Masters, W. H., & Johnson, V. E. (1970). *Human sexual inadequacy.* Boston: Little, Brown. The early work by these pioneering researchers delves into the roots of sexual problems.

Masters, W. H., Johnson, V. E., & Kolodny, R. C. (1985). *Human sexuality.* Boston: Little, Brown. This book represents a vast compendium of research on the sexual response.

Money, J. (1986). *Lovemaps: Clinical concepts of sexual/erotic health and pathology, paraphilia and gender transposition in childhood, adolescence and maturity.* New York: Irvington. This book introduces and describes Dr. Money's concept of the lovemap.

Money, J., & Lamacz, M. (1989). *Vandalized lovemaps: Paraphilic outcome in seven cases of pediatric sexology.* Buffalo: Prometheus. This study applies Money's lovemap concept to seven case studies.

UNIT 8

MOOD
DISORDERS

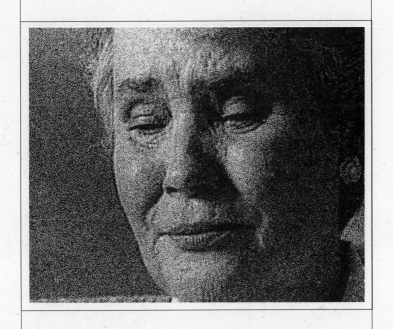

■ UNIT THEME

Moods are universal human experiences. But sometimes moods become the inappropriate, long lasting, or interfere with the ability to function. In short, they become mood disorders. This unit introduces mood disorders from mania to depressive stupor. It explores those factors that contribute to their onset, describes how they disrupt people's lives, and examines treatments that seem to work.

■ UNIT ASSIGNMENTS

Read: Unit 8. "Mood Disorders" in *The World of Abnormal Psychology Study Guide*, Toby Kleban Levine, editor (HarperCollins, 1992).

View: Program 8. "Mood Disorders" in THE WORLD OF ABNORMAL PSYCHOLOGY.

Read: Chapter 11. "Mood Disorders and Suicide" in *Abnormal Psychology and Modern Life*, Ninth Edition, by Robert C. Carson and James N. Butcher (HarperCollins, 1992).

■ GOALS AND OBJECTIVES

1. Describe several mild forms of normal depression and list three psychological variables that are involved with normal forms of depression.

2. List the dimensions customarily used to differentiate mood disorders and give examples of mood disorders from mild to moderate.

3. Describe the clinical manifestations of major depression and summarize what research tells us about the disorder.

4. Describe the symptoms of a bipolar disorder and summarize what research tells us about it.

5. Describe the symptoms of a schizoaffective disorder and explain why some psychologists find this diagnosis controversial.

6. Describe those biological and psychosocial factors that are related to mood disorders.

7. Discuss how sociocultural factors affect the incidence of certain types of mood disorders.

8. Describe several biological and psychosocial therapies that have been successful in treating mood disorders.

9. Describe the types of people who commit suicide, list some of their motives for ending their lives, and discuss how sociocultural variables are important for understanding this result of depression.

10. Discuss the ethical dilemma surrounding a person's right to end his or her own life and differentiate between cases that involve the terminally ill and cases that involve individuals whose wish to die is based on temporary depression.

UNIT OVERVIEW

by Edward S. Katkin, Ph.D.
State University of New York
at Stony Brook

All of us experience changes in mood. Sometimes we are blue; sometimes giddy. Our mood may be determined by an event: A relationship was broken off, we have just won a competitive tennis match, our favorite team has just won the Super Bowl. Or, we may just feel good or bad for no apparent reason. These ups and downs of daily life are normal; indeed, they are in some ways necessary, for without them our lives would be flat and emotionally dull.

Some people, however, experience moods that are so extreme and so unusually disruptive to normal living that they are said to have mood disorders. Although we all are capable of experiencing a wide variety of moods, modern psychology refers only to the dimension of happiness-sadness in its description of mood disorders. In the United States, about 10 percent of the population will experience a mood disorder at some time in their lives.

This unit covers the two broadest categories of diagnosable mood disorders, the **depressive** disorders and the **bipolar** disorders. Depressive disorders refer to those disturbances of mood that are unidirectional — that is, the patient suffers recurrent bouts of deep sadness. In bipolar disorders, the depressed periods alternate with periods of unusually exhilarated behavior, or manic states. For this reason bipolar disorder has been referred to as manic-depressive disorder, although this label is not currently in vogue, and it refers only to one form of bipolar disorder.

In both the depressive and bipolar disorders, the symptoms generally come and go of their own accord. Although they can be treated psychologically and medically, they frequently clear up in due time with no treatment at all. Unfortunately, without treatment, both the depressive and the bipolar disorders usually will recur frequently.

■ DEPRESSIVE DISORDERS

The depressive disorders are divided into two major categories, **major depression** and **dysthymia**. While your text discusses both types of depressive disorder and includes a special section on the relationship between depression and suicide, the video deals primarily with major depression and briefly considers one patient's contemplation of suicide. Major depression is a very serious disorder in which the patient not only feels extremely sad, but shows poor appetite, sleep disturbance, slowing of movement, loss of sexual drive, inability to concentrate, and extreme feelings of worthlessness and guilt that lead often to suicidal thoughts and acts. In extreme forms, major depression can deteriorate into **depressive stupor**, in which the patient retreats to bed or to a dark corner and becomes virtually nonresponsive to any stimulation.

Of all patients with mood disorders, about 10 percent will experience major depression. The video presents Phyllis, a woman who suffered with major depression for 40 years and had suicidal thoughts. Phyllis describes long periods in her life when her major depression interfered severely with her functioning and caused great stress within her family.

Dysthymia is another type of mood disorder in which a milder form of major depression is experienced, but persists for a period of at least two years.

■ BIPOLAR DISORDERS

Less than one percent of Americans suffer from bipolar disorder, a related but clearly different mood disorder. In bipolar disorder moods fluctuate between major depression and extreme excitement and exhilaration. In the video, Rodney describes severe manic episodes, in which he felt possessed and invulnerable. In such periods he was capable of being extremely dangerous to himself as well as to others. When people have recurrent mood swings, but they are not as severe or disruptive as Rodney's, they are said to be **cyclothymic**. Cyclothymia is not to be confused with recurrent episodes of dysthymia. The proper diagnosis of cyclothymia requires that the patient show recurrent episodes of both depressed and mildly manic, or **hypomanic**, mood.

■ CAUSES OF MOOD DISORDERS

No single cause of mood disorders is known, although a variety of psychological and biological theories are widely accepted. Bipolar disorders show a strong familial tendency, but it is difficult to know to what extent the disorder is transmitted genetically and to what extent it is the result of the family environment. The genetic evidence for bipolar disorders is suggestive, but not definitive; the genetic evidence for major depression is weaker still. Research suggests, however, that a basic malfunction of normal nerve function occurs in the central nervous system of depressed patients. Again, it is difficult to determine definitively if the neural malfunction precedes the depression or is a result of it.

Depression also may be caused by such severe life stresses as illness, the loss of a loved one, or loss of employment. Finally, some theorists believe that the cause of depression is deep-rooted, unconscious conflict, particularly conflict which results in turning anger inward on oneself. For each individual it is possible that one, some, or all of these may be causal factors.

■ TREATMENT

Mood disorders are generally treated with a combination of medication and psychotherapy, although some people may be treated with only one or the other. For bipolar disorder, standard practice is to administer **lithium carbonate**, a highly effective drug. The fact that lithium carbonate is relatively ineffective for major depression suggests that bipolar disorder and major depression are distinctly different syndromes.

For major depression, it is common to prescribe medications known as tricyclic **antidepressants**. These drugs have been demonstrated to be quite effective, but they must be taken continually, and they do not work quickly.

Some clinicians find that **cognitive therapy**, a specific form of psychotherapy, is uniquely effective with depression. The principles that guide cognitive therapy emerge from the view that depression may be caused and/or maintained by a set of ideas or thoughts that elicit bad feelings about the self. Cognitive therapists help the patient to discover what these negative thoughts and attitudes are and guide their patients in learning to substitute alternative ways of interpreting and thinking about their lives. Cognitive therapy focuses on current life experience and current thought patterns rather than on past relationships or childhood experiences.

Many therapists also practice more traditional forms of **psychodynamic therapy** with depressed patients. Traditional psychodynamic treatments focus on internal conflicts and their resultant emotions. Psychodynamic therapists assume that different parts of the patient's self (for instance, the unconscious and conscious selves) may be in conflict and that the alleviation of the depressed feelings depends upon discovering the conflict and resolving it. Psychodynamic therapy often focuses on the long-term development of the problem and emphasizes early childhood relationships with parents and other significant figures in the patient's life.

In certain cases of depression neither drugs nor psychotherapy are effective. As a treatment of last resort for such patients, **electroconvulsive therapy**, or ECT, may be employed. In

ECT, which you will see in the video, an electric current is passed through the patient's brain, causing a convulsion. Although no theory satisfactorily explains how this treatment works, it is highly effective in alleviating major depression.

KEY TERMS

The following terms are used in the text and/or the television programs.

Adjustment disorder with depressed mood	A maladaptive adjustment marked by depressive symptoms in response to an identifiable psychosocial stressor; it must have occurred within three months since the onset of the stressor and must not exceed six months in duration. This diagnosis assumes that the individual's problems will remit when the stressor ceases or when a new level of adjustment is achieved.
Adoption method of genetic research	A research method involving the psychiatric evaluation of people who were adopted out of their biological families, and the comparison of their disorders with those of their biological and adoptive family members.
Antidepressants	Drugs used primarily in the treatment of major depression, often effective in prevention as well as treatment for patients subject to recurrent episodes of depression.
Bipolar disorder	A mood disorder marked by one or more manic episodes, usually accompanied by one or more major depressive episodes, with periods of relative normalcy in between; the frequency of the cycling between manic and depressed episodes varies. Bipolar disorders are classified as depressive, manic, or mixed, according to their predominant pattern.
Cognitive therapy	A highly structured, systematic attempt to reeducate the patient in regard to the aberrant cognitions presumed to underlie and maintain the depressed state.
Cyclothymia	A mild mood disorder characterized by numerous hypomanic episodes and periods of depressed mood. These mood swings clearly are maladaptive but are not severe enough to be designated as a bipolar disorder.
Depression	An emotional state characterized by feelings of extraordinary sadness, dejection, worthlessness, and loss of hope.
Depressive stupor	The most severe form of depression in which the individual is completely unresponsive, withdrawn, and virtually immobile.
Dysthymia	A mood disorder in which an individual experiences symptoms of chronic depressed mood for at least two years (one year for children and adolescents). There must be no evidence of a major depressive episode in at least the preceding two years.
Electroconvulsive therapy (ECT)	Sometimes used to treat patients with major depression who present an immediate and serious suicidal risk. An electric current is passed through the brain, causing a convulsion. ECT is highly successful, but it can cause such serious side effects as memory loss, disorientation, and in some cases, irreversible brain damage. Also called electroshock therapy.

141

Familial concordance	The degree to which particular symptoms (or clusters of them) are shared by blood relatives; it is thought that symptom clusters that run in families are likely to help identify valid categories and subcategories of disorders, particularly depression.
Hypomania	An episode in which the individual experiences elevated, expansive, or irritable mood without marked impairment of functioning; similar to a manic episode but less severe and without delusions.
Interpersonal therapy (IPT)	A depression-specific psychosocial treatment used to address current problems rather than remote causal issues and directed at helping the patient develop a more stable long-range adjustment.
Lithium carbonate	A medication used to treat manic disorders to prevent the cycling between manic and depressive episodes.
Major depression	A mood disorder in which severe depressive symptoms are present, such as marked sadness, fatigue, and self-denunciation. In addition, decreased appetite, weight loss, decrease or agitation in mental and physical activity, and a preoccupation with death and suicide often occur. A majority of these symptoms must be present all day and nearly every day during two consecutive weeks for an individual to be diagnosed with major depression.
Mania	An emotional state characterized by intense and unrealistic feelings of excitement, euphoria, or irritability, which cause marked impairment of functioning. Symptoms can include inflated self-esteem, delusions, decreased need for sleep, psychomotor agitation, and lack of recognition of the consequences of certain activities. May require hospitalization to prevent harm to self or others.
Melancholic type	A major depression which involves loss of interest or pleasure in almost all activities, early morning awakenings and feeling worse in the mornings, no evidence of a personality disturbance prior to the first major depressive episode, and/or good response to antidepressant, biologically based therapies in any prior episodes.
Mood congruent	Disordered thinking or delusional ideas that are consistent with the predominant mood or emotional state in individuals with depression.
Mood disorder	A disorder involving states of persistent positive or negative emotion, or affect, of sufficient intensity as to be clearly maladaptive for significant periods of time.
Neurotransmitters	Chemical substances that transmit nerve impulses from one neuron — the brain's nerve cells — to another. Many think that depression and mania both may arise from disruptions in the delicate balance of biochemical substances that regulate and mediate the activity of neurons.
Normal depression	Depression occurring in anyone undergoing certain traumatic but rather common life events, almost always the result of recent stress. Some depressions are considered adjustment disorders in response to stressors rather than mood disorders.
Psychodynamic therapy	A treatment based on Freudian theory that seeks to understand and resolve disordered behavior through insight into a patient's unconscious conflicts.

Schizoaffective disorder	A disorder in which symptoms are similar to those of schizophrenia and mood disorders but do not meet the criteria for either. Symptoms can include manic or depressive episodes, as well as deranged mental and cognitive processes such as mood-incongruent delusions and hallucinations.
Seasonal affective disorder (SAD)	A mood disorder in which onset and remission or cycling are related to changes in seasons; individuals with this disorder usually are depressed in the fall and winter and normal or hypomanic in spring and summer.
Suicidal ambivalence	Recognizing that most people who contemplate suicide do not in fact kill themselves, researchers Farberow and Litman categorized the degree of suicidal intent into the following three categories: (1) "To be" group: individuals who do not wish to die but do wish to communicate a dramatic message to others concerning their distress and contemplation of suicide; (2) "Not to be" group: individuals intent on dying who leave little or no warning of their intent to kill themselves, arranging a suicidal situation so that intervention is not possible; (3) "To be or not to be" group: individuals ambivalent about dying who tend to leave the outcome of suicide attempts to chance or fate.
Unipolar disorder	A severe mood disorder in which only depressive episodes occur, as opposed to bipolar disorder in which both manic and depressive processes are assumed to occur.

VIDEO NOTES

■ INTRODUCTION

• Moods are universal experiences.

• It is part of being human to experience a wide range of moods.

• The determination of when a mood becomes a mood disorder depends on its extent, its severity, and its duration.

■ WHAT IS MAJOR DEPRESSION?
(Case Illustrations: Phyllis, Margarita)

• 15 million Americans will experience a major depression at some point in their lives.

• Symptoms include weight loss, insomnia, negative self-image, sometimes suicidal thoughts.

• Severity ranges from mild to severe:

Mildly depressed people may be able to work and function and hide their mood even though they are very unhappy.

Acutely or severely depressed people exhibit intensified psychomotor retardation, withdrawal from social contact, decreased motivation to work, and a sense that nothing is worthwhile.

Psychotic depression involves a break with reality and the experiencing of delusions.

In depressive stupor, people do not respond to the outside world at all.

■ WHAT IS BIPOLAR DISORDER?

(Case Illustration: Rodney)

• The mood swings of bipolar disorder include both depressive and manic episodes.

• Severity ranges from hypomanic to severe manic psychosis.

• Prevalence: 1.5 million Americans.

■ MAJOR DEPRESSION: CAUSAL FACTORS

• Freud postulated that depression occurs when someone is in conflict about angry or hostile feelings toward a significant other and, unable to express the anger for fear of losing the relationship, turns it inward.

• Others believe that the causes of depression are mixed. The risk-factor model says that when the combined risks get high enough, the person becomes depressed. Each person is affected idiosyncratically.

• Biological risks include genetic factors and other physiological conditions that create a predisposition to depression.

• Psychological factors include cognitive style and personality.

• Environmental factors include poverty, unemployment, drugs, homelessness, increasing amounts of violence, and lack of social support.

• Women are twice as likely to suffer from major depression as men and are more likely than men to come in for treatment. Reasons include: having lived in a long-standing socially disadvantaged role; being more affected by relationships (some theorists believe that losses in a relationship will be experienced more emotionally by women than men because women define themselves and their success in life through relationships); and hormonal differences. Also, men are much more likely to turn to alcohol as a means of treating their depression.

■ MAJOR DEPRESSION AND MANIC-DEPRESSION: BIOLOGICAL FACTORS

• A strong genetic component seems to exist, especially for people with bipolar disorder, although researchers have been unable to locate the specific gene that might be involved.

• How the brain works: Nerve cells in the brain carry information in the form of electrical impulses that travel along the length of the cell. For the information to be communicated to the next cell, the impulse must cross the synapse (the space between the cells). This is accomplished when a chemical called a neurotransmitter is released into the synapse. The neurotransmitters move across the space and lock into specific receptor sites on the next cell.

• Psychologists theorize that people with major depression may not have enough neurotransmitters at the synapse, and those who are manic may have too many.

■ MAJOR DEPRESSION: TREATMENT

• Some people with major depression are not treated because the episode runs its course, they are not properly diagnosed, or they just do not seek help.

• Psychotherapy and medication often are used together.

• In psychodynamic psychotherapy, clinicians try to uncover the unconscious conflicts that they believe to be at the heart of the depression. Therapy consequently focuses on the identification of the aggressive impulse and the understanding of how it is being rechanneled and conflicted so that the patient can accept the feeling and understand that it is appropriate.

• Newer, short-term therapies include cognitive, cognitive-behavioral, and interpersonal. They typically are used for a prescribed period of time, usually two or three months.

• Cognitive therapy is built on the belief that our feelings and behaviors are determined by the way we think about things. The depressed person tends to put a negative cast on events. Cognitive therapy identifies the thoughts a person is having, and evaluates whether alternative ways of thinking about the situation and behaving may yield different results.

• When patients are so severely depressed that they can no longer function, or they are suicidal and have not responded to drugs or other therapies, many psychologists see electroconvulsive therapy (ECT) as the treatment of last resort. In ECT a convulsion is produced by passing an electric current through the brain. In 80 percent of those who receive ECT, the depression lifts within weeks. A potential side effect of ECT is long-term memory loss.

■ BIPOLAR DISORDER: TREATMENT

• Treatment usually involves the administration of the drug lithium carbonate and some form of psychotherapy. Without proper treatment and without adherence to the medication schedule, the average risk of recurrence over five years is 80 percent. For those who take their medication as prescribed, only 20-30 percent will have a recurrence over a two-year period.

• In addition to medication and psychotherapy, self-help groups offer social support to people coping with mood disorders.

• The standard medications prescribed for depression (tricyclics and MAO-inhibitors) increase the availability of certain neurotransmitters.

• Medications are not effective for everyone and dosage must be carefully watched to preclude dangerous physical and psychological side effects.

■ VIDEO REVIEW QUESTIONS

1. Describe a variety of situations in which people exhibit normal moods. Tell why you call their moods normal.

2. Give an example of a situation in which a mood is inappropriate to the situation or where a mood has become so severe that it interferes with the person's ability to function.

3. Identify three ways in which Phyllis' and Rodney's mood disorders differ.

4. In the story about Susan and John, why does Dr. Knafo conclude that Susan's moods were entirely within the normal range?

5. What symptoms of depression does Margarita describe?

6. Differentiate between the following levels of depression: mild, severe, psychotic, and depressive stupor.

7. Using Jan as an example, discuss some ways in which depression affects those around the person with the disorder.

8. Discuss Freud's view of the love-hate relationship with respect to depression. How does Gary Edelstein apply Freud's theory to Margarita?

9. Dr. Fawcett says that "a person who is hypomanic may look like the American dream." What does he mean?

10. Describe the risk-factor model put forth by Dr. Young and identify at least two biological, psychological, and environmental factors that might contribute to the onset of depression.

11. What does Carol Gilligan's research suggest about why women experience depression more than men? How is this exhibited in the cases of Phyllis and Margarita?

12. Tell how unconscious conflicts, biological factors, genetic factors, and life events may have contributed to the onset of Rodney's illness.

 CASE STUDY

by Judith Rosenberger, C.S.W., Ph.D. Hunter College and Edith Gould, C.S.W. Postgraduate Center for Mental Health

Isabel

Isabel dreaded mornings. For the past two months she had been waking up at 5 a.m. unable to sleep. She would awaken with a jolt and within minutes be overcome by profound feelings of despair and anxiety. Her separation from Jack took place four months ago. She thought that she had worked through the usual phases of mourning accompanying the breakup of their relationship. But now the depression she was experiencing was severe. It seemed to have hit suddenly and appeared to have a relentless life of its own. Although she had an exhibition of her paintings scheduled in three months, she was unable to complete a painting. She felt paralyzed by feelings of hopelessness, worthlessness, and self-hatred. Her painting, which had always sustained her during difficult times, had lost all meaning for her. Any work she managed to do, she destroyed by the end of the day.

Isabel found herself spending an inordinate amount of time sitting, smoking cigarettes, and brooding about death. She flirted with the idea of suicide and was frightened by the thought. She was morbidly preoccupied with the state of her health, and every day she had a new terrifying fantasy that something was terribly wrong with her physically.

Her friends noticed the changes in Isabel. Recognizing that she was depressed, they came to see her and talk to her, but Isabel remained withdrawn and isolated, and rarely went out. She lost interest in food and consequently lost a good deal of weight. Isabel seemed to have lost her capacity to experience any pleasure.

Her five-year relationship with Jack had been close, but stormy. Their major conflict had centered around Isabel's ambition to be an artist. Jack wanted a more traditional relationship, envisioning Isabel at home caring for their children. Isabel's career had begun to soar in the past two years. She was terrified at the thought of children. She was afraid she would be suffocated if other people were dependent on her. She needed freedom to concentrate on art. That was her outlet and the area in which she felt control.

She told Jack she needed to delay marriage and mothering for at least eight years. Jack was devastated, and this finally precipitated their breakup. Although sad at first, Isabel asserted it was for the best. Then her depression set in. Isabel was plagued with guilt. She began to feel selfish. She heard through friends that Jack was still visibly upset. She began to feel she was responsible for ruining his life. Thoughts that she might be capable of throwing babies out of windows began intruding during the day. At night she had dreams of gruesome attacks on men and by men on herself. She could not stop crying. She felt her selfishness deserved punishment, and so could not envision any relief from the nightmare her life had become. Her hygiene deteriorated as she stayed in bed longer and longer each day, ruminating about her worthlessness and pain.

CLINICAL DISCUSSION

The case of Isabel clearly illustrates the depressed content of behavior, thought processes, and mood involved in major depression. Her downward spiral in self-care, productivity, cognitive themes, and overall mood is coherent. Two issues, related but not identical, are foremost in trying to understand and care for Isabel: How did this depressed state come about, and how can it be reversed? One hypothesis is that Isabel's diminishing daily functioning follows from her relentless self-attacks. That is, she feels like a bad person and therefore reacts as if shamed.

Many therapies address this self-attacking aspect of depression. Insight-oriented therapy tries to unravel why a small event in the present is linked to catastrophic remorse. The therapy focuses on revealing the hidden memories and associations that are sources of current pessimistic concerns. The goal of most cognitive therapy is to retrain the thought progressions that automatically and habitually connect small events to catastrophic implications so that alternative interpretations are acceptable. Both of these approaches focus on the thought content linked to depression. The aim is to change feelings and moods by changing the misguided or distorted patterns of thought that set them off.

Another way exists to look at the connections between thought, feelings, and behavior. Isabel's decline in functioning may be seen as having its basis in biochemical shifts that lower mood directly. Since people tend to seek a cohesive world view, depressing thoughts may be seen as reflections but not causes of lowered moods. It is a chicken/egg issue. What Isabel thinks may not drive her mood changes; rather, her mood changes may drive her thoughts. Treatment from this point of view involves addressing the depressed mood directly, primarily through medication. The expectation is that mood-congruent thinking and behavior can correct themselves as moods respond to biochemical intervention. In Isabel's case, medication would probably be used first. This is because Isabel is not just feeling depressed in the way we commonly use the term; her bodily processes also have become involved. These vegetative signs include disturbances in her sleep pattern, appetite, hygiene, and concentration. Isabel's general abandonment of caring for her body may mean she no longer cares about her physical being because of an overall numbing and disengagement within herself. Similarly, her unresponsiveness to people may reflect a clouding of her whole neuropsychological functioning, rather than a rejection of others because of angry feelings.

Major depression is especially worrisome due to the chance of suicide and often calls for aggressive intervention to reverse the downward spiral, regardless of whether the clinician sees it as starting from the mind or from the body. Since mind and body are inseparable, Isabel's self-hate and guilt could reflect her "explanations" of her sense of things being terribly wrong. Her psychotic features (beliefs she is a destroyer) take the form of mood-congruent delusions. Isabel builds a coherent world of depressed thoughts, feelings, and patterns of behavior that confirm her outlook of hopelessness.

Many theorists, beginning with Freud, see depression as anger turned against the self. In this case, Isabel may be angry with Jack for breaking off the relationship, but unable to admit or express that anger, she may turn it against herself, resulting in a devaluing of herself and thus depression. In certain cases of depression, submerged anger can be glimpsed. For instance, Isabel's behavior and mood-state make people living around her feel increasingly impotent and hopeless as she defeats their attempts to help her feel better. Their distress and anger at being made to feel this way themselves may contribute to Isabel's guilt and pessimism about the future. In the brief time since Isabel first became depressed, following the loss of her love relationship, we already can see the convergence of even more reasons for despair in her work problems, isolation, and feelings about hurting Jack. The therapist often provides one of the few relationships that can withstand the depressed person's anger and trend toward isolation. This can be a vital link back to normal relations once the worst depression is past.

Isabel's recovery from an earlier depression when a college romance failed is a good sign, although a family history of depression suggests a continuing risk that is not related to external life events alone. Professional intervention is needed to arrest the immediate symptom pattern and to help reverse the depression. Additionally, whether fueled by anger turned inward or by a biochemically based mood deterioration, the risk of suicide for Isabel and others in the midst of a major depressive episode cannot be ignored. Protective hospitalization may be required until medication and psychotherapy both can get underway.

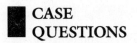

CASE QUESTIONS

1. Give an example of a vegetative sign of depression in Isabel's case. Using this example, explain both how her mind (thoughts) could be responding to her body, and how her body could be responding to her mind.

2. Explain what is meant by a mood-congruent delusion.

3. Does evidence of anger exist in Isabel's symptom picture? If we were to see concealed anger as a causative agent in Isabel's depression, what might she be angry about? Why might she conceal this?

4. If a person feels guilty, punishment in some form usually accompanies and relieves the guilt. Isabel feels guilty about rejecting Jack. Which behaviors (of Isabel's) could be seen as self-punitive in an attempt to alleviate her guilt?

SELF-TEST

1. Unipolar is to major depression as bipolar is to
   a) delusion-hallucination.
   b) introversion-extroversion.
   c) manic-depression.
   d) obsessive-compulsive.

2. All of the following are principal dimensions customarily used to differentiate the mood disorders EXCEPT
   a) duration.
   b) reality.
   c) severity.
   d) extent.

3. Aldin's friends say he has a lot of ups and downs. Sometimes he is "higher than a kite" while at others times he seems "lower than a snake's belly." His teachers say that his grades go in streaks with several As and Bs followed by several Ds and Fs. Aldin probably suffers from
   a) adjustment disorder with depressed mood.
   b) cyclothymia.
   c) dysthymia.
   d) manic-depressive psychosis.

4. All of the following are symptoms of major depression EXCEPT
   a) delusions of grandeur.
   b) diminished cognitive capacity.
   c) hypersomnia.
   d) loss of interest in pleasurable activities.

5. When a group of symptoms shows a strong relationship with each other but not with symptoms belonging to other groups, they are said to be a
   a) concordance.
   b) correlation.
   c) family.
   d) cluster.

6. Bipolar mood disorder is distinguished from major depression by
   a) at least one episode of mania.
   b) disturbance of circadian rhythms.
   c) evidence of earlier cyclothymia.
   d) evidence of earlier dysthymia.

7. All of the following are symptoms of the manic phase of bipolar mood disorder EXCEPT
   a) deflated self-esteem.
   b) euphoria.
   c) high levels of verbal output.
   d) notable increase in activity.

149

8. Elbert has been hospitalized for several months and his family never knows what to expect when they visit him. One time he will be so depressed that he can hardly speak and the next time he will talk elatedly about grandiose plans for his business and about becoming chairman of the board. Elbert is probably suffering from
   a) major depression.
   b) schizoaffective disorder.
   c) bipolar mood disorder.
   d) cyclothymia.

9. According to Wing and Bebbington, all of the following factors may reduce the risk of women developing mood disorders EXCEPT
   a) being employed.
   b) being religious.
   c) being unmarried.
   d) not having young children at home.

10. All of the following are true of research findings about hereditary factors in the development of mood disorders EXCEPT
   a) mood disorders show up more often in the biological than in the adoptive families of persons with mood disorders.
   b) the concordance rate for mood disorders is higher for adoptive families than for biological families.
   c) the concordance rate for mood disorders is higher for identical than for fraternal twins.
   d) the incidence of mood disorders is considerably higher among blood relatives of those with mood disorders than in the general population.

11. Biological causation of mood disorders remains a viable hypothesis because of all the following facts EXCEPT
   a) a predisposition to these disorders may be genetically transmitted.
   b) behavioral symptoms promptly abate with certain biological interventions.
   c) injections of serotonin are followed by manic behavior.
   d) profound alterations of bodily function frequently accompany the affective symptoms.

12. All of the following are risk factors in the development of serious mood disorders EXCEPT
   a) failing to develop a strong conscience.
   b) having a depressive parent.
   c) losing a parent early in life.
   d) possessing a "negative cognitive set."

13. Manic individuals try to escape the pain of their inner lives by
   a) attracting the attention and sympathy of others.
   b) expending vast amounts of energy so they can sleep and forget their troubles.
   c) hurting others whom they hold responsible.
   d) multiplying outer world distractions.

14. From a communication standpoint, depressive reactions often can be seen as attempts of a person to say, in effect,

    a) "I am unable to meet any of my own needs."

    b) "I do not think I have needs any more."

    c) "I have needs that you are failing to meet."

    d) "I am sorry that I have not been meeting your needs."

15. All of the following types of drugs are commonly used to treat severely disturbed manic and depressive patients EXCEPT

    a) antianxiety.

    b) antidepressant.

    c) antipsychotic.

    d) hallucinogens.

16. Lithium therapy has all of the following side effects EXCEPT

    a) decreased motor coordination.

    b) gastrointestinal difficulties.

    c) hyperactivity.

    d) kidney damage.

17. While the overall national suicide rate has increased slightly but consistently in recent years, disproportionate increases have occurred among

    a) females and the elderly.

    b) females and the young.

    c) males and the elderly.

    d) males and the young.

18. Durkheim, and Depue and Slater concluded that the greatest deterrent to committing suicide in times of personal threat is

    a) the number of unmet personal goals.

    b) the refusal to believe in life after death.

    c) a religious belief that suicide is a sin.

    d) a sense of involvement and identity with others.

19. All of the following are emphases of a crisis intervention counselor who is talking to a suicidal person EXCEPT

    a) fostering greater independence in the client.

    b) helping the client realize that the present emotional turmoil will abate.

    c) helping the client see alternatives other than suicide.

    d) helping the client understand that his or her judgment is impaired.

20. People suffering from a bipolar disorder, cycle

    a) with the seasons.

    b) several times per day.

    c) several times per year.

    d) idiosyncratically.

21. Freud believed depression is the result of

    a) a neurological disorder.

    b) a chemical imbalance.

    c) hostile feelings turned inward.

    d) a repressive society.

22. **Carol Gilligan's research suggests:**
   a) femininity is largely defined through relatedness.
   b) masculinity is largely defined through accomplishment.
   c) both a and b
   d) neither a nor b

23. **A deficit of neurotransmitters may result in**
   a) hypomania.
   b) depression.
   c) bipolar disorder.
   d) mania.

24. **Side effects of ECT include**
   a) insomnia.
   b) appetite loss.
   c) long-term memory loss.
   d) all of the above.

25. **The model positing psychological, environmental, and biological factors in the development of depression is called the**
   a) cognitive-behavioral model.
   b) psychodynamic model.
   c) risk-factor model.
   d) trifactor model.

[ANSWERS: 1-c, 2-b, 3-b, 4-a, 5-d, 6-a, 7-a, 8-c, 9-b, 10-b, 11-c, 12-a, 13-d, 14-c, 15-d, 16-c, 17-b, 18-d, 19-a, 20-d, 21-c, 22-a, 23-b, 24-c, 25-c]

SUGGESTED READINGS

Beck, A. T. (1990). *Depression: Causes and treatment* (12th ed.). Philadelphia: University of Pennsylvania Press. This book presents a fine review of the literature through the mid-1960s, covering the etiology, biology, and treatment of depression from a cognitive perspective.

Beck, A. T., Rush, A. J., Shaw, B. F., & Emery, G. (1979). *Cognitive therapy for depression.* New York: Guilford Press. This readable presentation of the history and techniques of the cognitive-behavioral approach to depression includes interesting case histories.

Berger, D., & Berger, L. (1991). *We heard the angels of madness: One family's struggle with manic depression.* New York: William Morrow & Co. The insightful and sensitive story of a mother and her manic-depressive son, as written by the mother and her sister.

Cohen, N. B., Baker, G., Cohen, R. A., Fromm-Reichmann, F., & Weigert, E. B. (1954). An intensive study of 12 cases of manic-depressive psychosis. *Psychiatry, 17,* 103-37. These case studies look at bipolar disorder from a psychoanalytic perspective.

Coyne, J. C. (Ed.) (1985). *Essential papers on depression.* New York: New York University Press. Part of a series of essential papers in several disciplines, this volume contains professional-level presentations by well-regarded theorists — for example, Freud, Beck, and Winokur — on various approaches to understanding depression, including the psychodynamic, behavioral, interpersonal/social, and biomedical theories.

Egeland, J. A., & Hostetter, A. M. (1983). Amish study: I. Affective disorders among the Amish. 1976-1980. *American Journal of Psychiatry, 140,* 56-61. This study examines the genetic history of an Amish community, in which a limited gene pool and well-documented pedigrees allowed the scientists to trace the inheritance patterns of mood disorders.

Freud, S. (1957). Mourning and melancholia. In J. Rickman (Ed.), *A general selection from the works of Sigmund Freud.* Garden City, NY: Doubleday. (Original work published 1909). In this seminal work, Freud defines depression as anger turned inward.

Goodwin, F. K., & Jamison, K. R. (1990). *Manic depressive illness.* New York: Oxford University Press. This handbook of bipolar disorder includes a historical look at its description from the patient's and professional's points of view. Among the topics covered are the epidemiology of manic-depression, the correlation of bipolar disorder and creativity and leadership, biological elements, including the role of genetics and neuroendocrinology, and treatment.

Jackson, S. W. (1986). *Melancholia and depression: From Hippocratic times to modern times.* New Haven: Yale University Press. From ancient Greece to the 20th century, this devastating and apparently ever-present disorder has evoked numerous explanations, which are reviewed in this fascinating history.

Rosenthal, N. E. (1989). *Seasons of the mind.* New York: Bantam. This book updates what is known about seasonal affective disorder.

Styron, W. (1990). *Darkness visible.* New York: Random House. The author of *Sophie's Choice* recounts his depression.

UNIT 9

THE
SCHIZOPHRENIAS

### ■ UNIT THEME	This unit explores what it feels like to live with schizophrenia, what factors are believed to contribute to its onset, and what is being done to treat it. The unit draws on the results of numerous research studies that have been conducted in the last decade to help explain this most devastating of disorders.

■ UNIT ASSIGNMENTS

Read: Unit 9. "The Schizophrenias" in *The World of Abnormal Psychology Study Guide*, Toby Kleban Levine, editor (HarperCollins, 1992).

View: Program 9. "The Schizophrenias" in THE WORLD OF ABNORMAL PSYCHOLOGY.

Read: Chapter 12. "The Schizophrenias and Delusional Disorders" in *Abnormal Psychology and Modern Life*, Ninth Edition, by Robert C. Carson and James N. Butcher (HarperCollins, 1992).

■ GOALS AND OBJECTIVES

1. Describe the symptoms that characterize the schizophrenias and explain and identify the criteria that are used in diagnosis.

2. Briefly summarize the case study of the Genain quads and explain why their schizophrenic breakdowns probably were due both to heredity and environment.

3. Distinguish between process (or chronic) and reactive (or acute) schizophrenia.

4. Identify and distinguish between paranoid, undifferentiated, catatonic, and residual schizophrenia.

5. Give several reasons for the difficulty in defining schizophrenic behavior and discuss some suggested solutions to this dilemma.

6. Summarize the evidence for a genetic basis for schizophrenia.

7. Explain why researchers believe that some biochemical factors may cause schizophrenia and evaluate the dopamine hypothesis.

8. Summarize the results of research on neurological and neuroanatomical factors that may cause or underlie schizophrenia.

9. Evaluate the evidence that early psychic trauma may increase a person's vulnerability to the schizophrenias.

10. Summarize the results of research concerning the possibility that some general sociocultural factors may contribute to the development of schizophrenia and explain why pathogenic family interactions cannot be the sole cause of this disorder.

11. Evaluate Laing's hypothesis that schizophrenia may be a social role and explain how this may be related to the insanity defense used in some criminal cases.

12. Summarize the success of biological, behavioral, and psychosocial interventions in the treatment of the schizophrenias.

13. List and describe the clinical symptoms of six types of delusional disorders and explain why formal diagnoses of these kinds of abnormal behavior are rare.

14. Discuss several major issues surrounding the schizophrenias and delusional disorders that remain unresolved.

UNIT OVERVIEW

*by Edward S. Katkin, Ph.D.
State University of New York
at Stony Brook*

The **schizophrenias** are a group of disorders that comprise the most severe form of mental disturbance. The term schizophrenia comes from the Greek word for split (*schizo*) mind (*phrenia*); this disorder is not to be confused, however, with split or multiple personality. In schizophrenia the patient has only one personality, and it is fragmented; the split refers to a lack of integration of the emotional and cognitive components of the patient's one and only personality.

Patients who suffer from schizophrenia show gross distortions of reality, characterized by **delusions, hallucinations**, and severe disturbances of normal thought. Delusions are defined as a systematic set of beliefs that has no foundation in reality. Often, schizophrenics have the delusion that they are being persecuted or threatened, usually by a conspiratorial group. Hallucinations are sensory experiences that are not related to reality. Although hallucinations can occur in any of the senses, causing people to see, feel, taste, or smell something that is not really there, the most common form of hallucination for schizophrenics involves the hearing of voices, usually telling the patients to do something or commenting critically on their behavior.

About one percent of all Americans will have a schizophrenic episode at some time in their lives. This rate is found in virtually every culture, and pertains to both men and women. Primarily because of its universality and the similarity of its symptoms across cultures, most experts assume schizophrenia has a biological basis. In the video you will see some of the modern brain imaging techniques that are being used to try to identify the changes in brain structure and function that are associated with schizophrenia.

■ PATTERNS OF SCHIZOPHRENIA

The official diagnostic manual of the American Psychiatric Association recognizes five separate patterns of schizophrenia, but bear in mind that they all are similarly characterized by severe disturbance of thought, perception, or emotional appropriateness. The five subtypes are:

1. Paranoid — Paranoid schizophrenia is characterized primarily by persecutory delusions, frequently with associated hallucinations. These patients may appear less disturbed than others because their delusional structure often is tightly constructed and they do not show as much social withdrawal as other subtypes. In the video you will meet two paranoid schizophrenic patients, Leslie and Janine. Leslie is quite articulate, and he appears to be quite able to describe his hallucinations vividly. Unfortunately, Leslie's "inner voices" ordered him to leap from a fifth-story window, resulting in a permanent deformity. Janine appears somewhat more disorganized than Leslie, and her symptoms are more clearly focused on delusions of persecution. She reports a chronic feeling of "being condemned" by others. Janine also denies her diagnosis and prefers to describe herself as suffering from posttraumatic stress disorder.

2. Undifferentiated — This subtype involves a mixture of the primary symptoms of all of the subtypes, often rapidly changing. These patients alternately appear very confused, disoriented, fearful, excited, delusional, or depressed. In the video you will meet Jeff, an undifferentiated schizophrenic patient who has been hospitalized for ten years. As you will see, Jeff sometimes sounds reasonably normal, and then he slips into strange and disconnected thoughts. It is important to note when watching Jeff that he has had the benefit of many years of treatment in a sheltered environment. It is likely that before treatment he appeared much more disturbed than he does now.

3. Catatonic — Alternating periods of extreme withdrawal and extreme excitement characterize this subtype. When withdrawn the catatonic patient may actually go into a state of suspended animation, appearing as still as a wax figure. This can last for days or sometimes even weeks. When extremely excited the catatonic patient may be dangerously aggressive.

4. Disorganized — These patients, the most seriously disturbed of the schizophrenics, show severely disturbed patterns of emotional distortion, peculiar mannerisms, and infantile behavior.

5. Residual — This label is reserved for those patients who are in remission after an episode of schizophrenia, but who, nevertheless, are significantly withdrawn from social contact and speak with unusual affect. In this type of schizophrenia, hallucinations, delusions, and thought disorders are not predominant.

It also is important to note that in all five categories, a diagnosis of acute or chronic may be used. **Acute schizophrenia** is sometimes described as **reactive schizophrenia**, because the patient shows acute symptoms of the disorder in reaction to some specific life stress and the symptoms continue for a relatively short period of time. Such individuals often show little or no sign of disturbance before the first reactive episode. The chronic patient often is described as a **process schizophrenic**, because the disorder is thought to develop gradually over a period of time, and the manifestation of symptoms is believed to be the end result of a chronic process. In the video, Jeff is the clearest case of a **chronic schizophrenic**. On the other hand, you will also meet Randy, a Vietnam War veteran who showed no signs of schizophrenia until he saw combat. The combat stress precipitated a schizophrenic reaction that has persisted for years but is under partial control by medication.

■ CAUSAL FACTORS AND TREATMENT

The causes of schizophrenia remain a mystery, despite extensive research from both the biological and the psychosocial perspective. Very strong evidence exists to support the view that schizophrenia is partly determined by genetic predisposition. The strongest evidence is derived from the observation that the concordance rate of the disorder in identical twins is five times greater than it is in fraternal twins. That means that in identical twins, as compared to fraternal twins, if one twin is schizophrenic the probability is five times greater that the other twin also will be schizophrenic. These differences in concordance rates argue strongly for a genetic transmission of the disorder. However, the fact that many identical twin pairs do not show concordance indicates that factors other than genetics may be important as well.

A popular belief is that the predisposition to become schizophrenic is inherited, but that specific environmental triggers must be present to elicit the disorder. These triggers may be biological or psychosocial. For instance, it has been suggested that intrauterine injury to the brain could be a biological trigger that causes subsequent schizophrenia. Perhaps only those who are genetically predisposed and who also suffer certain intrauterine injury will develop the disorder. Other biological evidence suggests that the brain of the schizophrenic may secrete an excess of **dopamine** at synapses, or may be too rich in dopamine receptor sites. This view is supported by the observation that the blocking of dopamine transmission with drugs relieves schizophrenic symptoms.

With respect to psychosocial triggers, those that have been investigated most extensively are the role of early parent-child interactions, communication patterns within families, excessive stress, and faulty social learning. So far little or no convincing evidence exists to support any of these factors as the sole cause of schizophrenia, and current beliefs are that the cause of schizophrenia is a complex chain involving genetics, biochemistry, and life experience.

The most widespread and successful treatment program for schizophrenia is antipsychotic medication. Yet it must be noted that no cure exists. Even the most successful drug treatments are primarily successful at reducing symptoms and allowing patients to leave hospitals and function reasonably well in the normal social world. Only rarely, however, will schizophrenics attain a fully integrated adjustment to society. Most treatment programs recommend both drugs and some form of supportive psychotherapy or counseling. The current state of the art in the treatment of schizophrenia is to try to control symptoms effectively and to help the patient to make a better adjustment to the world. Continued research may lead to a closer approximation of a cure.

■ KEY TERMS

The following terms are used in the text and/or the television programs.

Acute schizophrenia	A symptom pattern marked by confusion and intense emotional turmoil; also called reactive schizophrenia due to its sudden and dramatic onset brought on by significant stressors when little or no sign of symptoms existed before the first onset.
Adoption studies	Research studies that seek to separate heredity from environment. They compare concordance rates for the biological and adoptive relatives of individuals who have been adopted out of their biological families at an early age and have subsequently developed a disorder.
Amorphous (style)	A pattern of thinking and communicating within the family of an individual with schizophrenia that is characterized by a failure in differentiation in which attention toward feelings, objects, or persons is loosely organized, vague, and drifting.
Anhedonia	An inability to experience joy or pleasure; seen in more severe cases of schizophrenia. The individual appears to have no emotions; even the most dramatic events produce only an intellectual recognition, or the response is discordant with the situation.
Catatonic type schizophrenia	A subtype of schizophrenia marked by exaggerated motor symptoms that alternate between periods of extreme stupor and extreme excitement, which can be violent.
Chronic schizophrenia	A symptom pattern that develops gradually and tends to be long-lasting; also called process schizophrenia.

159

Computerized Axial Tomography (CAT)	A scanning technique used to obtain images of parts of the brain.
Concordance rate	The rate at which a diagnosis or a trait of one person is predictive of the same diagnosis or trait in relatives.
Delusional disorder	A disorder that features the presence of a persistent, nonbizarre delusion, specified by the type of delusion — persecutory, jealous, erotomanic, somatic, or grandiose.
Delusions	A systematic set of beliefs that has no foundation in reality. Most prominent are false beliefs that one's thoughts, feelings, or actions are being controlled by external agents, that one's private thoughts are being broadcast indiscriminately to others, that thoughts are being inserted into one's brain by alien forces, that events have an intended personal meaning, or that one's body has taken on grotesque changes.
Dementia praecox	A term first used by Morel, a Belgian psychiatrist, and Emil Kraepelin, a German psychiatrist, to describe a group of rather dissimilar conditions that feature mental deterioration beginning early in life.
Disorganized type schizophrenia	The most severe type of schizophrenia; symptoms include incoherence, loosening of associations, grossly disorganized behavior, and inappropriate affect. This type was formerly called hebephrenic schizophrenia.
Dopamine	A catecholamine neurotransmitter.
Dopamine hypothesis	A theory that schizophrenia is the product of an excess of dopamine activity at certain synaptic sites.
Double-bind	A faulty communications pattern in which family members communicate mutually incompatible ideas, feelings, and demands.
Echolalia	The mimicking of the phrases and speech of others; associated with catatonic schizophrenia.
Echopraxia	The imitation of the actions of others; associated with catatonic schizophrenia.
Erotomanic delusion type	A type of delusion in which the individual believes that some other person of higher status, frequently someone of considerable prominence, is in love with and wants to be sexually involved with the individual.
Expressed emotion (EE)	A form of negative communication directed at an individual with schizophrenia; often related to relapse after remission. Two components of EE are emotional overinvolvement with the individual and excessive criticism. EE also is associated with faulty communication.
Fragmented (style)	A pattern of thinking and communicating within the family of an individual with schizophrenia characterized by erratic and disruptive shifts in communication.
Grandiose delusion type	A type of delusion in which an individual believes he or she has extraordinary status, power, ability, talent, beauty, and other positive attributes.
Hallucination	A sensory experience that is not related to reality.

Induced psychotic disorder	A delusional system that develops in a second person as a result of a close relationship with a person who already has a psychotic disorder with delusions.
Jealous delusion type	A type of delusion in which an individual believes his or her sexual partner is being unfaithful.
Marital schism	Severe chronic discord in a family in which the continuation of the marriage is constantly threatened; thought to be a possible psychosocial factor in the onset of schizophrenia.
Marital skew	A situation in which family members accept as normal the maladaptive behavior of one or more members in order to maintain a sense of equilibrium.
Milieu therapy	An in-patient psychosocial therapy program in which patients share responsibilities and decision-making with a professional staff in preparation for life outside an institutional setting.
Negative-symptom schizophrenia	An absence or deficit of behaviors normally present in a person's personality, such as affective expression or reactivity to the environment.
Neuroleptics	Antipsychotic drugs that are effective in blocking dopamine action at the synaptic receptor.
Nuclear Magnetic Resonance Imaging (MRI)	A highly advanced internal scanning technique that allows visualization of the anatomical features of internal organs.
Paranoid type schizophrenia	A symptom pattern dominated by absurd delusions, with frequent auditory hallucinations, but a lack of symptoms characteristic of disorganized and catatonic types. Individuals with paranoid-type schizophrenia have a history of increasing suspiciousness and severe difficulties in interpersonal relationships.
Parent-child studies	Research that examines the incidence of a disorder among children raised by parents with the same disorder.
Persecutory delusion type	A type of delusion in which the predominant theme concerns unfair, harmful, or persecutory treatment of the patient or someone close to the patient.
Positive-symptom schizophrenia	A symptom picture in which something has been added to the normal repertoire of behavior and experience; may include marked emotional turmoil, motor agitation, delusional interpretation of events, or hallucinations.
Positron Emission Tomography (PET)	A scanning technology that assesses organ functioning by measuring metabolic processes.
Process schizophrenia	See *chronic schizophrenia*.
Psychosis	A severe psychological disorder involving loss of contact with reality and gross personality distortion.
Reactive schizophrenia	See *acute schizophrenia*.
Residual type schizophrenia	A category of schizophrenia used for people regarded as being in remission from schizophrenia but still manifesting some signs of the disorder.

Schizoaffective disorder	A disorder characterized by manic or depressive behavior concurrent with hallucinations or delusions that does not meet the diagnostic criteria for either schizophrenia or mood disorder.
Schizophrenias	A group of disorders characterized primarily by disorganization of thought processes, a lack of coherence between thought and emotion, and an inward orientation (split off) from reality. The splitting occurs within the intellect, between the intellect and emotion, and between the intellect and external reality.
Schizophreniform disorder	A diagnosis applied to an individual who shows schizophrenia-like psychoses of less than six months' duration.
Single Photon Emission Computed Tomography (SPECT)	A scanning technology that examines the brain's function; provides lower resolution quality than PET scans, but is less costly.
Somatic delusion type	A delusion in which the individual believes that he or she has a physical illness or disorder, often bizarre in nature, or an abnormality of appearance.
Tardive dyskinesia	A disfiguring disturbance of motor control, seen particularly in involuntary facial movements; a potential side effect of antipsychotic drugs that is irreversible and can develop even after medication is discontinued.
Twin studies	A form of research that examines the concordance rates for identical (monozygotic) and fraternal (dizygotic) twins; used to examine the relationship between genetics and the expression of disorders. In twin studies of schizophrenics, concordance rates have been found to be significantly higher for identical twins than for fraternal twins.
Undifferentiated type schizophrenia	A subtype of schizophrenia that does not clearly fit into one of the other categories because of a mixed symptom picture; symptoms include delusions, hallucinations, thought disorder, and bizarre behavior.

VIDEO NOTES

■ **THE SCHIZOPHRENIAS: WHAT THEY ARE**
(Case Illustrations: Leslie, Janine, William, Jeff, Randy, David)
• The schizophrenias are a group of disabling disorders that are considered the ultimate in psychological breakdown.

• Characteristics include gross distortion of reality, social withdrawal, and disorganization and fragmentation of perception, thought, and emotion. Symptoms include delusions (unusual thoughts that are not shared by others, e.g., belief that food is being poisoned); auditory and visual hallucinations (unusual perceptions); and disorganization of thoughts and speech.

• Onset may be acute (symptoms appear suddenly) or chronic (the disorder develops gradually and is long-lasting).

• About one percent of all Americans will develop schizophrenia in their lifetimes. Ten percent of people with schizophrenia need to be hospitalized permanently because they are either dangerous, disabled, or unable to care for themselves. People with schizophrenia occupy about 30 percent of all hospital beds in the U.S.

■ THE SCHIZOPHRENIAS: WHAT THEY ARE NOT

• The most salient characteristic of schizophrenia is not violence, it is withdrawal. But when violence occurs, it tends to be unpredictable and often is highly publicized.

• Multiple personality is not a characteristic of schizophrenia. The person with schizophrenia is fragmented within one personality, showing a disconnection between thoughts, feelings, and behavior (e.g., a sad thought might result in maniacal laughter).

• While some homeless people have schizophrenia, some of the bizarre behavior of homeless people may be due to the stress of homelessness, not to schizophrenia.

■ CAUSAL FACTORS

• The illness is thought to result from a variety of factors, probably working in combination.

• Brain science: Using brain imaging and scanning, scientists have found abnormalities in both brain structure and functioning in people with schizophrenia.

> The most common structural abnormality is an enlargement of the ventricular system.

> Functional abnormalities have been observed in acute schizophrenics in the prefrontal cortex, affecting thinking, decision-making, and planning.

> Some believe schizophrenia results from excessive activity of the neurotransmitter dopamine, because (1) drugs used to treat schizophrenia block dopamine receptors, suggesting that they are correcting an abnormality, and (2) drugs that increase dopamine transmission (amphetamines and cocaine) produce psychotic symptoms.

• Genetics: The rates of the disorder in a schizophrenic's immediate family are likely to be about ten times higher than in the general population. The closer the genetic relationship, the more likely it is that schizophrenia will occur.

• Environmental factors: Extreme stress may combine with a pre-existing vulnerability to trigger the initial onset. War, moving away from home, and the first sexual encounter are typical triggers. Onset under age 25 is more typical of men; onset for women tends to be later.

• Family dynamics: A traditional but controversial explanation for schizophrenia involves the schizophrenogenic family, one in which the parents, particularly the mother, are overprotective and rejecting.

> Recent theorists feel that the family may be reacting to the disorder, and that the presence of a person with schizophrenia alters the communication and mood pattern within a family.

> Positive family support also is seen as very important in the treatment of schizophrenia.

■ TREATMENT

• Prior to the 1960s, electroconvulsive therapy (ECT or shock treatment) was the treatment of choice. It rarely is used to treat schizophrenia today.

163

• Drug treatment (generally phenothiazine, an antipsychotic drug) has reduced the average hospitalization of schizophrenics from 353 days in the 1950s to 18 days in the 1980s, has cut relapse rates in half, and typically remits a schizophrenic episode within weeks.

> Drug therapy does not cure schizophrenia. It helps to normalize the thought process and increase the ability of the person to communicate, thus normalizing overt behavior.

> Side effects of antipsychotic drugs include mouth-dryness, muscle stiffening, tremors of the hands and legs, and tardive dyskinesia, a disfiguring disturbance of motor control, seen particularly in involuntary facial movements. Tardive dyskinesia is irreversible and can develop even after medication in discontinued.

• Psychotherapies ease the transition from hospitalization to out-patient treatment.

> Family therapy focuses on improving faulty communication patterns.

> Group therapy works on social interactions and relationships.

> Milieu therapy is an in-patient program in which patients share responsibilities and decision-making with a professional staff in preparation for life outside an institutional setting.

> Psychotherapy helps people with schizophrenia to understand their illness, manage their needs, and gain some control over both their thoughts and behavior. The goal of psychodynamic treatment is the development of a positive and trusting relationship between the therapist and the patient, rather than the development of insight by the patient.

VIDEO REVIEW QUESTIONS

1. Symptoms of schizophrenia include delusions, hallucinations, and disorganized thoughts and speech. Describe examples from the video in which each of these symptoms is illustrated.

2. What schizophrenic symptom prompted Leslie to fall out the window?

3. Develop a short scene that illustrates the disconnection between perception, thoughts, and feelings that is typical of schizophrenia.

4. What would you expect a painting by a schizophrenic to look like? Why?

5. What factors contribute to Dr. Kuehnel's conclusion that Jeff is ready to move back to the community? What role do memory exercises play in this regard?

6. Discuss the relationship between homelessness and schizophrenia.

7. What possible causes of schizophrenia have been identified and why do scientists think schizophrenia probably has multiple causes?

8. What role does the family play in the development and treatment of schizophrenia?

9. In the video, you saw interviews with a number of patients both on and off medication. Describe the differences in behavior that you observed between the two states.

10. What are the goals of psychodynamic psychotherapy in the treatment of schizophrenia? How does this differ from its use in the treatment of other psychological disorders?

CASE STUDY

*by Judith Rosenberger,
C.S.W., Ph.D.
Hunter College
and
Edith Gould, C.S.W.
Postgraduate Center
for Mental Health*

Janet

Three months into Janet's freshman year, her parents were summoned by the dean of the small out-of-town college she was attending to come and pick up their daughter. The dean said Janet was behaving strangely. She had begun to wander around the campus at night, barefoot and dressed only in a short nightgown. According to her roommate, Janet had "not been herself" for the past six weeks. She had stayed in her room continuously, hoarded food, wrote incessantly, and refused to attend classes except for one taught by Dr. M., an older, married man with whom Janet had become intensely preoccupied. She acted as if she were in her own world. She was unapproachable and was irritated by her roommate's attempts to converse. During the past few weeks, Janet had talked to herself frequently. It sounded to her roommate like one-half of a dialogue about what Janet and Dr. M. should do, and whether he was angry with her.

Janet's parents found their daughter in an extremely agitated state. She was dressed in a bizarre way, wearing all kinds of mismatched clothing that was inappropriate to the weather as well as to the setting. She was unkempt and obviously had not bathed. At first she was unresponsive and barely acknowledged her parents' presence. When she did speak she became overexcited. She explained repeatedly why she had to stay at college: because Dr. M. was passionately in love with her. She said he was unable to come to her because his wife kept him imprisoned at home at night. She reported that "voices" commanded her to unite with Dr. M. at any cost in order to save the world from destruction. Janet also was convinced that Dr. M.'s wife was reading her thoughts and now intended to harm her.

When Janet's parents told her they were taking her home, she became violent. She attacked them and wrecked her dorm room. Her words indicated that she was experiencing her parents' efforts as an attack by some dangerous beings, and she argued vehemently but incoherently with these persecutors. The police were called and Janet was taken to the emergency room of the local hospital. The threatening and acutely alarming nature of her hallucinations led staff psychiatrists to conclude that Janet was a danger to herself and others. Immediate hospitalization was advised. Upon admission, Janet was so out of control she had to be put in restraints until the medication she was given began to take effect. Janet was especially fearful that the hospital staff was collaborating with Dr. M.'s wife. She thought they were incarnations of evil forces intent on keeping Janet and Dr. M. apart so that they could not save the world. Janet became more subdued as her medication took effect, but she continued to be uncommunicative around the ward. Although the acute phase of her condition passed, the general prognosis for full recovery was guarded because of indications that this episode was only one part of a long and insidious process of deterioration.

■ CLINICAL DISCUSSION

Several features of the acute onset of Janet's disordered condition are typical of schizophrenia, including her rapid deterioration and its occurrence during her first major separation from home. Her parents reported that she always had been a shy and socially awkward and sensitive girl. For a time around age seven, she had refused to go to school. The whole family had undertaken a brief therapy designed to enable Janet to return to school. This seemed to clear up her behavior enough for her to attend school, but she was not happy. During early adolescence, Janet began to have frequent arguments with her mother. On several occasions, these arguments culminated in a self-destructive act. On one occasion Janet scratched her wrists with a razor blade in front of her mother, following which the school psychologist referred her to therapy. Janet refused to go, although her more provocative and worrisome behavior decreased after this episode. Janet continued to behave eccentrically, like needing to engage in complex rituals in order to go to sleep, or not wanting to be seen eating, but these behaviors were accommodated by her family and others. The depth of Janet's anxiety and the rigidity and fragility of her coping mechanisms, therefore, were masked while she remained at home. These quickly broke down, however, when she left the safety and supportive atmosphere of her accustomed surroundings and family.

Within her unfamiliar new environment, Janet found it impossible to feel safe. Her "substitute reality" enabled her to feel more secure. In her fantasies, she attained the special status of being desired by an important person, Dr. M. Also, dwelling exclusively on this one relationship helped limit her focus so that she felt less overwhelmed by all the new surroundings. She explained her anxiety about the imagined danger she was in as due to threats to her ties with Dr. M. She saw these threats as coming both from his wife and from the hospital staff. The pervasive sense of terror that accompanied her internal disintegration required a broader explanation, however, which became her conviction of impending world destruction. Her preoccupation with Dr. M. was a desperate attempt to save herself from this psychological catastrophe. The theme of salvation in her delusional system (Janet and Dr. M. were to unite to save the world) illustrates her hope of being rescued. Her parents, the dean, her roommate, and the hospital staff all were part of a threatening system that stood between Janet and the safer alternative reality she had constructed.

The elaborateness of Janet's alternative reality makes it a systematized delusion. In this complex story Janet uses a paranoid type of delusion to try to make sense of her anxiety and thereby to control it. Accompanying the delusional system is Janet's overall decline in hygiene, daily functioning, appearance, and ability to manage her impulses in response to being challenged. The broad sweep of these disruptions indicate that the delusional system was failing to contain her overall breakdown. The appearance of mistaken sensory perceptions (in this case hearing voices) indicates the presence of auditory hallucinations, which often are part of a schizophrenic process. While delusions reinterpret the meanings of things, hallucinations change the actual intake of reality through the perceptions. Janet's hallucinations instruct her about increasingly terrifying inner experiences (called command hallucinations). These, in turn, give rise to a concern that she might endanger herself or others because she is unable to use judgment and reality testing, and because she is fearful and reacts explosively to anything she views as a threat. This explains why she was hospitalized, even though she wasn't voicing a direct threat at the moment.

The outcome for Janet is unsure. While some of her more florid symptoms may be controlled by medication, indications of weakness in her adaptation are long-standing and began years before the onset of the acute schizophrenic phase. Her ability to resolve this crisis effectively is in doubt, less because of the presence of delusions and hallucinations than because of her long history of weakness in psychosocial functioning.

CASE QUESTIONS

1. What is the precipitating stressor event that probably triggered the onset of Janet's schizophrenic episode? What other factors may have contributed?

2. Identify Janet's primary delusion. How can we understand this as a way that Janet is trying to "make sense" of her collapsing world? How do her hallucinations fit together with her delusion?

3. Janet's hospitalization both makes her available for treatment and protects her and others. Explain the nature of danger to Janet and others that exists in her current acute condition.

SELF-TEST

1. **All of the following are characteristics of the schizophrenias EXCEPT**
   a) disorganization of perception.
   b) exceptional religiosity.
   c) gross distortions of reality.
   d) withdrawal from social interaction.

2. **Schizophrenic individuals occupy about _____ of the beds in mental hospitals because of their need for long-term care.**
   a) one-fourth
   b) one-third
   c) one-half
   d) two-thirds

3. **The differences in the schizophrenic disorders developed by the Genain quads must be ascribed to differences in their**
   a) environments.
   b) heredity.
   c) parents.
   d) temperament.

4. **Which of the following disorders has the best prognosis?**
   a) acute schizophrenia
   b) chronic schizophrenia
   c) poor premorbid schizophrenia
   d) process schizophrenia

5. **Which of the following would be typical of negative-symptom schizophrenia?**
   a) delusional interpretation of events
   b) hallucinations
   c) marked emotional turmoil
   d) unusual emotional flatness

6. **In cases of extreme withdrawal, some schizophrenics develop an elaborate inner world of fantasy unrelated to reality as others perceive it. This is usually called**
   a) amnesia.
   b) anhedonia.
   c) autism.
   d) mutism.

7. Mary is a schizophrenic patient in a state mental hospital. She has periods when she stands in the same awkward position for a long time and resists having that position changed. At other times she flies into a frenzy, trying to hurt others and herself. Her type of schizophrenia probably is
    a) catatonic.
    b) disorganized.
    c) paranoid.
    d) undifferentiated.

8. Some catatonic patients will imitate the phrases of others. This is known as
    a) echolalia.
    b) echopraxia.
    c) psychotometric language.
    d) reintegration.

9. Which of the following types of schizophrenia is considered the last stop on the downward path of process schizophrenia?
    a) catatonic
    b) disorganized
    c) paranoid
    d) undifferentiated

10. Freud used the memoirs of Dr. Daniel Paul Schreber in developing his theory that paranoid thinking is due to
    a) a malfunction of the superego.
    b) being fixated in the latency stage.
    c) repressed homosexuality.
    d) unrepressed guilt.

11. The results of twin studies of hereditary factors in the development of schizophrenia show
    a) equal concordance rates for identical and fraternal twins.
    b) higher concordance rates for fraternal twins.
    c) higher concordance rates for identical twins.
    d) higher incidence of schizophrenia among twins than among others.

12. According to the dopamine hypothesis, schizophrenia is the product of a(n)
    a) excess of dopamine activity at certain synaptic sites.
    b) shortage of dopamine in the central nervous system.
    c) suppressive effect dopamine has on norepinephrine.
    d) suppressive effect that norepinephrine has on dopamine.

13. Use of CAT-scanning devices has produced evidence that many chronic schizophrenic persons have
    a) an abnormal enlargement of the brain's ventricles.
    b) an abnormally small medulla.
    c) atrophy of the prefrontal lobes of the cerebrum.
    d) misshapen parietal lobes of the cerebrum.

14. The concept of the schizophrenogenic mother has been largely abandoned because
    a) motherhood is sacred in the United States.
    b) the same maternal characteristics have been causally implicated in many other disorders.
    c) the statistical methods used in the research were not appropriate.
    d) the subjects of the research were not representative of the schizophrenic population.

15. Sam's mother always is telling him that she loves him but quickly pushes him away when he tries to hug her. Bateson described the effect of this pattern as a
    a) bidirectional relationship.
    b) double-approach conflict.
    c) double-bind.
    d) double-jeopardy interaction.

16. Jimmy believes he can never do anything right. When he and his brother Tim say the same thing, their parents agree with Tim and disagree with Jimmy. In Martin Buber's terminology, the authenticity of
    a) Jimmy is being confirmed.
    b) the parents' communication is being disconfirmed.
    c) Tim is being confirmed.
    d) Tim is being disconfirmed.

17. In the sexual sphere, schizophrenic individuals' problems are often complicated by
    a) highly moralistic attitudes toward sexual behavior.
    b) highly permissive attitudes toward sexual behavior.
    c) incestuous behaviors between siblings.
    d) sexual incompatibility of the parents.

18. Laing has suggested that the "madness" labeled schizophrenia is a(n) _____ created as a protection from the destructive social expectations and demands of the outside world.
    a) elaborate symbol of self-destruction
    b) mental illness
    c) social role
    d) threatening demeanor

19. In paintings by schizophrenics, which is most likely?
    a) Content is sexually explicit.
    b) Primary colors predominate.
    c) Inanimate objects take on human characteristics.
    d) Form is highly representational.

20. Dr. Shulman's experience with Maureen in the Emergency Room demonstrates that
    a) a part of every schizophrenic is healthy.
    b) schizophrenics are prone to violence.
    c) schizophrenics have a low tolerance for frustration.
    d) schizophrenics always seem bizarre.

169

21. The voice telling Leslie that "nobody wants you anymore" is a(n)
    a) auditory hallucination.
    b) visual hallucination.
    c) disorganization of speech.
    d) auditory delusion.

22. A schizophrenic is someone who has
    a) two to four separate personalities.
    b) fragmentation within one personality.
    c) mood-congruent behavior.
    d) an ego-dystonic personality.

23. SPECT and PET scans have revealed functional abnormalities in the activity of the _____ of acute schizophrenics.
    a) prefrontal cortex
    b) left hemisphere
    c) right hemisphere
    d) cerebellum

24. The incidence of schizophrenia among family members of an individual who has been diagnosed with schizophrenia is likely to be
    a) two times higher than in the general population.
    b) five times higher than in the general population.
    c) ten times higher than in the general population.
    d) 20 times higher than in the general population.

25. Skills training teaches people with schizophrenia to
    a) learn skills they failed to learn from their families.
    b) develop specific job skills.
    c) develop the executive functions of the prefrontal cortex.
    d) all of the above.

[ANSWERS: 1-b, 2-c, 3-a, 4-a, 5-d, 6-c, 7-a, 8-a, 9-b, 10-c, 11-c, 12-a, 13-a, 14-b, 15-c, 16-c, 17-a, 18-c, 19-c, 20-a, 21-a, 22-b, 23-a, 24-c, 25-c]

SUGGESTED READINGS

Andreasen, N. C. (1984). *The broken brain: The biological revolution in psychiatry*. New York: Harper & Row. This important work by a leading proponent of the biological perspective examines what's gone wrong in the brain in schizophrenia, depression, and other major mental disorders.

Gottesman, I. I. (1991). *Schizophrenia genesis: The origin of madness*. New York: W. H. Freeman & Co. This wide-ranging history of schizophrenia includes personal accounts, a discussion of genetics and twin studies, psychosocial and environmental stressors, the role of social policy, and a look at the future including an examination of the decade of the brain program at NIMH.

Greenberg, J. (Hannah Green). (1964). *I never promised you a rose garden*. New York: Penguin. This fictionalized account describes the author's personal experience with schizophrenia.

Laing, R. D. (1960). *The divided self*. London: Tavistock Publications.
Laing, R. D. (1967). *The politics of experience*. London: Tavistock Publications. These two books present Laing's experiences with schizophrenics and his contention that in order to understand and treat them the therapist must learn to view the world from the schizophrenic's point of view. Challenging and provocative reading.

Torrey, E. F. (1988). *Surviving schizophrenia: A family manual* (rev.). New York: Perennial Library/Harper & Row. One of the foremost researchers in the field discusses all aspects of schizophrenia, including who has it, what it is like, its diagnosis, prognosis, and course, potential causes, treatment, and its effect on the family and society.

UNIT 10

ORGANIC MENTAL DISORDERS

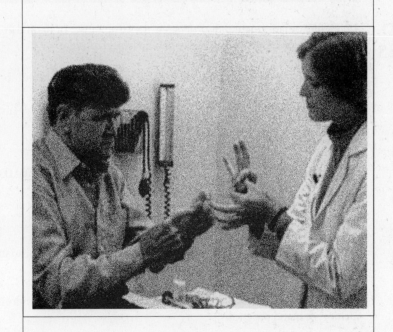

| **UNIT THEME** | Organic mental disorders refer to psychological and behavioral problems that follow physical damage to the brain. This unit focuses on organic mental disorders that result from three causes: physical trauma, disease, and exposure to toxic substances. Assessment, treatment, and prognosis all are addressed. |

UNIT ASSIGNMENTS

Read: Unit 10. "Organic Mental Disorders" in *The World of Abnormal Psychology Study Guide*, Toby Kleban Levine, editor (HarperCollins, 1992)

View: Program 10. "Organic Mental Disorders" in THE WORLD OF ABNORMAL PSYCHOLOGY.

Read: Chapter 13. "Organic Mental Disorders" in *Abnormal Psychology and Modern Life*, Ninth Edition, by Robert C. Carson and James N. Butcher (HarperCollins, 1992).

GOALS AND OBJECTIVES

1. Define organic mental disorders, list the basic causes of brain damage, and discuss those factors that contribute to the behavioral deficits involved.

2. List and discuss behavioral changes that may be associated with brain damage.

3. Discuss organic mental disorders in terms of a computer hardware/software analogy.

4. Describe the four organic symptom syndromes.

5. Discuss what is known about the symptoms and treatment of AIDS dementia complex.

6. Define tumor, describe some symptoms of tumors in various areas of the brain, and indicate the nature of treatment.

7. Discuss some common effects of brain damage incurred in head injury and identify factors that indicate a favorable prognosis in head injury cases.

8. Differentiate between Alzheimer's disease and Korsakoff's syndrome with respect to memory loss and prognosis.

9. Describe the typical symptoms of dementia of the Alzheimer type and summarize what is known about its causal factors.

10. Discuss the basic goals and approaches to treatment for patients and caregivers in cases of dementia of the Alzheimer type.

11. Discuss the significance of the extent and location of brain damage and give examples of resulting behavioral changes due to impairments in specific parts of the brain.

UNIT OVERVIEW

*by Edward S. Katkin, Ph.D.
State University of New York
at Stony Brook*

Generally in this course, we discuss behavioral problems that are defined as "functional" disorders — that is, although the individual appears to function abnormally, examination reveals no clear evidence of physical illness, injury, or disease. Such mental disorders may have some underlying genetic or biological foundation, but as yet no evidence for that has been found. Other mental disorders, however, are directly linked to physiological or biological malfunctioning. These disorders, caused by any one of a number of discrete biological causes, are collectively referred to as **organic mental disorders**. Organic mental disorders are differentiated from purely psychological disorders in that they involve both biological and psychological conditions.

Organic mental disorders result from many diverse causes including brain **tumor**, such infections as AIDS and syphilis, tumors of the nervous system, disorders of the endocrine glands, and impaired circulation from stroke and digestive disease. They also may occur in association with injury to the brain, toxic exposure in the workplace, substance abuse, or as yet unknown environmental hazards and physiological processes. In each of these cases, the distinguishing characteristic that leads to a diagnosis of organic mental disorder is the appearance of more or less specific alterations of mental capacities or of behaviors associated with brain dysfunction.

This unit focuses on three types of organic mental disorders, all of which are related to brain dysfunction: disorders associated with traumatic brain injury; disorders associated with brain disease; and disorders associated with or arising from a nutritional deficiency. The program also briefly considers an instance of dysfunctional behaviors afflicting a large population of Michigan residents after a **neurotoxin** was accidentally released into the food chain. All of the patients we will see manifest some common neuropsychological symptoms; yet each set of symptoms is sufficiently specific to differentiate it for purposes of diagnosis, treatment, and prognosis.

Patients with mental disorders of organic origin have sustained alterations in brain processing that interfere with normal functioning. Their mental disorder often is complex: along with changes in how their brain works, their reactions to these changes can create additional psychological problems. Thus, some dysfunctional behavior may be a direct, or primary, manifestation of the organic disease; other, secondary problems may reflect an emotional reaction to experiencing the world in an altered, less com_ .ent way.

■ INJURY

The video presents Nick Crane, a young man who suffered traumatic brain injury when he fell from a swing. He sustained both motor deficits and mental changes. Motor deficits are apparent in his poor physical coordination and articulation problems. Mental changes include problems in handling his emotions and an inability to deal with social needs and leisure time creatively. Note also that Nick has had frequent bouts of depression. Depression can be a primary symptom of brain injury, but this is not a common occurrence. More likely, Nick's depression is secondary — that is, a reaction to his neuropsychological impairments and his resulting social isolation and emotional distress. In some cases, depression may arise both from brain dysfunction and as a secondary reaction.

Nick's case of traumatic brain injury represents a frequent source of brain dysfunction. Auto accidents, diving board accidents, and a frighteningly large number of cases of traumatic brain injury in abused children contribute to many and different kinds of neuro-psychological syndromes. Nick's case would be considered moderately severe; the most severe cases remain bedridden in comatose or near-comatose states; the mildest would have sustained some diminution in mental efficiency, at least initially, but can maintain themselves quite adequately in society.

■ ALZHEIMER'S DISEASE

Larry Gorrell suffers from **Alzheimer's disease** — a progressive disease of the brain involving changes in brain substance that result from a continuing abnormal loss of brain cells. These losses disrupt the normal patterns of communication in the brain. This disease rarely occurs before middle age, and it affects about 4,000,000 Americans, mostly among people who are over 65 years of age. Although Alzheimer's disease begins discretely, ultimately it involves most of the cerebral cortex and underlying structures so that virtually all aspects of functioning may be affected in the end stages of the disease. The most dramatic symptoms of early Alzheimer's disease are the loss of the ability to think clearly, to learn or recall information readily, and to appreciate and behave appropriately with respect to social situations and personal experiences. As you will hear, for instance, Larry Gorrell thinks his feet are children.

Larry Gorrell is a good example of a person with a relatively mild dementia. Unfortunately, however, his symptoms can be expected to progress. As more people live to be 70 and older, the number of Alzheimer's patients will continue to increase.

■ KORSAKOFF'S SYNDROME

Wyatt Ingram suffers from **Korsakoff's syndrome**, a mental disorder that is associated with fairly extreme alcohol abuse with attendant disregard for and disinterest in maintaining adequate nutrition. Because of inadequate nutrition, the patient may suffer from a severe deficiency of the B-complex vitamin thiamine. This nutritional deficiency leads to a pattern of subcortical brain damage characterized by a significant memory disorder and emotional dulling. Korsakoff's patients may be distinguished from Alzheimer's patients both by their behavioral history and by the nature of their symptoms. In Korsakoff's syndrome, the patient has a history of severe alcohol abuse, usually for a prolonged time period. The Korsakoff symptoms are relatively circumscribed, and if proper nutrition is restored and maintained, no further deterioration will occur; in some cases, minor improvement will be seen. In Alzheimer's disease, on the other hand, the symptoms ultimately involve all psychological systems, and they progressively grow worse. Finally, Korsakoff's syndrome is due to nutritional deficiency, whereas the etiology of Alzheimer's disease remains unknown.

Wyatt Ingram is a member of a very rare group. The incidence of Korsakoff's syndrome is quite low, and with education aimed at preventing it through dietary supplements, it can decrease. Wyatt also manifests a fairly mild form of his disease, and if he continues to abstain from alcohol he is not likely to show any progressive deterioration.

KEY TERMS

The following terms are used in the text and/or the television programs.

AIDS dementia complex (ADC)	A generalized deterioration of brain substance that can accompany acquired immune deficiency syndrome (AIDS). Clinical features usually begin with psychomotor slowing and problems with concentration, memory, and motor abilities; later phases can include behavioral regression, confusion, psychotic thinking, apathy, and marked withdrawal.
Alzheimer's disease (dementia of the Alzheimer type)	A dementia syndrome with an onset usually after age 65 and a slow but progressively deteriorating course ending in death.

Amnestic syndrome	An impaired ability to learn new material (short-term memory) and to recall material that was known in the past (long-term memory).
Delirium	A set of behaviors characterized by inattentiveness, disorganized thinking, which may be exhibited in rambling or incoherent speech, sensory misperceptions, and disorientation. Onset is usually rapid and duration is brief.
Dementia	A disorder characterized by impairment in short- and long-term memory as well as by impaired thinking and judgment that can interfere with work and relationships.
Hallucinosis	A disorder characterized by the persistent occurrence of hallucinations due to an organic factor, most commonly alcohol use.
Infarct	An interruption of the blood supply to parts of the brain because of arterial disease; commonly known as stroke.
Korsakoff's syndrome	A disorder that involves amnestic syndrome — impairment in short- and long-term memory — due to thiamine deficiency associated with long-term alcohol abuse.
Multi-infarct dementia	A dementia due to a series of cerebral infarcts (strokes).
Neurotoxin	A poison that affects the nervous system and the brain, potentially resulting in psychological impairment.
Organic anxiety syndrome	A condition in which panic attacks or anxiety is due to organic causes.
Organic delusional syndrome	A syndrome that features delusions that result from a specific organic factor.
Organic mental disorders	A group of disorders caused by significant impairment or damage to the normal brain, resulting in a loss of functioning that may range from limited behavioral deficits to severe psychopathology.
Organic mood syndrome	Manic or depressive states caused by an organic factor; symptoms resemble those of either depressive or manic mood disorders.
Organic personality	A change in a person's general personality style following brain damage.
Petechial hemorrhage	Hemorrhaging in the brain that involves small spots of bleeding.
Retrograde amnesia	An inability to recall events immediately preceding an injury.
Simple deterioration	A condition exhibited in dementia of the Alzheimer type in which the person gradually loses mental capacities; deterioration begins with memory and progresses to disorientation, poor judgment, neglect of personal hygiene, loss of contact with reality, and limited mature functioning.
Subdural hematoma	The accumulation of a large amount of blood behind the skull as the result of a head injury; may exert a significant amount of pressure on neighboring regions of the brain; can damage brain functioning and produce permanent neuronal damage.
Syndromes	A group of symptoms that tend to cluster together.
Tumor	A growth involving an abnormal enlargement of tissue. In the brain, malignant tumors destroy the brain tissue in which they arise; benign tumors exert pressure on the brain and can interfere with normal functioning.

177

VIDEO NOTES

■ INTRODUCTION

• Organic mental disorders involve mental or behavioral aberrations which are assumed to be associated with physical damage to the brain.

• Organic mental disorders fall into three categories:

Physical trauma: injuries from falls, accidents, or blows to the head

Medical problems: Alzheimer's disease, Parkinson's syndrome, AIDS, or stroke

Toxic substances: environmental pollutants, drugs, and alcohol

• The brain controls all behavior; if any part is damaged or becomes dysfunctional, behavior and personality may be altered, weakened, or destroyed. Injury to the left temporal lobe, for example, can impair speech; injury to the frontal lobe can impair problem-solving ability.

• Communication of information within the brain is accomplished by means of electrical impulses between cells (neurons). Neurons communicate across gaps (synapses) by releasing chemicals (neurotransmitters). Neurotransmitters lock onto receptor sites on neighboring neurons. Damage to this communications infrastructure can impair functioning and lead to intellectual and emotional problems.

■ HEAD TRAUMA

(Case Illustrations: Phineas P. Gage, Stephen Baker, Nick Crane, Tracy, Celia, Mark)
• Over two million Americans suffer a head injury each year; 500,000 require hospitalization.

• Psychological effects of head trauma can range from minor and transitory to devastating and permanent.

• Some head trauma victims suffer neuropsychological deficits so severe they can no longer live in mainstream society.

• In addition to neurological deficits, head trauma victims may experience psychological problems.

Such problems as social withdrawal, memory loss, anxiety, impulsiveness, depression, lack of initiative, and difficulties with planning and judgment can be a direct result of damage to the frontal lobe of the brain.

Some emotional problems, such as depression, may be an indirect result of brain damage stemming from the patient's realization that he or she will never be quite the same again. This is called a secondary or reactive depression.

• Head trauma victims may learn skills for coping with emotional problems. Treatment often focuses on compensatory strategies that make it possible to live a relatively normal life in mainstream society.

• One treatment program shown in the video leads patients through six stages of a resocialization process:

Stage 1: Maximize concentration and motivate the desire to be rehabilitated.

Stage 2: Increase the individual's awareness of the problems resulting from the injury without creating demoralization.

Stage 3: Evaluate the person's potential to learn new skills that compensate for losses.

Stage 4: Help the individual accept that the brain injury cannot be reversed (the brain cannot be "rewired").

Stage 5: Provide occupational training appropriate to the individual's rehabilitative capacity.

Stage 6: Place the trainee/patient in a mainstream workplace.

■ MEDICAL PROBLEMS
(Case Illustration: Larry Gorrell)
• Some four million Americans have Alzheimer's disease. The disease afflicts nearly 10 percent of those over age 65 and almost half of those over 85. The number of cases is expected to rise as the population ages.

• Early it its course, Alzheimer's typically affects the parietal and temporal lobes, causing language and memory difficulties. When the frontal lobe is affected, behavioral changes, such as depression or belligerence, may occur.

• It is believed that Alzheimer's may be caused by the development of protein fibers or plaques that attach to and destroy neurons. In addition, certain neurotransmitters may be lost.

• The damaging process can occur in different areas of the brain, resulting in a variety of symptoms linked to the disease.

• People with Alzheimer's frequently withdraw from society and regular activities, and they become more dependent on other people.

• Other brain diseases may cause similar mental impairments, which makes Alzheimer's disease difficult to diagnose. To assist in the diagnosis, clinicians utilize various assessment tools that test specific areas of the brain known to be affected by Alzheimer's.

• Caregivers are said to be the second patient in Alzheimer's disease because of the great stress involved in caring for an Alzheimer's patient. For this reason, caregivers frequently need support services.

■ TOXIC SUBSTANCES
(Case Illustrations: 1973 Michigan toxic poisoning, Wyatt Ingram)
• Historical footnote: The phrase "mad as a hatter" and The Mad Hatter, the Alice in Wonderland character, was based on the erratic personality traits frequently exhibited by 19th-century workers in the hat-making trade. These traits where found to result from lengthy exposure to mercury released in the process of making felt.

• Neurotoxins are substances found both in some workplaces and in the environment that can adversely affect a range of physical and psychological processes.

• In 1973, a toxic substance accidentally mixed into cattle feed in Michigan worked its way through the food chain and caused such behavioral problems as oversleeping, depression, inability to concentrate, and memory loss among thousands of people.

• Alcohol is a neurotoxin that can cause permanent changes in personality and mental ability in long-term abusers. Effects range from mild to moderately severe and tend to relate to the length of time over which an individual has abused alcohol. They include losses in conceptual abilities, problem-solving, and perceptual abilities, as well as some memory deficits.

• Korsakoff's syndrome is a neurological impairment caused by a thiamine deficiency that is related to the malnutrition that alcoholics suffer. The thiamine deficit affects the thalamus of the brain and impairs processing of new information. The Korsakoff's patient is unable to learn and recall new information. While this condition does not progress, provided that adequate nutrition is maintained, it is likely to be permanent.

• In some respects, Korsakoff's is similar to such other diseases as Alzheimer's; diagnosis can require a variety of mental status tests to determine the specific deficit, i.e., short-term memory loss.

• A person with a relatively permanent short-term memory deficit needs to rely on a familiar and highly structured living environment.

■ SUMMARY

• Physical damage to the brain can directly and indirectly cause behavioral and emotional problems. The detection and treatment of these disorders must rely on both medical science and on psychology, the science of human behavior.

• Medical research continues to provide new information about the brain's structure and function. It is unlikely that all psychological problems will prove to have neurological contributions, however. Most psychological disorders have multiple causes, including genetics, environment, and interpersonal interactions.

■ VIDEO REVIEW QUESTIONS

1. What are some primary functions of each of the following parts of the brain: the cortex, the limbic system, the frontal lobe, the temporal lobes, and the occipital lobe?

2. When Nick Crane fell off the swing, he injured the left side of his head. What problems are likely to result from an injury to the left side of the brain and how do they differ from those you might expect from damage to the right side of the brain?

3. Using Nick Crane as an example, differentiate between depression that is a direct result of head injury and depression that is secondary or reactive.

4. What does Dr. Russo mean when he says, "It's the client's worst behavior, not his best behavior, that will determine his future"? How would this apply to Nick?

5. What is the purpose of a mental status exam?

6. Which of Larry Gorrell's behaviors suggest that he has Alzheimer's disease? Relate each of these behaviors to a part of the brain.

7. Discuss the ways in which Larry Gorrell's memory loss differs from Wyatt Ingram's memory loss in terms of their respective abilities to recall previously learned information, their current abilities to learn and store new information, and their prognoses.

8. What do we learn about organic mental disorders from the phrase "to be mad as a hatter"?

9. When doctors first examined Wyatt Ingram they thought he had Alzheimer's disease. Which of Wyatt's behaviors caused them to rule out this diagnosis?

10. What is the most likely reason Wyatt Ingram developed Korsakoff's syndrome?

CASE STUDY

by Diane Howieson, Ph.D.
Oregon Health Sciences
University

Bob

Bob made an appointment with his neuropsychologist to discuss his future. He believes he has completely recovered from the brain injury he received in an automobile accident two years ago. In particular, he wants to control his own finances. Currently, his mother serves as his financial conservator.

Bob doesn't like having his mother pay his bills and feels that he would have no difficulty handling his own affairs. After all, he worked and lived independently before his accident, and he's been responsible with the $100 he receives each month from subleasing a garage on his rental property.

His three attempts to return to work this year failed, he says, because his supervisors were "bozos" and were jealous because he was a better worker than others. Furthermore, he sees no need to begin a program of vocational rehabilitation because he plans to accept a friend's offer to work full-time paving roads as soon as the weather improves. When work begins, he will give up his Social Security disability income.

He also claims considerable progress overcoming an alcohol abuse problem. He had been an alcohol abuser before the accident and had been drinking when the accident occurred. Afterwards he tried to stop drinking because his doctors told him that it could cause him to have seizures. Many of his friends socialized at taverns, however, and one evening when he went out with them, he became intoxicated and had a seizure. This caused him to lose his driving license because state law requires that people who have had a seizure be seizure free for one year before driving again. He learned his lesson, albeit the hard way, and has not resumed drinking. He has just become eligible to drive again.

He now lives in his own apartment with his girlfriend and is looking forward to getting on with his life. In the meantime, he spends his time watching television and lifting weights.

He is concerned, however, that the neuropsychologist won't be fair to him because he believes that all health-care professionals are against him. He still hasn't forgiven them for tying him in his bed in the early weeks following his accident. At every turn they tell him what he can and cannot do. He hasn't been treated like this since he was a child. Why can't they let him be?

CLINICAL DISCUSSION

At age 23, Bob, a high school graduate with average grades, had held a variety of manual labor jobs. For the six months prior to the accident, he was employed repairing automotive radiators. His accident resulted in two broken limbs and a head injury with bleeding in the right frontal lobe. He was unconscious for 12 days and required surgery to remove blood collecting on his brain. After regaining consciousness, he repeatedly attempted to get out of bed despite his broken leg and had to be restrained. He was unaware of his medical problems and could not remember from hour to hour explanations given to him by the medical staff. Like most people with serious head injury, he had no memory of being in an accident. After remaining in the hospital for eight weeks, he was discharged to a nursing home and then to the care of his parents.

Like many people with right-hemisphere brain damage, he is unable to understand that he has been having problems with his memory and judgment. Beginning three weeks after the accident, Bob has had periodic neuropsychological evaluations, which have shown gradual improvement of his mental functioning. The present evaluation was conducted nearly two years after the accident.

Bob did not arrive for his scheduled appointment. When he was located in a different part of the hospital, he stated that he had not known where to go, so he went to his previous unit to visit. His affect was positive throughout the evaluation, and he repeatedly commented on how well he was getting along. At two points he burst into song and, noting that he was a "great" singer, persisted until he wanted to stop. During the neuropsychological testing he frequently began a task before the directions were completed or attempted to change the task demands to meet his expectations. Despite his poor self-regulation, once engaged in a task, he appeared to put forth good effort.

A comparison of his test performance with normal people of his age group shows that he has difficulty in a number of areas. His greatest area of strength is on visual constructional tasks such as copying complex geometric designs and reconstructing designs with blocks. His approach to these tasks was relatively well organized and less impulsive compared to many other tests. This suggests that he has the basic skill to perform construction work tasks. On other types of tests, he showed mild deficits in common sense reasoning and judgment, reading comprehension, and memory. His greatest difficulty is with problem solving and flexibility of thinking. He was unable to perform a task in which he was to solve problems using feedback about the correctness of his performance as he gained experience with the task. He persisted with his preferred, although incorrect, solutions despite ample feedback about their incorrectness. Although he knew he was performing poorly on this task, he tended to blame the task rather than modify his approach.

Bob also demonstrated a number of behavioral problems including impulsivity, poor self-regulation, self-centeredness, poor judgment, and a poor appreciation of his problems. His personality assessment suggests that he struggles with behavioral control and low frustration tolerance. These problems frequently occur in patients with right-hemisphere brain damage.

His prognosis for independent living is fair. His behavioral problems and poor insight are major limitations, and he is not motivated to change his behavior or to take recommendations from others because he is unaware that he is having mental problems from his brain injury. It will take considerable time for him to learn that he has new limitations. This process would be facilitated if he entered a brain-injury rehabilitation program.

His mother and the neuropsychologist agreed to give Bob a chance to handle his own finances by making him responsible for the monthly payments on his cable television subscription. He will need to demonstrate that he can save the amount of the fee from an increase in his allowance, keep track of the bill, and pay it in a timely fashion. They felt that Bob would be highly motivated to maintain his cable television and would make a maximum effort to succeed. If he can handle this financial responsibility, more and more may be turned over to him on a trial basis.

CASE QUESTIONS

1. What evidence exists that Bob is having problems with his judgment?

2. What problems might arise if Bob is given control of his finances?

3. Bob says he can handle more responsibility. Keeping in mind the nature of his injury, do you think he can? Why?

SELF-TEST

1. Impaired social judgment, decreased emotional and impulse control, and an inability to sustain goal-directed activity all may occur as a result of brain damage. These are symptoms of
   a) amnestic syndrome.
   b) dementia.
   c) organic mood syndrome.
   d) organic personality syndrome.

2. In adults, brain tumors occur with greatest frequency between the ages of
   a) 18 and 25.
   b) 26 and 35.
   c) 40 and 60.
   d) 70 and 80.

3. A benign brain tumor causes abnormal behavior because it
   a) attracts and destroys spinal fluid.
   b) changes the electrical nature of the brain's pathways.
   c) destroys the brain tissue in which it arises.
   d) exerts pressure on the brain.

4. Patients with brain tumors who have some insight into the seriousness of their condition tend to become
   a) depressed.
   b) euphoric.
   c) expansive.
   d) paranoid.

5. Approximately _____ individuals in the USA suffer significant brain damage from head injuries each year.
   a) 3,000
   b) 30,000
   c) 300,000
   d) 3,000,000

6. If a head injury is sufficiently severe to result in unconsciousness, the person may experience retrograde amnesia or an inability to recall
   a) events immediately following the injury.
   b) events immediately preceding and following the injury.
   c) events immediately preceding the injury.
   d) names or faces of friends.

7. All of the following indicate a favorable prognosis in cases of head injury EXCEPT
   a) a long period of unconsciousness.
   b) a nonstrategic location of the brain lesion.
   c) a well-integrated preinjury personality.
   d) a strong motivation to recover.

8. Which of the following is the most common behavioral manifestation of Alzheimer's disease?
   a) jealousy delusions
   b) paranoid orientation
   c) psychopathological symptoms
   d) simple deterioration

9. Because of its somewhat similar clinical picture, multi-infarct dementia is sometimes confused with _____.
   a) dementia of the Alzheimer type
   b) AIDS dementia complex
   c) hallucinosis
   d) organic personality syndrome

10. The impairment of functioning due to brain damage is a result of
    a) the extent of brain damage and not the location of the damage.
    b) the location of the brain damage and not the extent of the damage.
    c) the extent and location of the brain damage.
    d) the extent and location of the brain damage but rarely an interaction of the two.

11. Depression among brain-injured individuals often is the result of
    a) the injury itself.
    b) the realization of one's limited condition.
    c) diminished self-esteem.
    d) all of the above.

12. The extent to which damage to the brain results in behavioral deficits depends upon all of the following EXCEPT the
    a) location and extent of the damage.
    b) nature of the individual's life situation.
    c) premorbid personality of the individual.
    d) relative size of the person's brain.

13. All of the following are true of delirium EXCEPT
    a) attention, perception, memory, and thinking are severely impaired.
    b) it is caused by a general disturbance in brain metabolism.
    c) information processing is impaired.
    d) it is usually associated with chronic brain disturbances.

14. A noteworthy deterioration in intellectual functioning occurring after the completion of brain maturation is called
    a) amnestic syndrome.
    b) confabulation.
    c) delirium.
    d) dementia.

15. Which of the following is the most common cause of dementia?
    a) alcoholism
    b) Alzheimer's disease
    c) drug toxicity
    d) intracranial tumors

16. In the early stages of dementia
    a) semantic memory is most severely impaired.
    b) memory for events from childhood is more impaired than is memory for recent events.
    c) loss of emotional control is the most noticeable symptom.
    d) an individual is alert and fairly well attuned to events in the environment.

17. Multi-infarct dementia involves a(n)
    a) appearance of senile plaques.
    b) continuing recurrence of small strokes.
    c) increase in neurofibrillary tangles.
    d) loss of neurons in the basal forebrain.

18. The first stage in Dr. Ben-Yishay's rehabilitation program involves motivating the patient to want to rehabilitate. This stage is called
    a) engagement.
    b) awareness.
    c) compensation.
    d) rehabilitation.

19. The case of Phineas P. Gage is important because it shows
    a) how schizophrenia often results from a head injury.
    b) how even minor head injuries can result in death.
    c) how an individual can suffer a severe head injury and show almost no cognitive problems.
    d) the psychological difficulties that can result from severe head injuries.

20. In Alzheimer's disease, the caregiver is often considered the second patient because
    a) Alzheimer's disease is contagious.
    b) caregivers accompany patients to treatment sessions and therefore seem like patients.
    c) caregivers frequently suffer extreme stress from watching a loved one deteriorate.
    d) none of the above.

21. Behavioral and cognitive skills training seeks to help the brain-injured individual recover some losses by

    a) retraining the injured parts of the brain.

    b) enhancing neural efficiency.

    c) identifying and utilizing the least damaged parts of the brain.

    d) building new neurotransmitter pathways.

---

22. Korsakoff's syndrome is usually

    a) progressive and chronic.

    b) chronic and irreversible, but not progressive.

    c) reversible with surgery.

    d) controllable with medication.

---

23. A systematic way of assessing brain function using questions and tasks to test different skills is called a(n)

    a) CAT scan.

    b) mental status exam.

    c) EEG.

    d) EKG.

---

24. Korsakoff's syndrome typically develops from deterioration of what part of the brain?

    a) frontal lobe

    b) parietal lobe

    c) thalamus

    d) hyperthalamus

---

25. The actual cause of Korsakoff's syndrome is thought to be

    a) the toxins in alcohol.

    b) a thiamine deficiency.

    c) an iron deficiency.

    d) genetic in nature.

[ANSWERS: 1-d, 2-c, 3-d, 4-a, 5-c, 6-c, 7-a, 8-d, 9-a, 10-c, 11-d, 12-d, 13-d, 14-d, 15-b, 16-d, 17-b, 18-a, 19-d, 20-c, 21-c, 22-b, 23-b, 24-c, 25-b]

SUGGESTED READINGS

Bloom, F. E., Lazerson, A., & Hofstadter, L. (1985). *Brain, mind, and behavior*. New York: W. H. Freeman. This beautifully illustrated book — the companion to the television series THE BRAIN — provides a general overview of the workings of the brain and its relationship to behavior.

Diagram Group, The. (1983). *The brain: A user's manual*. Berkeley, CA: Berkeley Books. This comprehensive look at the anatomy of the brain and the nervous system also focuses on the senses, instincts and feelings, awareness and thought, and damage and disease. In addition, it includes discussions of the physiological correlates of the troubled mind, the effects of drugs, and the power of mind over matter.

Frank, J. (1985). *Alzheimer's disease: The silent epidemic*. Minneapolis: Lerner Publications. Case histories help explain the progressive brain deterioration of Alzheimer's and describe the problems faced by families.

Franklin, J. (1987). *Molecules of the mind: The brave new science of molecular psychology*. New York: Dell. This book examines the chemistry of the brain and its relationship to behavior.

Holland G. B. (1985). *For Sasha, with love: An Alzheimer's crusade — The story of Anne Bashkiroff*. New York: Dember Books. This moving and intimate book portrays how this couple, Anne and Sasha Bashkiroff, dealt with Sasha's Alzheimer's, and ultimately, how Anne coped with his death.

Sacks, O. (1987). *The man who mistook his wife for a hat and other clinical tales*. New York: Perennial Library. These case histories describe various psychological symptoms of people with neurological disorders.

Sacks, O. (1990). *Awakenings*. New York: Harper Perennial. The basis of the popular film, this is the moving and informative collection of case histories of patients "awakened" from encephalitis-induced catatonia.

BEHAVIOR
DISORDERS
OF
CHILDHOOD

■ UNIT THEME

The classification of childhood disorders as separate from adult disorders is a relatively recent distinction that recognizes the biological and psychosocial factors that affect a child's emotional development. This unit focuses on three types of children's disorders: developmental, primarily autism; disruptive, including attention-deficit hyperactivity disorder and conduct disorder; and emotional, primarily separation anxiety disorder. The text includes the broader topic of mental retardation.

■ UNIT ASSIGNMENTS

Read: Unit 11. "Behavior Disorders of Childhood" in *The World of Abnormal Psychology Study Guide*, Toby Kleban Levine, editor (HarperCollins, 1992).

View: Program 11. "Behavior Disorders of Childhood" in THE WORLD OF ABNORMAL PSYCHOLOGY.

Read: Chapter 14. "Mental Retardation and Developmental Disorders."
Chapter 15. "Behavior Disorders of Childhood."
Abnormal Psychology and Modern Life, Ninth Edition, by Robert C. Carson and James N. Butcher (HarperCollins, 1992).

■ GOALS AND OBJECTIVES

1. List several ways in which childhood disorders are different from those of other ages and explain the special vulnerabilities of childhood.

2. Describe attention-deficit hyperactivity disorder and summarize what is known about causal factors and treatment.

3. Describe conduct disorder and discuss various potential causes and treatment options.

4. Identify several forms of delinquency, differentiating among their causal factors.

5. Describe and evaluate different ways in which Americans deal with delinquency.

6. Describe separation anxiety disorder and discuss causal factors and potential treatment strategies.

7. Identify several biological and sociocultural factors that can lead to mental retardation.

8. Discuss the current situation regarding treatment for mentally retarded individuals, including availability and access, and evaluate several forms of treatment.

9. Describe two contemporary goals in the prevention of mental retardation and explain the three-pronged, broad spectrum approach to providing a more supportive sociocultural setting for children.

10. Summarize what is known about the causes and treatment of autism.

11. Discuss the clinical picture of learning disability and summarize what is known about causal factors.

UNIT OVERVIEW

by Edward S. Katkin, Ph.D.
State University of New York
at Stony Brook

Scientific attention to the unique mental health problems of children is a relatively recent development in the history of abnormal psychology. Traditionally, psychiatry focused little energy on the problems of children; even when it did, these problems were not well understood. In recent decades, however, it has become clear that childhood disorders are widespread (surveys suggest that about one in seven children manifest signs of maladjustment) and that they are characteristically quite distinct from adult disorders.

The nature of specific childhood disorders can be influenced by a number of biological and environmental factors. In addition, developmental patterns must be understood in evaluating childhood disorders in that each stage of development includes a normal range of behaviors. Some behaviors that may be perfectly normal at age three, however, would be considered abnormal if manifested at age six. The clinician who works with children, therefore, must understand the normal process of development and be familiar with the range of expected behavior.

The video presents children who exemplify some of the most pervasive disorders of childhood — **attention-deficit hyperactivity disorder** (ADHD), **conduct disorder**, **separation anxiety disorder**, and **autism**. These are only some of the varied problem behaviors that afflict children and adolescents.

The textbook assignment also covers **mental retardation**, which is included here because it usually appears in the early years of life. Both organic and sociocultural factors play roles in the causation of mental retardation, which can range from mild to profound. While certain preventive measures are possible, treatment does not focus on cures. It primarily involves training individuals who are developmentally disabled to function up to their potential in their community; some individuals, however, may require lifelong institutionalization.

■ ATTENTION-DEFICIT HYPERACTIVITY DISORDER

In the video, you will meet James, an 11-year-old boy who appears to enjoy such normal activities as video games. When James has to deal with problems that are less stimulating, however, such as schoolwork, his behavior breaks down. Here is a very clear example of the importance of evaluating the degree of disruption in evaluating abnormality. It is perfectly reasonable and normal for 11-year-old children to prefer video games to homework. One would not consider it abnormal if such a child showed signs of boredom or restlessness when asked to do tasks that were uninteresting. In the case of James, however, this restlessness is far beyond expectation. He shows an extreme inability to concentrate or focus his attention and becomes impulsive and unusually agitated.

What is the cause of this disorder? Many experts believe the root cause of ADHD lies within the frontal lobe of the brain. Yet, while this theory is widely accepted, the exact nature of the specific frontal lobe malfunction has not been fully explained. Most experts believe that the brain deficit underlies a motivational deficit; that is, children with ADHD cannot maintain their attention at motivational levels that would be sufficient for normal children, and they need higher levels of motivation to engage their attention.

The treatment of ADHD is complex and often requires several interventions, including medicine, family counseling, and behavior modification. Among the pharmacological approaches to treatment, the most popular has been the use of such stimulant drugs as Dexedrine or Ritalin. That these drugs have a calming effect on hyperactive children is somewhat paradoxical, because these drugs are stimulants and would cause a normal person to become hyperactive. It is believed that in hyperactive children the deficient area of the frontal lobe, and its connections to more primitive parts of the brain, is underaroused.

191

When aroused by medication, this part of the frontal lobe serves a normal inhibitory function, restraining the hyperactivity. Even with advanced medical and behavioral treatments, it is estimated that 80 percent of hyperactive children will not be cured, and that they will have adjustment problems throughout adolescence and adulthood.

■ CONDUCT DISORDER

Conduct disorder is a label assigned to older children who exhibit such antisocial or otherwise socially disruptive behavior as fighting, stealing, property destruction, and truancy. Most children with conduct disorder are boys. Typically, they are low in self-esteem, unpopular with peers, and unsuccessful at most activities. Unlike the ADHD child, the conduct-disordered child is not assumed to have a brain function deficit, nor can his symptoms be alleviated by stimulant drugs. Rather, the conduct disorder is thought to result from poor parenting, an unstable family life, and unsuccessful parent-child relationships.

No sure ways to treat conduct disorder exist, and frequently such children are dealt with by the legal system rather than the mental health system. It is estimated that up to 70 percent of juvenile crime is committed by children who have conduct disorder, for example. One attempt to treat these children consists of training foster parents to provide the child with a stable and intensive family experience while his real parents receive counseling and parent training. After about six months the conduct-disordered child and his parents are reunited. In the video, Paul, a conduct-disordered child, and his mother describe their participation in such a program.

■ SEPARATION ANXIETY DISORDER

It is normal for almost all young children to become frightened when they are separated from their parents. It also is normal for children to learn to overcome the anxiety as they mature. Yet, about three percent of children experience separation anxiety disorder, which is associated with unreasonable fear, and sometimes panic, at the thought of being separated from loved ones, particularly the mother. In the video you will meet Amanda, a girl who has been suffering from separation anxiety for a number of years. She discusses a period of her life when she was afraid to leave her home for school, a visit to a friend's house, a movie, or a restaurant. Her abnormal anxiety interfered with normal activity and prevented her from participating in the normal social life of children her own age.

The causes of separation anxiety are not fully understood, and a number of competing theories attempt to explain it, including psychodynamic, learning, and biological theories. Psychodynamic theorists believe that the anxiety reflects an unconscious anger that the child feels toward the parents. This anger, while unconscious, can be so intense, it is suggested, that the child develops a conscious sense that the parent is in danger and may be harmed or even killed.

Learning theory suggests that the fearful behavior is learned through a process of reinforcement. That is, if the child once expresses symptoms of separation anxiety and the parents rush back to provide comfort, the child learns to express anxiety as a way of controlling the parents' behavior and reducing his or her own fear. In short, the expression of the fear serves to bring the child results that are desirable, and then the fearfulness becomes habitual.

Biological theorists suggest that some children are born with temperaments that are prone to fearfulness and that such children may elicit negative reactions from their parents, which increases their fears. It also has been argued that such children may have their fears exacerbated by specific traumatic events.

The treatment of separation anxiety is varied and usually is tailored to the individual child's needs. Among the most common forms of treatment are family therapy, in which the entire family unit deals with the problem; behavior modification, in which the child is helped to confront directly the object of his or her fears; and traditional forms of child therapy, including play therapy. Amanda underwent a multiple treatment program that included traditional therapy and behavior modification.

■ AUTISM

The most profound and debilitating form of childhood disorder is called autism. This is a disorder characterized by three primary symptoms: a lack of responsiveness to other people; impaired communication skills; and a limited number of stimuli to which the child will respond. In the video you will see Wesley, an autistic child with severely impaired communication skills, as well as other autistic children with a variety of symptoms. The common underlying cause of autism is believed by most professionals to be a neurological defect, but the precise location and nature of such a defect have yet to be determined.

In early infancy the symptoms of autism may go undetected because they are subtle; yet the experienced professional can detect the difference between an autistic infant and a normal one. In the video, you will see two babies, Ryan and Callum, who appear normal when viewed individually. When their responses to the environment are compared, however, it becomes evident that Callum probably is autistic.

No cures for autism have been found, but some dramatic improvements in treatment have emerged that can alleviate the most disabling of its symptoms. It is no longer considered necessary to institutionalize autistic children, as it once was. Among the innovative treatments are highly structured classroom environments and behavior modification programs that aim to eliminate the most disruptive behavioral manifestations of the disorder. Extremely noncommunicative autistic children, like Wesley, can use new electronic computerized keyboards to communicate their thoughts without having to speak. The use of such techniques has taught us that some autistic children are capable of high levels of learning and comprehension, even when they are not able to communicate that knowledge through normal channels.

■ KEY TERMS

The following terms are used in the text and/or the television programs.

Attention deficit-hyperactivity disorder (ADHD)	A disorder characterized by maladaptive behavior that interferes with effective task-oriented behavior in children; specifically includes impulsivity, excessive motor activity, exaggerated muscular activity, and difficulty maintaining attention.
Autism (autistic disorder)	A pervasive developmental disorder occurring in infancy or childhood whose central features are qualitative impairment in reciprocal social interactions and communication and a restricted repertoire of activities and interests.
Childhood depression	A behavior pattern that may include withdrawal, crying, avoidance of eye contact, physical complaints, poor appetite, retarded mobility, apathy, and aggressive behavior. In DSM-III-R depression among children is not a separate category but is included within the adult diagnostic system.

193

Conduct disorder	The persistent, repetitive violation of rules and a disregard for the rights of others. Characteristic maladaptive behavior includes fighting, defiance, disobedience, destruction of property, attention-seeking, and inattentiveness.
Cretinism	A form of mental retardation in which the thyroid has either failed to develop properly or has undergone degeneration or injury, resulting in a deficiency in thyroid secretion, which in turn causes brain damage.
Cultural-familial retardation	A form of mental retardation that occurs as a result of an inferior quality of interaction with the cultural environment and with other people. Although children whose mental retardation is cultural-familial in origin are usually only mildly retarded, they constitute the majority of people labeled as mentally retarded.
Developmental disorder	A problem rooted in deviations in the developmental process, such as a disturbance in the acquisition of cognitive, language, and motor skills.
Down syndrome	The most common of the clinical conditions associated with moderate and severe mental retardation; results from a defective, or extra, chromosome, which distorts the growth process both physically and intellectually.
Dyslexia	A developmental reading disorder involving impairment in word recognition and reading comprehension skills.
Echolalia	The mimicking of the speech of others; common among autistic children.
Functional encopresis	Encopresis is the involuntary passage of feces; functional encopresis is not organically caused and occurs after age four.
Functional enuresis	Enuresis is the involuntary discharge of urine after age five; functional enuresis refers to habitual involuntary or intentional bed-wetting that is not organically caused.
Hydrocephalus	An organic retardation syndrome in which the accumulation of an abnormal amount of cerebrospinal fluid within the cranium causes damage to the brain tissues and enlargement of the cranium.
Juvenile delinquency	The commission of illegal acts by people under the age of 16, 17, or 18 (depending on state law).
Macrocephaly	An organic retardation syndrome involving neurological problems and an increase in brain and skull size.
Mainstreaming	The practice of placing mentally retarded children in regular school classes for at least part of the day.
Mental retardation	A level of intellectual functioning that is significantly below average, that exists concurrently with deficits in adaptive behavior, and is manifested during the developmental period (based on the American Association on Mental Deficiency definition, 1973).
Microcephaly	An organic retardation syndrome resulting from impaired development of the brain and a consequent failure of the cranium to attain normal size.

Overanxious disorder	A childhood disorder characterized by excessive worry and anxiety, preoccupation with trivial problems, and self-consciousness. The anxiety may be expressed in such somatic ways as stomach pain, shortness of breath, dizziness, headaches, and sleeping problems.
Pervasive developmental disorders	A subclass of disorders characterized by qualitative impairment in social interaction, communication skills, and imaginative activity; can include a restricted repertoire of activities.
Phenylketonuria (PKU)	An organic retardation syndrome in which a baby lacks a liver enzyme needed to break down phenylalanine, an amino acid found in many foods. An accumulation of phenylalanine eventually produces brain damage.
Separation anxiety disorder	A childhood disorder characterized by excessive anxiety about separation from people to whom the child is attached. Symptoms include unrealistic fears, oversensitivity, self-consciousness, nightmares, and chronic anxiety.
Sleepwalking (somnambulism)	A sleep disorder involving repeated episodes of a person leaving bed and walking around without being conscious of the experience or remembering it later.
Specific developmental disorders	A subclass of disorders characterized by inadequate development in academic achievement, language, speech, or motor skills, not due to any demonstrable physical or neurological defect.
Specific learning disabilities	A group of specific developmental disorders involving academic skills; in the DSM-III-R, these are categorized as academic skills disorders.
Structural therapy	An approach to treating autistic children that involves a highly structured environment; stimulation is provided in order to make the children more aware of and related to their environment.
Tic	A persistent, intermittent muscle twitch or spasm, usually limited to a localized muscle group, occurring most frequently between the ages of 6 and 14.
Token economies	A type of behavior therapy in which appropriate behaviors are encouraged and may be rewarded with tangible reinforcers in the form of tokens that can be exchanged for desired objects or privileges.
Tourette's syndrome	An extreme tic disorder involving multiple motor and vocal patterns, accompanied by uncontrollable head movements and such sounds as grunts, clicks, yelps, sniffs, or words.

VIDEO NOTES

■ INTRODUCTION

• Approximately one in seven children has a psychological or physical disorder. Children's psychological disorders include disruptive disorders, emotional disorders, and developmental disorders.

• Some psychological disorders experienced by children are similar to those experienced by adults; others are unique to childhood. But the criteria for diagnosing abnormal behavior in children differ from those used in assessing adults.

195

- Whether a child's behavior is considered normal or abnormal depends on its frequency, intensity, duration, and the age of the child at the time the behavior occurs. Children who cry occasionally when they are frustrated, for example, are less likely to be considered disordered than children who cry intensely for long periods of time whenever they are frustrated.

■ DISRUPTIVE BEHAVIOR DISORDERS: ATTENTION-DEFICIT HYPERACTIVITY DISORDER (ADHD)
(Case Illustration: James)
- Roughly three percent of children may have ADHD.

- Among the symptoms of ADHD are developmentally inappropriate inattention, impulsivity, and hyperactivity. Frequently these behaviors lead to problems both at home and at school.

- Dr. Russell Barkley describes how such children are assessed at the Center for ADHD at the University of Massachusetts Medical Center.

> Behavior rating scales (questionnaires) completed by parents and teachers enable doctors to compare what adults say about troubled children with what they say about normal children. This provides a measure of just how far from normal a particular child falls.

> ADHD children often score well when asked to perform in clinical environments, a phenomenon that makes diagnosis difficult. To overcome this problem, psychologists try to create situations that are relatively uninteresting and of sufficiently long duration to see if ADHD behavior will emerge. In the video, James participates in a restricted academic situations task, in which he is asked to work on math problems for 15 minutes. Shortly after beginning the task, his ADHD behavior appears, and he abandons the math problems.

■ CAUSAL FACTORS AND TREATMENT
- For more than 50 years, the precise cause of ADHD has remained unknown although several theories have been put forth.

- Some have suggested that the disorder develops out of poor social circumstances pertaining primarily to bad parenting or the degree of stress and change in our society.

- Dr. Barkley believes that ADHD has it roots in the brain. He feels that the centers of the brain that control motivation and sensitivity to surroundings do not work well in some children, a phenomenon he refers to as a "biological deficit." Barkley believes the successful use of stimulants (e.g., Dexedrine or Ritalin) in the treatment of ADHD supports the hypothesis that these drugs stimulate the otherwise sluggish motivational centers of the brain.

- Family and/or individual therapy also may be appropriate in cases of ADHD so that family members may understand the child's problem and learn the best methods to use in managing the child. Family therapy also helps parents understand that the problem is not their fault.

- The methods used to help parents cope with and better manage children with ADHD are typically based on behavior modification concepts.

One common method is called a token economy, in which a child is given a reward, such as poker chips, for good behavior. The method is most effective when the chips are given immediately following the behavior. These tokens may be cashed in for treats, toys, or privileges.

Such techniques are important for teachers because a child with ADHD runs the risk of a multitude of problems with schoolwork, teachers, and other students.

• Pat Henningson, who works with children with ADHD, teaches them to continuously stop and think about situations and to plan their response. She sees this primary focus on encouraging them to behave properly as a means of helping them focus and as a way to cut down their impulsivity. She also frequently reminds children about the specific behaviors on which she wants them to focus.

• Despite advances in understanding ADHD, only about one in five children will outgrow the disorder. Those who do not may be vulnerable to a range of problems including school difficulties, employment problems, relationship problems, and substance abuse. About one in four may develop into adults with antisocial personality disorders.

• Dr. Barkley believes that how a family treats a child with ADHD is more important than the severity of the disorder in determining whether the child will become a functional adult.

■ DISRUPTIVE BEHAVIOR DISORDERS: CONDUCT DISORDER
(Case Illustration: Paul)
• Among the symptoms of conduct disorder are violent, disruptive, and often criminal behavior, poor relationships, and a general lack of respect for authority. Many of these behaviors cause the child to be rejected by both adults and peers.

• Conduct disorder affects many more boys than girls. It usually begins to appear by the time children are 10 or 11 years old and typically affects about one in 12 boys. Studies indicate that between 50 and 70 percent of juvenile crime is committed by young people with conduct disorder.

■ CAUSAL FACTORS AND TREATMENT
• Although some evidence has been found to suggest a genetic connection, conduct disorder typically results from a neglectful, harsh, or unstable family life. Treatment of conduct disorder, therefore, must involve the parents as well as the child.

The video visits a program run by the Oregon Social Learning Center that combines individual counseling, family therapy, and parent training. Children with conduct disorder live with specially trained foster parents for up to six months. During that time, the child's negative behaviors are modified through behavior management techniques, often including a token economy approach. Foster parents receive intensive supervision and meet weekly to discuss their child's progress. During the time the child is living in the foster home, the natural parents work with counselors to develop better parenting skills.

■ EMOTIONAL DISORDERS: SEPARATION ANXIETY
(Case Illustration: Amanda)
• Separation anxiety disorder is one of the most common emotional disorders of childhood. It affects about three percent of all children.

• While all children experience some separation anxiety when they must be away from their parents, children with separation anxiety disorder experience extreme anxiety and fear to such an extent that it interferes with the kind of behavior expected from a child of a particular age.

Diagnosis is sometimes difficult, particularly because some children experience the feelings of anxiety but never show it or act on it.

■ CAUSAL FACTORS AND TREATMENT

• Many psychologists believe that normal separation anxiety has contributed to the survival of the human species in the evolutionary process because when children need care, they cry and their parents come to care for them.

• Many psychologists have offered explanations for more acute separation anxiety.

Some believe that children who have experienced an unpredictable, unavailable, or rejecting parent are more prone to separation anxiety.

Learning theory would explain the development of separation anxiety by suggesting that it is reinforced by its aftermath. Some parents exhibit their own anxieties about separation to their children, for example. Some reinforce and reward the behavior that children exhibit when anxious.

Psychologists also generally agree that children differ temperamentally at birth.

Traumatic childhood events, a long illness, a death in the family, even an extended parental vacation may exacerbate normal childhood fears.

Some psychodynamic theorists see children's unconscious anger at their parents at the heart of separation anxiety disorder. Others, such as those of the object-relations school, view separation anxiety as arising from the child's fear that it cannot relieve its own pain.

• Treatment for separation anxiety can involve traditional play therapy, family therapy, or exposure therapy in which the child is encouraged to confront anxious situations in a supervised step-by-step process.

■ DEVELOPMENTAL DISORDERS: AUTISM
(Case Illustrations: Wesley, Carley, Callum, Ryan)
• Autism is a profound developmental disorder that typically involves three symptoms: a lack of responsiveness to other people, impaired verbal and nonverbal communication skills, and responsiveness to a limited number of stimuli. Ann Donnellan describes autism as a "profound deficit in two-way social interaction and communication."

• All symptoms typically appear within the first 30 months of life and may range from mild to severe. Early symptoms may be extremely subtle.

■ CAUSAL FACTORS AND TREATMENT
• For 15 to 20 years, parental behavior was blamed directly or indirectly. Most experts now agree the disease is organic in nature.

• Treatment of autism must be matched to the severity of the behavior. Some children with autism can be mainstreamed into regular school classes; others cannot.

Children who are severely autistic often have been thought to be retarded. Current research indicates that this is not necessarily true. Wesley, who is severely autistic, shows how he uses an electronic keyboard to communicate through typed messages. Wesley's success with this technology is all the more amazing in that Wesley was never taught to read or write, and prior to his work with this device, no one knew he could.

VIDEO REVIEW QUESTIONS

1. Identify three types of psychological disorders that afflict children and give one example of each.

2. What criteria would you use to determine if a child had a psychological disorder or just was developmentally different from other children of the same age? Apply these criteria to some specific behaviors.

3. In what ways did James exhibit the symptoms of attention-deficit hyperactivity disorder?

4. How does Dr. Barkley explain ADHD?

5. Describe how you would use a token economy program to help a child with ADHD.

6. Differentiate between ADHD and conduct disorder with regard to cause.

7. What have you learned about the typical behavior exhibited by youngsters with conduct disorder that explains why such a high percentage of juvenile crime is attributed to them?

8. Why do you think Dr. Patterson recommends that children with conduct disorders be placed in foster homes for a period of time?

9. What were some of the ways Amanda exhibited her separation anxiety?

10. Give three explanations for separation anxiety and name the psychological approach taken in each.

11. The video identifies three primary symptoms of autism. Identify each and describe how each might manifest itself in terms of a child's behavior.

CASE STUDY

by Judith Rosenberger, C.S.W., Ph.D. Hunter College and Edith Gould, C.S.W. Postgraduate Center for Mental Health

Tommy

I'm nine years old. I hate school. When my mom brings me, she comes to the classroom door and then leaves. I watch her walk away, but she never looks back. She just disappears. I can't help it. I start to cry. Seeing her disappear like that is scary. I don't know why, but it makes me feel really bad, like sick to my stomach. My teacher is nice and tries to make me feel better, but she can't. She takes me into the classroom and tells me I have to go to my seat. Sometimes I have to run to the bathroom.

The school day is very, very long, and all I can think about is going home to be with Mom. Mom complains about me following her around all the time, but I just need to be close to her. She doesn't even have to talk to me or anything — I just need to be able to see her. Sometimes I pretend I have stomachaches so Mom will let me stay home from school. I really do have stomachaches a lot.

Mom thinks I have a lot of problems. She took me to a lot of doctors because I couldn't stop wetting my bed. They said there was no real problem, so Mom said I have to try harder. I really tried to stop. But in the night, when I'm cozy in bed, it happens. I know I should be waking up, but I'm scared to see the dark, and it's cold and scary walking to the bathroom. I start to get upset, but then I feel the warm, wet feeling, and I know it's too late. I feel bad, but then I can go back to sleep until it's light out.

Lots of things scare me and give me butterflies in my stomach. I saw a dead dog once, and a bird. Dying scares me. I can't stop thinking about it. I try to imagine what it would feel like to be dead. I get so scared when I think about that at night. I start to cry, and Mom has to come into my room and sit by my bed until I go to sleep. I hate the dark, so she says it's okay to leave the light on. If my room has shadows I see monsters with big claws coming to kidnap me. Even when I tell myself there are no real monsters, they feel real to me. I also worry about being kidnapped. I saw this TV show once where this little boy was kidnapped. They stole him from his school and tied him up and wouldn't give him anything to eat.

I have a lot of bad dreams about Mom dying, and then I'm all alone. Whenever I dream that, I wake up and my bed is wet. Sometimes I go into Mom and Dad's bed, but then they start to argue. Mom tries to be nice, but Dad gets angry and tells me I have to get out. The other night I fell asleep sitting on the floor with my head resting on their bed. Mom says she thinks I have all of these problems because I'm sensitive, but I don't really know what that means. All I know is I want to be next to my mother all the time.

Other kids are braver than I am. They can do sleep-overs. When I tried to sleep at my friend Danny's house I got so upset and cried so hard that his mom called my mom to come and get me. I don't want to get laughed at by the other kids but I can't help it. I don't know what to do. Even if I made myself sleep over, I might wet the bed and then everyone would know! I would never, never go to sleep-away camp. I just wish I weren't so scared all the time.

CLINICAL DISCUSSION

The fear that Tommy shows by his inconsolable crying and clinging to his mother upon being left at school used to be thought of as a school phobia. As customs have changed and children are sent more frequently to preschool programs, day care, and other out-of-home activities, it has become clear that what a child like Tommy fears is not the place to which he is going, but rather being separated from his primary caretaker. Protesting and avoiding separation are now recognized as symptoms of separation anxiety disorder.

Tommy feels anxious that something dreadful will happen when his mother's protective presence is unavailable. His fears of the dark, dying, and kidnapping all reflect this theme of not being able to reach her. As Tommy's case also demonstrates, other kinds of symptoms like enuresis (bed-wetting), sleep disturbances, and somatic complaints that are hard to pinpoint often accompany the primary anxiety of separation.

The roots of the anxiety may be in many sectors of development. Anything that creates cognitive disruptions, such as learning disabilities, medical conditions that induce disequilibrium, and poor nutrition, may heighten a child's potential for anxiety. These also may increase his or her dependence on a trusted adult to provide protection and interpretation of complex situations like school. Tommy's mother, for example, might be helping him to understand and cope with a variety of confusing stressors. If this is so, his separation anxiety is linked to his own functional deficits and his mother's role in compensating for them rather than to an excessively emotional attachment to his mother.

A traumatic experience or chronically difficult life situation also may cause children to exhibit an unusual readiness for alarm in new situations. Predictability of life circumstances gives children a chance to learn how to manage their feelings and cope effectively. Children from chaotic homes will need extra time and assistance to resolve the anxieties that might otherwise compromise their education process. Only then can normal anxiety become a spur to action rather than alarm. The social climate into which a child is introduced also is crucial in keeping anxiety tolerable. Even if his teacher is kind, if Tommy is faced with a chaotic educational setting that confuses him, and perhaps has to cope with bullying or teasing that threatens his safety and self-esteem, any feelings of vulnerability he has will be amplified.

The issue most commonly suspected to be the underlying basis of a separation anxiety like Tommy's is the nature of the mother-child relationship itself. Why does Tommy need his mother so consistently? Why can't his father or teacher substitute? What creates the fear he feels in her absence? His concerns about death may be a clue. Does he fear she will die? Does he, therefore, need the constant reassurance of seeing her to know that she is still alive and available to him?

Assuming there is no factual basis for Tommy's concern about his mother's death, what does his concern symbolize? The feeling that he will lose her unless he holds on tightly can have many origins. It might result, for example, if Tommy's mother were depressed, overanxious, psychotic, or otherwise psychologically preoccupied and not available to him in a consistent way. Fear of her imminent disconnection also could stem from her hidden rejection of Tommy for any number of reasons lodged in her own personal history. In this case, his anxiety would be responding to signals from his mother of which even she may be unaware. In addition, Tommy's anger with or rejection of his mother, which might result, could be turned into apparent overconcern and overattachment.

Another possible origin is the mother-son relationship. The inability of his teacher or father to be acceptable substitutes suggests an ongoing dynamic between mother and son. Social customs certainly promote this link by assigning the jobs of child care and teaching sensitivity to feelings of others almost exclusively to mothers.

Tommy's mother took him to the doctor in response to his bed-wetting. A possible medical basis for enuresis was explored, but was ruled out. So, in Tommy's case, we can assume a psychological explanation. Tommy explains his bed-wetting as a result of his fear of awakening alone in the night and having to walk to the bathroom in the dark. He struggles to avoid the fear by staying asleep too long. He gets a primary gain from this pattern by avoiding the dreaded anxiety of being alone. A secondary gain comes in the form of extra concerns and attention shown by his mother, which could reinforce the behavior. The process may also symbolically parallel gaining warmth and relief when rejoining mother after some distress occurs in waking life. The way Tommy's parents do or do not work together to handle his bed-wetting will add to his store of symbolic meanings over time. Is it a chance to win mother's attention for himself? Does it make him special in some way compared to siblings?

The goal from Tommy's point of view is singular and clear: to be with mother. Any threat to this access will set off anxiety. Desperate efforts to recover her presence will be made. Pressure, rules, admonitions to try harder, kindness by others, and even punishments are irrelevant to him in his frantic state of need once separation anxiety starts. Decoding the experience of separation for Tommy, in terms of all psychological, physical, and social aspects, is a complex assessment task made more complex by the fact that the symptomatic child wants not understanding but relief.

CASE QUESTIONS

1. What conditions at home and in other situations could contribute to Tommy's anxiety?

2. How is Tommy's enuresis linked to his anxiety? Why would he not be able to solve it by trying harder?

3. School problems and peer-relationship problems are often secondary to separation anxiety. How could you see each type of problem occurring in Tommy's case?

4. Give an example of how his mother could react to his bed-wetting in a way that would reinforce the behavior by providing secondary gains.

SELF-TEST

1. **Generally, IQ tests measure an individual's predicted level of success in dealing with**
   a) conventional schoolwork.
   b) economic problems.
   c) personal frustration.
   d) social interaction.

2. **Mental retardation is defined both in terms of _____ and _____ competence.**
   a) cognitive/behavioral
   b) intellectual/social
   c) moral/spiritual
   d) physical/mental

3. **All of the following are true about the abilities of Down syndrome children EXCEPT**
   a) their greatest deficit is in visual-motor coordination.
   b) they remain relatively unimpaired in their appreciation of spatial relationships.
   c) they show deficits in language-related skills.
   d) they show deficits in verbal skills.

4. **All of the following are true of ADHD EXCEPT**
    a) between three and five percent of elementary school-aged children manifest hyperactive symptoms.
    b) hyperactivity occurs six to nine times more often in boys than in girls.
    c) it is the most frequent referral to mental health facilities.
    d) it occurs with greatest frequency after age 8.

5. **All of the following are true of hyperactive children EXCEPT they**
    a) are highly distractible.
    b) are viewed negatively by their peers.
    c) commonly show specific learning disabilities.
    d) usually show deficits in intelligence.

6. **All of the following are true of the use of amphetamines to quiet hyperactive children EXCEPT**
    a) the medication is thought to stimulate areas of the brain that control impulsivity.
    b) the medication decreases children's overactivity and distractability.
    c) the medication increases children's attention and ability to concentrate.
    d) the medication increases IQ by about five points.

7. **Children and adolescents who persist in committing acts of aggressive or antisocial behavior are usually diagnosed as having**
    a) anxiety disorder.
    b) attention-deficit hyperactivity disorder.
    c) conduct disorder.
    d) juvenile delinquent disorder.

8. **Concerning the frequency of conduct disorders, which of the following is true?**
    a) An equal number of boys and girls are diagnosed.
    b) More boys than girls are diagnosed.
    c) More girls than boys are diagnosed.
    d) Only after puberty do differences appear between boys and girls.

9. **Beatrice, a 10-year-old, often was in the principal's office for things like pinching, biting, and bullying her classmates. Several times she was caught with stolen goods from her classmates' lockers. Beatrice probably has**
    a) antisocial personality disorder.
    b) an anxiety disorder of childhood.
    c) attention-deficit hyperactivity disorder.
    d) conduct disorder.

10. **The family setting of the conduct-disordered child is typically characterized by all of the following EXCEPT**
    a) consistent discipline.
    b) general frustration.
    c) harsh discipline.
    d) rejection.

11. **Therapy for a conduct-disordered child is likely to be ineffective unless**
    a) genetic factors have been ruled out.
    b) the child has reached puberty.
    c) the child's environment is modified.
    d) the intrapsychic conflict can be specified.

12. **Punishment of the conduct-disordered youth appears to**
    a) cause a highly cohesive gang structure to develop.
    b) cause them to be more devious about their misbehavior.
    c) improve subsequent behavior markedly.
    d) intensify their aggressive behaviors.

13. **Which of the following types of therapy appears to be most effective in treating conduct-disordered children?**
    a) behavioral
    b) gestalt
    c) humanistic
    d) psychodynamic

14. **Children who suffer from anxiety disorders usually cope with their fears by**
    a) becoming overly dependent on others.
    b) denying the existence of fearful things.
    c) developing compulsive behaviors.
    d) indulging in "guardian angel" fantasies.

15. **All of the following are causal factors in the development of childhood anxiety disorders EXCEPT**
    a) early illnesses or accidents.
    b) failure to learn ego-defense mechanisms.
    c) overanxious parents.
    d) unusual constitutional sensitivity.

16. **Bed-wetting that is not organically caused is termed functional**
    a) dysphagia.
    b) encopresis.
    c) enuresis.
    d) rectalgia.

17. **Tourette's syndrome, an extreme tic disorder, typically involves all of the following EXCEPT**
    a) involuntary grunts, clicks, or yelps.
    b) involuntary sniffs or words.
    c) uncontrollable head movements.
    d) antisocial behavior.

18. **Autistic children show deficits in all of the following areas EXCEPT**
    a) language development.
    b) perceptual functioning.
    c) relationships to things.
    d) relationships to other people.

19. **Most investigators believe that autism begins with**
    a) a cold, unresponsive mother.
    b) a strong hereditary predisposition.
    c) an inborn defect that impairs perception.
    d) significant endocrinological pathology.

20. In using parents as change agents for their disordered children, therapists train them to do all of the following EXCEPT

 a) punish children for maladaptive behavior.

 b) reinforce adaptive behavior.

 c) understand their child's behavior disorder.

 d) withhold reinforcement for undesirable behavior.

21. When a clinical evaluation of ADHD is being made it is important for the clinician to remember that

 a) the ADHD child might pay greater attention and score better in the laboratory than he/she would under normal circumstances.

 b) clinical evaluations are not useful for ADHD evaluations.

 c) a family history is critical since ADHD is transmitted through the mother's family.

 d) ADHD often is confused with developmental lag.

22. Dr. Barkley believes the medication prescribed for ADHD works by

 a) inhibiting the part of the brain that controls motor activity.

 b) blocking the overactive responses of the nervous system regulation of activity level.

 c) activating the part of the brain responsible for inhibiting behavior and focusing concentration.

 d) none of the above.

23. Typically, parents of children with separation anxiety

 a) want to keep their children close to them.

 b) themselves suffered from separation anxiety as children.

 c) have a difficult time letting go of their children and unconsciously resent progress the children make in therapy.

 d) cannot bring themselves to inflict pain on their children by insisting that they leave them.

24. In the video segments of Ryan and Callum playing with shaving cream and watching their dads leave the room

 a) neither boy shows emotion when the fathers leave.

 b) no differences between them can be seen.

 c) one of the boys is unable to pay attention to the shaving cream for a sustained period of time.

 d) the boys exhibit different levels of nonverbal communication.

25. Wesley's use of an electronic communicating device demonstrates that

 a) autism and mental retardation are linked.

 b) he is more aware of what is going on around him than his affective behavior indicates.

 c) autistic individuals are unable to communicate either verbally or nonverbally.

 d) he is unable to use written symbols such as those found in words.

[ANSWERS: 1-a, 2-b, 3-a, 4-d, 5-d, 6-d, 7-c, 8-b, 9-d, 10-a, 11-c, 12-d, 13-a, 14-a, 15-b, 16-c, 17-d, 18-c, 19-c, 20-a, 21-a, 22-c, 23-d, 24-d, 25-b.]

SUGGESTED READINGS

Apter, S. J., & Conoley, J. C. (1984). *Childhood behavior disorders and emotional disturbances.* Englewood Cliffs, NJ: Prentice Hall. Written for special education students and teachers, this book presents an historical and theoretical overview of childhood psychopathology.

Barkley, R. A. (1990). *Attention-deficit hyperactivity disorder: Handbook for diagnosis and treatment.* New York: Guilford Press. This book describes how the diagnostic criteria for this disorder developed and discusses treatment programs.

Donnellan, A. M. (Ed.). (1985). *Classic readings in autism.* New York: Teachers College Press. Each classic paper in this collection is followed by a commentary by a contemporary authority.

Robins, L., & Rutter, M. (Eds.). (1990). *Straight and devious pathways from childhood to adulthood.* New York: Cambridge University Press. This collection of conference papers presents findings from major longitudinal studies examining the development of childhood disorders and their implications in adulthood.

PSYCHOTHERAPIES

■ UNIT THEME

Clinicians select from a wide range of therapeutic approaches to treat psychological disorders. In the video portion of this unit, clinicians demonstrate various types of psychologically based therapies (psychodynamic, cognitive-behavioral, and experiential) and show their applications with both individuals and groups. The text includes a discussion of biologically based therapies.

■ UNIT ASSIGNMENTS

Read: Unit 12. "Psychotherapies" in *The World of Abnormal Psychology Study Guide*, Toby Kleban Levine, editor (HarperCollins, 1992).

View: Program 12. "Psychotherapies" in THE WORLD OF ABNORMAL PSYCHOLOGY.

Read: Chapter 17. "Biologically Based Therapies."
Chapter 18. "Psychologically Based Therapies."
Abnormal Psychology and Modern Life, Ninth Edition, by Robert C. Carson and James N. Butcher (HarperCollins, 1992).

■ GOALS AND OBJECTIVES

1. List and explain several reasons why people enter psychotherapy and describe three types of mental health professionals who are trained in the identification and treatment of mental disorders.

2. List and describe four basic techniques of psychoanalysis and discuss the manner in which the psychodynamic approach is used to treat maladaptive behavior.

3. Identify and describe several forms of behavioral therapy and explain some advantages that behavioral therapy has over other psychotherapies.

4. Define cognitive-behavioral therapy, describe several techniques for using it to treat mental disorders, and compare the outcomes of cognitive-behavioral therapy with other psychotherapies.

5. Describe the humanistic-experiential therapies, with particular attention to gestalt therapy, and list some contributions and criticisms of these therapies.

6. Describe several approaches to interpersonal therapy, in particular couple counseling.

7. Discuss the issue of integrating different psychological treatment approaches.

8. Describe group therapy, discuss the therapist's role, and identify some advantages of group therapy for the therapist and the patient.

9. List five sources of information necessary to evaluate the effectiveness of treatment and describe some of the limitations these impose on the process.

10. Briefly summarize the history of attempts at biological intervention and describe some of the more controversial biological therapies.

11. Define psychopharmacology, list four types of chemical agents commonly used in therapy for mental disorders, and describe their effects and side effects.

12. List some of the advantages and disadvantages of using pharmacological therapy for treating behavior disorders.

 UNIT OVERVIEW

*by Edward S. Katkin, Ph.D.
State University of New York
at Stony Brook*

Throughout this course we have examined the world of abnormal psychology and have seen many examples of mental health professionals trying to alleviate people's distress. Sometimes they prescribed medicine; sometimes they recommended changes in life situation; frequently, they provided some sort of interpersonal advice and guidance, or just sympathetic conversation. These interpersonal interventions, with individuals or groups, are referred to generically as **psychotherapy**. The video in this unit focuses on three specific kinds of individual psychotherapy and introduces **couples therapy** and **group therapy**.

Each approach to psychotherapy possesses unique attributes, but all share some important elements. In each, the therapist is totally committed to the welfare of the patient and to communicating that sense of caring to the patient. Some theorists have suggested that the communication of concern and a caring attitude are the most effective features of psychotherapy, and that the specific techniques and styles of therapeutic practice are less important than the attention that the patient receives.

In the video, a professional actor plays the role of Tom, a middle-class man with some emotional problems. Tom will be treated first by Dr. Cooper, a **psychodynamic** therapist, and then by Dr. Morris, a **cognitive-behavioral** therapist. In addition, you will see Deborah, a volunteer, participate in a session with Alan Cohen, a **gestalt** therapist.

In addition to discussing an array of psychologically based therapies, the textbook assignment covers biologically based therapies. Early attempts at biological intervention were, at best, often misguided. Frequently, such invasive methods as **electroconvulsive therapy** (ECT) and **prefrontal lobotomy** resulted in serious damage to the patient. The past few decades, however, have seen the increasing application of psychopharmacology (the use of medications in the treatment of mental disorders), as well as a refinement in the technology and use of ECT. As we have witnessed throughout this course, drug treatment has proven to be very successful in many cases and has significantly reduced the use of the earlier invasive and dangerous biological interventions.

■ PSYCHODYNAMIC THERAPY

The basic principle of psychodynamic therapy is that people have thoughts and feelings that are unconscious, or out of awareness. These thoughts and feelings exert powerful influences on our conscious lives and may create conflict or motivate undesirable behavior. Sigmund Freud, who first developed and articulated psychodynamic theory, believed that people must uncover these unconscious conflicts and make them conscious. Freud developed a form of therapy, called **psychoanalysis**, to discover the unconscious thoughts and feelings that underlie current conflicts.

The psychodynamic therapist's responsibility is twofold: to create a climate of comfort and safety, and to recognize and interpret the signs of unconscious conflict when they are expressed. As you will see in the video, Tom comes to therapy and presents complaints about his supervisor and fears about losing his girlfriend. Dr. Cooper does not focus on these presenting problems, but instead asks general, open-ended questions, allowing Tom to say whatever comes to his mind. This is a specific psychodynamic technique known as **free association**, which is based on the principle that if the patient is comfortable and feels safe, then unconscious conflictual material will be expressed. As Tom describes a traumatic event from his childhood, Dr. Cooper interprets a link to his current behavior.

In addition to interpreting free associations, the psychodynamic therapist also looks for signs of unconscious conflict in slips of the tongue, in the content of dreams, and in the patient's fantasies. Another major feature of psychodynamic therapy is the analysis of

transference. It is assumed that patients will transfer unconscious feelings about important people in their lives, such as parents, to the therapist. An analysis of this transference of feelings is believed to help the patient to become conscious of the meaning of these feelings.

■ COGNITIVE-BEHAVIORAL THERAPY

The cognitive-behavioral approach to therapy is not concerned with unconscious thoughts and feelings or with past experiences or early childhood relationships, but rather focuses on an individual's current thinking and behavior. The aim of the therapy is to change faulty thinking and alter unproductive behavior patterns.

In the video, Tom presents the same complaints to Dr. Morris that he had presented to Dr. Cooper. Dr. Morris, however, chooses to focus on Tom's relationship with his supervisor. She engages Tom in a process called **cognitive restructuring**, a technique used to help the patient replace self-defeating or faulty thinking with new ways of thinking about problems. After Tom succeeds in cognitive restructuring, Dr. Morris leads him through **role-playing**, or rehearsal of the new ways of thinking about his problem. Dr. Morris asks Tom to act out the new way he will behave with his supervisor. Note that Dr. Morris does not discuss Tom's childhood or his early family experiences, although she says that in some instances such a discussion may help broaden understanding.

■ GESTALT THERAPY

Whereas cognitive-behavioral therapy focuses on present thought patterns, gestalt therapy focuses on present feelings. Gestalt therapy trains the patient to become aware of emotions and body feelings as they are experienced. This is shown in the video by Alan Cohen, a gestalt therapist, working with Deborah. At the core of this approach is the idea that the emotional state directly affects body states. Thus, awareness of the body state can help the patient become more aware of emotions.

Gestalt therapy also uses a specific variant of role-playing called the **empty-chair technique**. In this technique, the therapist asks the patient to visualize another person sitting in an empty chair, and then to role-play an interaction with that person. In the video, Deborah has a dialogue with her mother in the empty chair, and then she assumes the role of her mother and has a dialogue with herself. Sometimes a gestalt therapist will ask the patient to imagine part of herself in the empty chair and to have a dialogue between different parts of the self.

Although these three forms of individual psychotherapy appear to be distinct, in practice it is likely that therapists of different persuasions borrow techniques from other approaches that they find useful. Sometimes the therapist decides that a patient's most critical problem involves a particular relationship. If that is a marital relationship then couples therapy may be called for; if it is a general difficulty in relating to others, group therapy may be indicated.

■ COUPLES THERAPY

In couples therapy, or in family therapy, the focus of the sessions is on the relationship among the participants rather than on the individual problems of each of them. In the video, Dr. Rivas-Vazquez works with actors who portray Wanda and Harry Jakes, a couple with marital problems. As you will see, the problems they bring up appear to be quite trivial, but they reflect a deeper sense of communication failure and mutual despair in the relationship.

When Dr. Rivas-Vazquez finds that the relationship between Harry and Wanda may be complicated by Harry's individual problems, she sees him separately in individual therapy. While the focus of these individual sessions may be on Harry's unique problems of adjustment, the focus of the joint sessions always is on the relationship.

■ GROUP THERAPY

In group therapy the patients are not usually members of the same family. The focus of treatment is on the use of the group as a model of interpersonal relations in the real world. Group therapy may be organized around any one of a number of theoretical orientations, including those that are used in individual therapy. The focus of group therapy, however, is on the here and now functioning of each member of the group. Group therapy helps participants to have new experiences with people in a safe environment; members can count on the group to help them learn how they are perceived by others, and what their impact on others may be.

The video will introduce you to Dolores McCarthy, a group therapist, and a group of young adults (in this case, these are actual group members). One of the great advantages of group therapy is that the therapist does not have to depend only on the patients' reports of how they behave but can see how a patient really acts in relationships with others. An additional important feature of group therapy is that each participant has a dual responsibility, that of patient and also that of helper to the other patients. That is, the group takes on a cohesive role as a helping agent for the individual members of the group.

■ CONCLUSION

After 100 years of therapeutic practice, psychology is divided by theoretical disputes among a great many different approaches to therapy. As psychologists and other mental health specialists continue to research therapeutic processes and outcomes, it is likely that the field will continue to grow and change. It also is likely that the differing theoretical approaches will begin to merge, selecting the most effective aspects of each and creating a new, integrated form of therapy.

■ KEY TERMS

The following terms are used in the text and/or the television programs.

Antianxiety drugs	Used to treat anxiety disorders, these drugs basically have a sedating effect and reduce tension and anxiety. The three major classes of antianxiety drugs are barbiturates, propanediols, and benzodiazepines.
Antidepressant drugs	Medications used to treat depression; they have generally shown short-term effectiveness. The two basic classes of antidepressant drugs are monoamine oxidase (MAO) inhibitors and tricyclics.
Antipsychotic drugs	Used with such major disorders as the schizophrenias to alleviate or reduce the intensity of such psychotic symptoms as delusions and hallucinations and to make withdrawn or immobile patients more active and responsive. Drugs of the phenothiazine family are most commonly used, though there are several alternatives. Most work by blocking dopamine receptors. The antipsychotic drugs can involve troublesome side effects.

211

Assertiveness therapy	A form of behavioral therapy used to develop more efficient coping techniques to overcome anxieties that prevent people from asserting themselves; involves practice in overcoming inhibitions and openly expressing oneself first in a therapy setting, and then in real-life situations.
Aversion therapy	A form of therapy that modifies maladaptive behavior by removing desired reinforcers; techniques include the use of such aversive stimuli as negative imagery or mild electric shock to reduce the temptation value of stimuli that elicit undesirable behavior.
Behavioral contracting	A technique in which two parties, such as a client and therapist, agree in a contract on the behaviors that need to be changed. The contract specifies both the client's obligations to change and the responsibilities of the other party to provide something the client wants in return, such as tangible rewards, privileges, or therapeutic attention.
Behavioral therapy	A therapeutic approach that modifies behavior by extinguishing or counterconditioning maladaptive reactions.
Biofeedback	A technique that enables a person to influence his or her own physiological processes by monitoring feedback about bodily changes as they occur.
Client-centered therapy	A form of therapy developed by Carl Rogers that focuses on self-acceptance and the alteration of a constraining and hostile self-concept; client-centered therapy encourages the expression of real feelings and thoughts in an environment in which they will be unconditionally accepted, understood, and valued.
Clinical psychologist	A mental health professional with a doctorate in clinical psychology and specialization in personality theory, abnormal psychology, psychological assessment, and/or psychotherapy.
Cognitive-behavioral therapy	A therapeutic approach based on the belief that cognitive processes influence motivation, emotion, and behavior, and that learning principles can be applied to alter cognitions.
Cognitive restructuring	A cognitive-behavioral technique designed to help a patient replace maladaptive thinking with more productive thought patterns.
Countertransference	The transference of feelings that a therapist may have to a client.
Couples therapy (marital therapy)	Therapy in which members of a couple participate together and focus on clarifying and improving their interactions and relationship.
Electroconvulsive therapy (ECT)	An electric current passed through the brain, causing a convulsion; sometimes used in treatment of patients with major depression who present an immediate and serious suicidal risk. ECT is highly successful, but it can cause such serious side effects as memory loss, disorientation, and in some cases, irreversible brain damage. Also called electroshock therapy.
Empty-chair technique	A gestalt therapy role-playing technique in which the patient imagines someone to be sitting in a chair and interacts with that person.
Existential therapy	A humanistic-experiential therapy that applies existential thought to understanding human problems, emphasizing the uniqueness of each person. During the therapy session, therapists also share their feelings, values, and experiences.
Extinction	A behavioral therapy method that eliminates maladaptive behavior by removing its reinforcer.

Family therapy	A form of therapy developed from the idea that an individual's problems may reflect a larger family problem; focuses on improving faulty communications, interactions, and relationships among family members.
Flooding	A behavioral therapy method that repeatedly exposes individuals to real-life anxiety-arousing situations to show that the feared consequences do not occur. The goal is to extinguish the individual's conditioned avoidance of anxiety-arousing stimuli.
Free association	A basic method in Freudian psychoanalysis in which the individual says whatever comes to mind. The therapist's interpretation may help patients overcome inner obstacles to remembering and discussing problems.
Gestalt therapy	A humanistic-experiential approach that emphasizes the unity of mind and body and the need for integration of thought, feeling, and action to increase self-awareness and self-acceptance.
Humanistic-experiential therapies	A group of therapeutic approaches that focus on self-awareness and human potential.
Implosion	A behavioral technique in which the client imagines aversive scenes in order to elicit increased anxiety — an implosion. With repeated exposure in a safe setting, the stimulus loses its power to provoke anxiety and the avoidance behavior is extinguished.
Latent content	The latent content of dreams is composed of ideas that seek expression but are so unacceptable they are disguised. In Freudian dream analysis, the therapist seeks to uncover these hidden meanings.
Manifest content	The content of a dream as it appears to the dreamer. In Freudian dream analysis, the therapist studies the manifest content to assess a dream's hidden meaning.
Modeling	A form of behavioral therapy in which one learns skills by imitating another person.
Pharmacology	The science of medicines.
Prefrontal lobotomy	A psychosurgical procedure used in the treatment of nervous system disorders in which the frontal lobes of the brain are severed from the deeper centers underlying them, resulting in permanent brain damage and sometimes other undesirable side effects. The procedure was largely supplanted by the use of antipsychotic drugs and is rarely used today.
Psychiatric social worker	An individual who holds a master's of social work (M.S.W.) or a doctorate from a school of social work. Graduate training usually involves coursework in family evaluation, psychotherapy, and supervised field experience.
Psychiatrist	A physician who has had further training in psychotherapy. A medical degree qualifies the psychiatrist to prescribe drugs and to administer such somatic therapies as electroconvulsive therapy.
Psychoanalysis	A system of therapy, developed by Freud, that is based on four basic techniques: free association, analysis of dreams, analysis of resistance, and analysis of transference.
Psychodynamic therapy	A treatment based on Freudian theory that seeks to understand and resolve disordered behavior through insights into a patient's unconscious conflicts.

Psychosurgery	Brain surgery used in the treatment of functional or central nervous system disorders.
Psychotherapy	The treatment of mental disorders by psychological methods to bring about more adaptive ways of perceiving, evaluating, and behaving.
Rational-emotive therapy (RET)	A form of cognitive-behavioral therapy that attempts to change maladaptive thought processes by restructuring a person's belief system and self-evaluation.
Resistance	In psychodynamic therapy, an unwillingness or inability to talk about certain thoughts, motives, or experiences during free association. Therapists analyze resistance to uncover the threatening material that is prevented from entering awareness.
Response shaping	A method of establishing a response that is not initially in an individual's behavior repertoire by gradual approximation; often used with children who have behavioral problems.
Role-playing	A procedure in which an individual plays a part in a hypothetical situation to try out a new behavior or to allow observation by a clinician.
Stress-inoculation therapy	A cognitive-behavioral treatment that focuses on changing how individuals think about stressors. It involves three stages: cognitive preparation, skill acquisition and rehearsal, and application and practice.
Structural family therapy	A type of family therapy based on the assumption that the family system itself is more influential in producing abnormal behavior than individual personality or intrapsychic conflicts. The goal is to change the organization of the family so that the family members behave more positively and supportively toward each other.
Systematic desensitization	A form of behavioral therapy that teaches the individual to relax in the presence of an anxiety-producing stimulus. In a safe setting, the individual is gradually and repeatedly exposed to an anxiety-producing stimulus until it loses its power to elicit anxiety, thus extinguishing the need for avoidance behavior.
Token economies	A type of behavioral therapy in which appropriate behaviors are encouraged and may be rewarded with tangible enforcers in the form of tokens that can be exchanged for desired objects or privileges.
Transference	In Freudian terminology, a process that occurs between a client and therapist in which the client carries over attitudes and feelings from other relationships to the relationship with the therapist.

VIDEO NOTES

■ THERAPISTS AND PATIENTS

• A variety of treatments are available for people with psychological disorders.

• An essential element of the change process involves the unique relationship that develops between the therapist and the client.

> The therapist provides the patient with undivided attention and has a total commitment to the welfare of the patient.

> The communication of concern, attentiveness, and interest to the client may, in itself, be quite therapeutic.

214

■ PSYCHODYNAMIC THERAPY

(Case Illustration: "Tom")

• The fundamental principle of psychodynamic therapy is that thoughts and feelings lie outside of awareness in the unconscious and create conflicts.

> Freud believed that unresolved conflicts from crucial childhood years exert a powerful influence on adult behavior. Psychodynamic therapy seeks to resolve these conflicts, which have been forced out of awareness to protect the person against the anxiety that would surface if they were conscious.

> As therapy progresses, the clinician helps the patient to discover these conflicts and how they relate to childhood. These interpretations help the client see how the past influences the present through an impact on feelings and behavior.

• Psychodynamic methods include free association, interpretation of dreams and fantasies, interpretation of slips of the tongue, analysis of transference, and the understanding of defense mechanisms.

> Free association encourages the patient to say anything that comes to mind, no matter how bizarre or irrelevant it may seem to be. It rests on the assumption that information about the conflict may emerge in the process.

> In transference the patient plays out or transfers onto the therapist emotions and conflicts from important relationships, such as with a mother, father, or sibling. By pointing out the transference, the therapist helps make the conflict conscious.

> Defenses are methods people adopt to keep painful ideas out of consciousness, e.g., projection, repression, rationalization, denial, overcompensation, displacement. Therapy helps people become less afraid of the anxiety that might result if they dropped the defenses.

■ COGNITIVE-BEHAVIORAL THERAPY

(Case Illustration: "Tom")

• The cognitive-behavioral model tries to understand factors in the present that are influencing and maintaining dysfunctional thinking and behavior. The model draws both on cognitive theory, which believes that faulty thinking causes maladaptive behavioral and emotional problems, and on behavioral theory, which emphasizes the importance of altering current behavior rather than focusing on the past. The past may be a source of information for how a problem developed, but it is not the focus of the therapy.

• The role of the cognitive-behavioral therapist is to help the patient develop new thought patterns that lead to more productive behavior and to practice more appropriate behaviors in the safety of the therapeutic setting.

• One method used is cognitive restructuring.

> In cognitive restructuring, the goal is to change faulty or nonproductive thinking. Once the patient has learned to recognize and reevaluate faulty thinking, thereby reducing emotions that interfere with productive action, the therapist and patient role-play or rehearse these new actions.

■ GESTALT THERAPY
(Case Illustration: Deborah)

• Gestalt therapy is concerned with the present. It focuses on becoming aware of and expressing current emotions. It has roots in psychodynamic therapy but concerns the idea that a person's emotional experiences have an impact on the body.

• Gestalt therapists believe that people limit access to parts of themselves (e.g., intelligence, emotions, energies, creativity, desire, needs, wants, abilities) and that the active intervention of a therapist can reduce these limitations or inhibitions. Gestalt therapists seek to help individuals become aware of how they maintain a status quo and provide opportunities to try out and experience new behaviors.

• Gestalt therapy is very attuned to what is going on physically with the patient. It includes such techniques as exploration of dreams, creative visualization, and body-centered awareness.

> A technique called the empty-chair technique — a role-playing exercise in which a patient conducts an imaginary interaction with a significant person — helps patients understand how key people have influenced them and contributed to their personality and experience.

■ INTEGRATION OF THERAPIES

• In practice, most present-day psychotherapists draw from a variety of therapeutic orientations in order to meet the particular needs of the patient.

■ COUPLES THERAPY
(Case Illustration: "Wanda," "Harry")

• In couples therapy, the clinician operates under the assumption that the disagreement that brought a couple into therapy often is only a reflection of an underlying agenda. In the majority of cases, the hidden agendas involve two major issues: control and love (or the absence of love).

• In family therapy, the clinician needs to understand the family's stage of development and to recognize that each member may have personal issues that need to be addressed as well as issues that involve the couple or family as a unit.

• Sometimes, both people are trying to get what Dr. Rivas-Vazquez calls their "neurotic needs" met. If one person goes to therapy and works through neurotic needs, the marriage may fail because a neurotic balance no longer exists.

■ GROUP THERAPY
(Case Illustrations: Paul, Debbie, Jean, Michael)

• In the group setting, each person comes with his or her own problems. Group therapy offers the opportunity to discuss and work through common issues as well. It does so in a safe atmosphere in which people can take risks expressing their feelings, try out new behaviors, and give and receive honest feedback.

• In group therapy it is the cohesion of the group, rather than the relationship between patient and clinician, that is key. The way individuals see the group often is the way they see the world.

- Group therapy enables the therapist, who may also see members individually, to see how a patient acts with other people. It is a living laboratory. The group also gives people a sense of sharing and of not being alone.

- Group therapists may use a variety of therapeutic orientations.

VIDEO REVIEW QUESTIONS

1. Identify the major foci of psychodynamic, cognitive-behavioral, and gestalt therapies and differentiate among them.

2. The actor, "Tom," goes to two therapists with different orientations. How do their orientations differ? Discuss how these differences can be seen in the way they work with Tom.

3. Differentiate between the role of the therapist in individual therapy and in group therapy.

4. If Tom had gone to the gestalt therapist as well, what aspects of his story do you think would have drawn the therapist's attention? How might a gestalt therapist have applied the empty chair technique in Tom's case?

5. What buried thoughts and feelings did Dr. Cooper help Tom become aware of?

6. What function does the use of free association play in psychodynamic therapy?

7. Discuss how cognitive restructuring was applied in Tom's case.

8. Dr. Goldfried says that gestalt therapy tries to help patients "become aware of what is going on in their body and how they are experiencing it." How does this apply to the work that Alan Cohen does with Deborah?

9. Dr. Goldfried says that the two most typical issues in couples therapy are love (or the absence of it) and control. What do you learn about these issues in reference to Harry and Wanda?

10. Why do you think Dr. Rivas-Vazquez suggests that Harry undergo individual therapy?

11. Dr. Rivas-Vazquez talks about why a marriage may break up after one spouse successfully undergoes therapy. Discuss why this happens.

12. What are the particular strengths of group therapy? Illustrate your thoughts with reference to Debbie.

CASE STUDY

*by Judith Rosenberger,
C.S.W., Ph.D.
Hunter College
and
Edith Gould, C.S.W.
Postgraduate Center
for Mental Health*

Sam

I'm a research virologist, and last year I started a new job working for an international pharmaceutical company. The job represents the culmination of years of hard work. It's a real achievement in my field, and sometimes I feel almost too lucky to have gotten it. Since the company I work for has its main research facility in Europe, I frequently am called upon to travel abroad. On the first few trips in my new position, I was very surprised by the fuss that my hosts made over me. I thought this would make the trips a real treat.

About six months ago, however, a few days prior to one of my flights to Europe, I became aware of a growing sense of uneasiness. I had never experienced any anxiety about plane travel before, so my nervousness seemed particularly odd to me. I couldn't sleep the night before, and I was jittery all the way to the airport. As I stepped onto the plane, I felt scared. I didn't exactly panic, but my hands became cold and sweaty, and I had to control my breathing to avoid hyperventilating. I couldn't understand the reasons for this sudden outbreak of anxiety. The plane seemed cramped and claustrophobic, and the impossibility of escaping once we took off became truly unbearable. It was ridiculous, but I just could not make this trip! Claiming I was suddenly ill and had to postpone the trip, I quickly left the plane. As soon as I was outside and on my way home, my anxiety subsided, and I could breathe easily once again.

The humiliation of having to lie to my boss about being unable to make this trip because of illness was almost intolerable. Worse still was the fact that this was not an isolated event. For several months, each time I got close to travelling, I became more anxious. I spent more and more time worrying about getting on planes and found myself thinking more and more about all the terrible things that could happen to me. Even movies or stories about airplanes made me upset, and I started checking before I went out to be sure that no references to planes would come up. I also found myself putting a lot of energy into avoiding business trips I really should have taken. This became increasingly cumbersome to manage. It started to affect my relationships at work and my overall productivity. I had to spend more and more time covering up and avoiding anything that would expose my inexplicable fears.

It was clear to me that my problem was a full-blown phobia related to flying. Thus began my search for treatment. Due to the nature of my work and the travel requirements involved, this was a symptom I had to resolve as quickly as possible. As I began to investigate the therapeutic options, I was faced with myriad possibilities.

My first therapy interview was with a psychodynamic psychotherapist who informed me that I had been unable to master the outbreak of anxiety I had on the plane because the motivations and meanings of my phobia were outside of my awareness. In other words, they were unconscious. According to this therapist, his treatment would be psychoanalytic, involving an in-depth exploration of my childhood experiences and how they connected with my current problem. He also told me we would analyze my dreams to gather clues about what was going on in my unconscious mind. He suggested I come in three times a week and that the treatment would take from one to three years. Although I responded well to this therapist, and the idea of an extensive psychoanalytically oriented psychotherapy intrigued me, my situation was urgent. I felt I needed a more immediate resolution.

The second therapist I consulted was a behavioral therapist who specialized in treating my kind of problem. She informed me that the treatment would take a few months, during which time I would engage in systematic desensitization. She would guide me through exercises that would consist of a gradual approach to the object of my phobia — taking a plane trip. I would use visual imagery like imagining myself making a reservation, then going to the airport, and finally moving toward actually getting on a plane and taking a flight. She suggested that in addition to my individual work with her, I participate in a short-term group therapy experience where I could meet with other people who suffered from the same fear.

My third consultation was with a psychiatrist who specialized in psychopharmacology. He listened to my concerns and recommended that I begin taking antianxiety medication a few days before a flight. Since my next trip was scheduled for the following week, I decided to try this approach. I managed to get through the flights and successfully complete my business abroad, but I could still feel the underlying buzz of my fear while I was flying.

When I returned home, I decided to try the behavioral therapy approach. I prefer to lick the problem itself, rather than take medication on a continual basis to cope with the fear. So far, after three sessions, it's going quite well. But I'm still perplexed. How did this happen? And why now? The main thing that I want relief from is the phobia. That's what I'll work on. In the future, I may want to explore how this happened so I won't be wondering when some new phobia might erupt.

CLINICAL DISCUSSION

Sam's symptom is clear: a phobia linked to a specific situation — flying — that does not seem to be intruding into other areas of functioning. The phobia expresses itself in his seemingly inexplicable fear. The more gradual onset and the spread of avoidant strategies, which themselves become the main encumberance, distinguishes his fear from a full-blown panic attack, which is more catastrophic. Why the symptom appeared then and there is a mystery. The treatment options involve varying degrees of conscious participation on Sam's part. Consequently, they require varying amounts of time and money and have entirely different formats. Will Sam be able and willing to regain mastery over his fear through medication that blocks the anxiety reaction itself? Will he need to augment or substitute a learned pattern of anxiety reduction by steering his cognitive processes away from fearful thoughts? Will he want or require a more in-depth understanding of the origins and meanings of the fear that strikes him at just that time and place so that he can master his anxiety by placing it in a comprehensible context?

Practitioners of each of these treatment options assume that the method practiced is linked to the source of the symptom. Psychopharmacologists assume that panic like Sam felt — sudden, without apparent cause — may be a biological event devoid of meaning. Untreated, or treated too slowly, the anxiety can return or accelerate and become more complicated as the person struggles to make sense of what may be a senseless biochemical phenomenon. The advantages of quick and inexpensive symptom reduction via medication have to be weighed, however, against its total efficacy and possible side effects. Although Sam does report residual anxiety even while taking medication, he does not report side effects. Since he can function with some persisting discomfort, he elects behavioral therapy as the next least complicated remedy.

The behavioral therapist assumes Sam's fear of being on an airplane is triggered by an association that was made in the instant he felt panic. His original source of panic may never be known and is not vital to know in this model. The dysfunction in Sam's life revolves around his anticipation of that distress, which he has attributed to being in an airplane. Unlearning the association is necessary to avoid a recurrence of the panic that now would be self-induced. Sam will be helped by this therapist to unhook all the cues linked to airplane travel from the anxious feelings that now rise up at the very idea of being in that situation again. Besides being able to fly again, Sam will acquire a way of working with whatever his mental images and thought processes are that can escalate discomfort into full-blown terror. The relief of functional mastery may reassure Sam in a way that more broadly reduces his vulnerability to anxiety.

The psychodynamic psychotherapist assumes that Sam's panic was triggered by a hidden connection he made between some aspect of being on that airplane at that time and another set of circumstances, probably in early childhood, in which his panic would have been appropriate. Depending on the model of the mind the psychodynamic therapist was using, varying ways of looking for and representing the hidden connections might be applied. The common aim would be to bring to Sam's awareness that the way he was reacting in the present was based on unconscious associations from the past. In this way, Sam's symptom would be seen as having some meaning, and Sam himself seems inclined to search for understanding of this kind. The shared exploration of anxiety in the long-term psychodynamic relationship also would provide an antidote to the helplessness that accompanied Sam's panic on the plane. From the psychodynamic perspective, Sam's anxiety and need for escape could reemerge in other forms unless the unconscious reasons why he should have such an inexplicable reaction were brought to light in a context in which he could safely explore whatever he might feel.

Sam's self-designed treatment approach works for him. Step by step he works toward restoring self-confidence. As a consumer of therapy who is functioning well overall and is not financially limited, he can decide about priorities. He starts with direct symptom relief, moves into symptom deconstruction, and anticipates symptom understanding as the final step.

CASE QUESTIONS

1. How does each of the three treatment models explain the origin of Sam's fear of flying?

2. How does the method used by the psychopharmacologist connect to his assumption about what caused Sam's symptom?

3. How does the method used by the behavioral therapist connect to her assumption about what caused Sam's symptom?

4. How does the method proposed by the psychodynamic psychotherapist connect to his assumptions about what caused Sam's symptom?

5. Apart from the theoretical model of cause and effect that each therapist uses to treat Sam's symptom, what other factors relate to the type of treatment chosen?

SELF-TEST

1. In electroconvulsive therapy (ECT), the shock immediately causes the patient to show all of the following symptoms EXCEPT
   a) a lengthy series of contractile seizures.
   b) excruciating pain.
   c) loss of consciousness.
   d) marked extensor seizure of the muscles.

2. All of the following are side effects of prefrontal lobotomy EXCEPT
   a) a 1 to 4 percent death rate.
   b) loss of the use of short-term memory.
   c) permanent inability to inhibit impulses.
   d) unnatural "tranquility."

3. Antipsychotic, antidepressant, antianxiety, and lithium compounds are all referred to as _____ drugs.
   a) hallucinogenic
   b) mind-expanding
   c) narcotic
   d) psychotropic

4. The unique quality of antipsychotic drugs is their ability to
   a) calm patients down.
   b) put patients to sleep.
   c) reduce patients' anxiety.
   d) reduce the intensity of delusions and hallucinations.

5. Virtually all of the antipsychotic drugs accomplish the same biochemical effect, which is
   a) blocking dopamine receptors.
   b) blocking the production of noradrenalin.
   c) stimulating the production of endorphins.
   d) stimulating the production of glutamic acid.

6. It is currently believed that most antidepressant compounds
   a) block dopamine receptors.
   b) block the production of noradrenalin and stimulate the production of adrenalin.
   c) increase the concentrations of certain neurotransmitters in pertinent synaptic sites in the brain.
   d) increase the production of endorphins.

7. A major thrust of current research and treatment for severe psychopathology is
   a) combining chemical and psychological forms of therapy.
   b) combining chemical and sociocultural therapies.
   c) limiting therapy to psychological methods.
   d) limiting therapy to psychotropic drugs.

221

8. **All of the following are goals of psychotherapy EXCEPT**
   a) changing maladaptive behavior patterns.
   b) improving interpersonal competencies.
   c) preventing mental disorders from developing.
   d) resolving disabling inner conflicts.

9. **Which of the following mental health professionals always has an M.D.?**
   a) clinical psychologist
   b) counseling psychologist
   c) psychiatric social worker
   d) psychiatrist

10. **All of the following are key dimensions that can be used to describe various approaches to psychotherapy EXCEPT**
    a) cognitive change/behavior change.
    b) directive/nondirective.
    c) individual/group.
    d) successful/unsuccessful.

11. **All of the following are basic techniques of Freudian psychoanalysis EXCEPT analysis of**
    a) behavior.
    b) dreams.
    c) resistance.
    d) transference.

12. **In Freudian psychoanalysis, the therapist uses the patient's dreams to uncover repressed motives and conflicts by**
    a) analyzing the latent content to find the manifest content.
    b) analyzing the manifest content to find the latent content.
    c) analyzing the resistance apparent in the manifest content.
    d) hypnotically inducing dreams that bring out latent conflicts.

13. **Behaviorists believe maladjusted people exhibit all of the following EXCEPT**
    a) their faulty patterns are being maintained by some kind of reinforcement.
    b) they have failed to learn competencies needed for coping with life's problems.
    c) they have inner conflicts that must be made extinct.
    d) they have learned faulty coping patterns.

14. **Both implosive therapy and flooding focus on**
    a) bombarding maladaptive behavior with aversive stimuli.
    b) exploding inner conflicts.
    c) extinguishing the conditioned avoidance of anxiety-arousing stimuli.
    d) inundating a person with positive reinforcement.

15. **Marva felt awkward in social situations because she didn't know how to initiate conversations with others. Her therapist demonstrated several techniques that she tried later at parties. Bandura would call this therapeutic technique**
    a) identification.
    b) induction.
    c) modeling.
    d) shaping.

16. According to Ellis' rational-emotive therapy (RET), all of the following are core irrational beliefs EXCEPT

    a) happiness can be achieved by taking action.

    b) it is better to avoid life's problems than to face them.

    c) it is horrible when things are not the way we would like them to be.

    d) one should be loved by everyone for everything one does.

17. In stress-inoculation therapy, all of the following take place in the "cognitive preparation" phase EXCEPT

    a) agreeing on a new set of adaptive self-statements.

    b) exploring the client's beliefs about the problem.

    c) practicing more adaptive self-statements.

    d) understanding how the client's self-talk can influence later performance.

18. The primary objective of Rogerian client-centered therapy is to resolve the incongruence between the client's

    a) ego and superego.

    b) "good me" and "bad me."

    c) self-concept and actual experiencing.

    d) self-concept and self-ideal.

19. The main goal of gestalt therapy is to

    a) change the "shape" of a person's motives.

    b) increase the client's positive self-talk.

    c) increase the client's self-awareness and self-acceptance.

    d) reduce the congruence between self-concept and self-ideal.

20. The rate of improvement given in most studies of therapy outcome, regardless of approach, is usually about _____ percent.

    a) 20

    b) 40

    c) 60

    d) 80

21. In the psychodynamic therapy session with Tom, the therapist tried to make clear to Tom that his current lack of self-expressiveness has its roots in

    a) illogical thought patterns.

    b) countertransference.

    c) childhood experiences.

    d) maladaptive behavior patterns.

22. Changing faulty or nonproductive thinking is the goal of

    a) cognitive restructuring.

    b) psychodynamic therapy.

    c) mindmapping.

    d) gestalt restructuring.

23. After Tom learned to recognize and reevaluate faulty thinking, he and the cognitive-behavioral therapist began to

    a) work on transference.

    b) investigate repressed motives and conflicts.

    c) role-play or rehearse new, productive actions.

    d) construct a hierarchy of possible responses.

24. **Psychodynamic is to insight as gestalt is to**
    a) thinking.
    b) experiencing the body.
    c) behavior.
    d) dream analysis.

25. **In couples therapy two major issues frequently underlie the problems the couple is having. These are issues of**
    a) money and sex.
    b) money and control.
    c) jealousy and control.
    d) control and love.

26. **In group therapy it is the _____ of the group that is parallel to the therapeutic relationship.**
    a) make-up
    b) duration
    c) cohesion
    d) honesty

[ANSWERS: 1-b, 2-b, 3-d, 4-d, 5-a, 6-c, 7-a, 8-c, 9-d, 10-d, 11-a, 12-b, 13-c, 14-c, 15-c, 16-a, 17-c, 18-c, 19-c, 20-d, 21-c, 22-a, 23-a, 24-b, 25-d, 26-c]

SUGGESTED READINGS

Brenner, A. (1973). *An elementary textbook of psychoanalysis* (rev. ed.). New York: Anchor Books. This basic text on contemporary psychoanalysis covers psychopathology, the hypothesis of psychic determinism, the structure of the psyche, dreams, and drives.

Corsini, R. (Ed.). (1979). *Current psychotherapies* (2nd ed.). Itasca, IL: Peacock. This book describes numerous psychotherapeutic approaches.

Dryden, W., & DiGuiseppe, R. (1990). *A primer on R-E-T.* Champaign, IL: Research Press. This book describes the theory and practice of the therapeutic techniques of rational emotive therapy.

Haley, J., & Hoffman, L. (1967). *Techniques of family therapy.* New York: Basic Books. This collection of interviews gathers the thoughts of a number of family therapists about how they conduct therapy.

Lindner, R. (1954). *The fifty-minute hour: A collection of true psychoanalytic tales.* New York: Delta. This still fascinating look at the practice of psychoanalysis includes accounts of a rapist/murderer and patients with obsessive personality, bulimia, and schizophrenia.

Norcross, J. C., & Goldfried, M. R. (Eds.). (1992). *Handbook of psychotherapy integration.* New York: Basic Books. This compendium records past and current attempts to integrate various forms of therapy, and considers the issues involved in doing so.

O'Leary, K. D., & Wilson, G. T. (1987). *Behavior therapy: Application and outcome* (2nd ed.). Englewood Cliffs, NJ: Prentice Hall. This description of the developments and major concepts in behavioral therapy also includes a discussion of the application of behavioral therapy techniques to specific problems of children and adults.

Satir, V. (1983). *Conjoint family therapy* (3rd ed.). Palo Alto: Science and Behavior Books. This classic on treating the individual within the context of the family is easy reading and interesting because it includes transcripts of many therapy sessions.

UNIT 13

AN OUNCE
OF
PREVENTION

■ **UNIT THEME**	Mental disorders can emerge at any point in the life span. Can they be prevented? This unit examines several community-based projects that focus on specific life stages. Each example uses a unique combination of strategies to lessen the effects of known psychological, sociocultural, environmental, and biological risk factors in the hope that the development of psychological disorders can be averted.

■ **UNIT ASSIGNMENTS**	*Read:*	Unit 13. "An Ounce of Prevention" in *The World of Abnormal Psychology Study Guide*, Toby Kleban Levine, editor (HarperCollins, 1992).
	View:	Program 13. "An Ounce of Prevention" in THE WORLD OF ABNORMAL PSYCHOLOGY.
	Read:	Chapter 19. "Contemporary Issues in Abnormal Psychology" in *Abnormal Psychology and Modern Life*, Ninth Edition, by Robert C. Carson and James N. Butcher (HarperCollins, 1992).

■ **GOALS AND OBJECTIVES**

1. Define primary, secondary, and tertiary prevention and list several interventions that are examples of each.

2. Evaluate the programs visited in the video and explain how they represent efforts at primary, secondary, or tertiary prevention.

3. Discuss the programs visited in the video in terms of the theoretical orientation from which they approach mental health, e.g., psychodynamic, cognitive-behavioral, biological, etc.

4. Explain and give examples of how mental health professionals are able to reach a larger group through consultation and the education of intermediaries.

5. Explain the milieu and social-learning approaches to treatment and compare them to traditional mental hospital treatments.

6. List four conditions that must be met before involuntary commitment to a mental institution can occur and describe the legal process that follows.

7. Discuss the dilemmas involved in assessing the degree to which a patient is dangerous and explain the implications of the Tarasoff decision.

8. Explain what is meant by the insanity defense in criminal cases, describe four established precedents defining this plea, and discuss the "guilty but mentally ill" alternative.

9. Define deinstitutionalization, briefly describe its history, and identify factors that are associated with successful programs.

10. List several examples and describe the roles and functions of governmental and other national and international organizations in the mental health field.

11. Discuss the need for social planning in the mental health field, describe several opportunities that individuals have to contribute to the advancement of mental health, and list five priorities to keep in mind in those endeavors.

228

by Edward S. Katkin, Ph.D.
State University of New York
at Stony Brook

"An ounce of prevention is worth a pound of cure," goes the saying. Is it true for mental health? Can the devastating toll that mental disorders take on individuals and society be prevented? If so, are preventive efforts more efficient and less costly than treating the disorders? These issues will be considered in this unit.

Psychological researchers have addressed prevention by trying to reduce or eliminate risk factors that predispose people to mental disorders. These risk factors include child abuse, poverty, social isolation, and such stressful life events as joblessness or the death of a loved one. The video visits four prevention programs, each of which targets a different population in the life span: early childhood, adolescence, adulthood, and old age. Each of these programs is designed to prevent the mental disorders that might arise from life crises unique to different age groups and social situations. Each has developed preventive intervention strategies for its target population and for the family members of that population.

In addition, the textbook considers prevention strategies incorporated into the treatment of people who already have developed mental disorders. These include programs in mental hospitals as well as aftercare treatment for individuals who have left hospitals and are readjusting to life in the community. The textbook also covers legal issues and the mentally ill, including commitment to mental institutions and the insanity defense.

■ EARLY CHILDHOOD: THE AVANCE PROJECT

One of the greatest risk factors for early childhood behavior disorders is incompetent or inadequate parenting skills. Diane Mendes and her family live in a public housing project in San Antonio. Diane's first child, Vanessa, was the source of great difficulty for the family, largely because Diane was unprepared for the responsibilities of motherhood and unaware of the range of normal childhood behaviors. Consequently, Diane neglected Vanessa's needs. Diane is now involved in a preventive intervention project called Avance, which is directed by Mercedes Perez de Colon and was founded by Gloria Rodriguez. The main purpose of Avance is to train adults to concentrate on their role as parents thereby reducing risks to their children. Avance has many subsidiary goals also. Among these are to stabilize the family structure; to provide therapeutic help to the parents, many of whom were emotionally deprived as children; and to provide education and job skills training for the families, in an attempt to break the cycle of poverty.

Avance involves both mothers and fathers in the training program. Mike, a single father of six children, and other fathers in the project have participated in training programs focused on teaching them the significance of their role in the upbringing of their children, and the importance of having positive experiences with their children.

Research data collected from the Avance project indicate that the children of families who participate in the program have a lower chance of becoming delinquent, failing in school, or developing conduct disorders. Moreover, the parents become more involved in educational opportunities and are more likely to achieve a high school equivalency diploma, thereby increasing their chance of breaking out of the cycle of illiteracy and poverty that is a primary cause of many of their adjustment problems.

■ ADOLESCENCE: THE SOCIAL DEVELOPMENT PROJECT

Gang fights, alcohol and drug abuse, sexual assault, conduct disorder, depression, suicide: these are common problems facing adolescents. Early adolescence is a time when people make choices about how to behave, how to channel the emerging energy that is released at puberty, and how to use the freedoms of adulthood that are quickly becoming available. In most cases, adolescents depend upon their families for guidance, but all too often, adolescents find either that they have no intact family or that the family they have is incapable of providing the guidance needed to prevent bad choices.

In the video you will see how an interdisciplinary team of psychologists, psychiatrists, and school teachers in New Haven, Connecticut, work together in the Social Development Project to try to prevent the development of seriously disturbed behavior in a group of early adolescents at risk. Dr. James Comer and Timothy Shriver provide adolescents with systematic instruction in critical thinking skills and problem-solving strategies. A critical component of these programs is the creation of a cooperative climate between the school and the families. Once the climate of cooperation is established it serves to deter transgressions and influences each of the students to conform to its expectations.

Research results show that the incidence of delinquency among the students who participated in the New Haven project was unchanged, but a matched group of students who did not participate showed a significant increase in delinquency. Further, the behavior of the students in the program was characterized by cooperation rather than fighting, and they had better peer relationships, less anxiety, and more self-control. The project shows that preventive intervention in adolescence may minimize the risks associated with this turbulent time of life.

■ ADULTHOOD: THE MICHIGAN JOBS PROJECT

Although adulthood is less filled with turmoil and crises than adolescence, it still has its share of stressful and often unpredictable life stresses. One of the most critical of these is the loss of a job. Job loss not only threatens the financial security of a family but also disrupts social relationships at work, undermines self-esteem, and often has a devastating impact on normal mental health. In order to help prevent major psychological setbacks after the loss of a job, Dr. Richard Price and his colleagues set up the Michigan Jobs Project, targeted at recently unemployed workers. The primary purposes of this program are to prevent depression and other psychological disorders, and to help clients develop the skills necessary to find new jobs.

In the video you will meet Joanna, Dennis, and other recently unemployed adults. These participants meet as a group with the trainers for five consecutive days, and they engage in role-playing to practice handling some of the difficult problems they will have to face. Research studies have been conducted to evaluate the effectiveness of this project. In general, it appears that participants in the program differed from those in a control group in several important ways. They showed lower levels of anxiety and depression and were more likely to find satisfying employment. Even for those who did not find new jobs, depression was reduced and confidence was greater.

■ OLD AGE: AUSTIN GROUPS FOR THE ELDERLY

Old age presents a number of challenges, often including the loss of one's competence, the loss of a spouse, and the erosion of the ability to cope with daily needs. Often older people find themselves without the social support they had earlier in life and sometimes isolated from their children, who may live far away. In such cases the elderly are highly susceptible to depression as well as to other psychological disorders. In Austin, Texas, social and psychological services have been organized by Austin Groups for the Elderly (AGE). This program — a model for avoiding competition among agencies — coordinates the efforts of a variety of social service agencies in order to help the elderly avoid sometimes frustrating and complex bureaucracies and to provide them with alternatives to institutionalization. Among the services AGE provides is to give the elderly a sense of community through mutual help groups. You will see a program called Grandparents Raising Grandchildren, for instance, whose members have had to cope with the stress of raising their abandoned or abused grandchildren. The group provides them with an opportunity to meet others in the same situation and to share their experiences.

Other programs allow the elderly to work directly with children who need day care and with younger parents who need help and guidance to become better parents. The common theme in all of these programs is the integration of the elderly into meaningful relationships with others of their own age as well as with younger people. This socialization and opportunity to be active and involved is a significant preventive intervention to protect the elderly against psychological decline associated with their aging.

■ SUMMARY

All of the prevention programs are aimed at helping to develop needed social skills, alleviating or preventing depression, and reducing the unique stresses that may elicit disorders. The evidence indicates that these programs work and that they are far less expensive for society than the alternative of not preventing disorder and then having to provide treatment.

■ KEY TERMS

The following terms are used in the text and/or the television programs.

Aftercare	A tertiary prevention program designed to smooth the transition from institutional to community life and to maintain therapeutic gains.
Commitment	The process by which individuals are voluntarily or involuntarily placed in mental institutions. Generally, in involuntary commitment procedures, an individual must be shown to be dangerous to himself or herself, incapable of providing for basic physical needs, unable to make responsible decisions about hospitalization, and in need of hospital care.
Crisis intervention	A secondary prevention effort that responds with immediate help in stressful situations, such as disasters. Two modes of crisis intervention have been developed: short-term crisis therapy and the telephone hot line.
Deinstitutionalization	The process of taking chronic patients out of mental institutions, integrating them into the community, and, ideally, treating them with continued psychiatric care.
Forensic psychology (forensic psychiatry)	The field that examines the legal rights of mental patients and/or the legal rights of members of society to be protected from disturbed individuals.
Insanity defense	A plea used in criminal trials to claim that the defendant is innocent by reason of insanity. It frequently means that the defendant committed the criminal act but should not be held criminally responsible.
Milieu therapy	An inpatient psychosocial therapy program in which patients share responsibilities with a professional staff in preparation for life outside an institutional setting.
Primary prevention	Prevention aimed at reducing the possibility of disease by altering conditions that contribute to mental disorders and establishing conditions that foster positive health.

Secondary prevention	Prevention programs that emphasize early detection and prompt treatment. These include (1) crisis intervention and (2) consultation with and education of such intermediaries as teachers or police who learn skills and develop sensitivity for dealing with people under stress.
Short-term crisis therapy	Brief therapy focused on the immediate problem with which an individual or family is having difficulty; a form of secondary prevention.
Social-learning program	A hospital treatment program that uses learning principles and such techniques as token economies to shape socially acceptable behavior.
Tarasoff decision	A California court decision that ruled that if a patient in therapy threatens the life of another person, the therapist has a duty to warn that person.
Telephone hot line	A telephone line staffed by persons who assist callers undergoing stress. Hot lines have been set up to help people considering suicide, rape victims, runaways, and people experiencing other kinds of stress.
Tertiary prevention	A program directed at reducing the long-term consequences to individuals who have had a disorder or serious psychological problem; includes treatment in mental institutions and aftercare programs.

VIDEO NOTES

■ INTRODUCTION

• Prevention is difficult to conceptualize because when you prevent something, nothing happens.

• Poverty, child neglect, social isolation, and major life stressors all are risk factors that can contribute to severe dysfunction, conduct disorder, major anxiety, substance abuse, personality disorders, and depression.

• Since the early 1960s, researchers have focused on how to prevent psychological disorders by decreasing such risk factors. Psychologists also have identified ways to increase such protective factors as positive role models, specific coping skills, and good parenting.

■ EARLY CHILDHOOD

(Case Illustration: Avance, San Antonio, Texas)
• Children who are neglected often show impaired cognitive development, aggressive behavior, and extreme difficulty relating to others.

• Avance is a prevention project for low-income Mexican-American families that works to stabilize families, educate them, and motivate them so that they can improve their parenting.

Many Avance parents were themselves emotionally deprived as children. Further, 95 percent live below the poverty line, 75 percent did not graduate from high school, and 30 percent have abused drugs and alcohol. Such adults often find it impossible to give emotional sustenance to their children.

Avance helps parents overcome their emotional and economic problems through a structured process. Parents learn about child development, effective parenting, and

232

appropriate forms of discipline and are given opportunities to try out new behaviors with their children. They complete their education, receive job skills training, and get assistance with job placement.

• A research study about the effectiveness of Avance found that parents who were in the program were more likely than those who were not to be less restrictive, less punitive, more emotionally encouraging, less aggravated by their children's behavior, and to have an intellectually enriched home environment. The first wave of families involved in the program also were found to be more likely to go on and complete high school.

■ ADOLESCENTS

(Case Illustration: The Social Development Project, New Haven, Connecticut)
• Young adolescents are, almost by definition, at risk for many disorders, including substance abuse, conduct disorder, dangerous sexual behavior, and depression, regardless of the social and economic environment in which they have grown up. The Social Development Project in New Haven attempts to keep such problems from developing by teaching students how to make effective, healthy decisions.

> The program believes that youngsters can be taught to make healthy choices in the same ways they are taught math and reading and that systematic, classroom-based instruction in critical thinking skills and problem solving must be included throughout the curriculum beginning in kindergarten.
>
> All adults involved in the schools use problem-solving techniques and work collaboratively in school planning and management teams.
>
> Mental health teams also bring adults together to focus on the emotional and social climate of the schools and on the ways in which it contributes to student success or failure.
>
> Specific problem-solving models are taught to children throughout the grades and are applied not only to academic problems but to social problems and emotionally stressful situations. At the teen level, for example, when approaching drug-related issues, programs focus on ways to promote health-enhancing behaviors and beliefs and on teaching techniques that enable students to try out different behaviors and decisions in a risk-free environment. Among the prevention strategies is a weekly meeting of students who have experienced the recent death of a loved one.

• Research has demonstrated that the Social Development Project is having a positive impact on the students' behavior. While the level of delinquent behavior among the students in the project was unchanged, it was significantly less than that of a matched group of students not in the project, whose delinquent behavior increased by 40 percent. Research also has shown that students who were involved in the program for two years did better than those who were involved for only one year.

■ ADULTS

(Case Illustration: The Jobs Project, Ann Arbor, Michigan)
• The Jobs Project is based on the premise that the developmental process does not end at age 18 but continues throughout life. It also acknowledges that difficult transitions will occur throughout life. One of these involves the loss of a job.

• Many unemployed people become depressed and anxious. In severe cases, unemployment can result in stress-related illnesses like high blood pressure and such behaviors as substance abuse, family violence, or suicide.

• The goals of the Jobs Project are to help people maintain their strength through this stressful period and to give special skills to those in need. Ultimately, the Jobs Project tries to get people back into good jobs and to prevent such psychological disorders as depression and anxiety from emerging.

> Role-playing is one technique used. This gives individuals an opportunity to identify potential obstacles and to plan alternative courses of action. The program also provides a great deal of peer support to individuals during a period in which they might be feeling increased isolation. And, through group problem solving, participants learn to anticipate setbacks and devise means of coping with them.

• Follow-up studies have shown significant differences between participants and a control group. Participants showed lower levels of anxiety and depression and were more likely to be reemployed in higher-paying, more satisfying jobs. Participants also were earning more money and thus paying more state and federal taxes. The increase in tax revenue actually meant that the project was paying for itself in about seven months.

■ OLDER ADULTS

(Case Illustration: Austin Groups for the Elderly — AGE — Austin, Texas)
• Old age often revolves around problems and losses. Elderly people who lack a strong support system are especially vulnerable to depression and other psychological disorders.

• In a single building, AGE houses more than 15 agencies that serve older adults. Among these are the Gray Panthers, the Seniors' Respite Service, Elderhaven (a day-care center for adults), Grandparents Raising Grandchildren (a support group), and Information and Referral for Older Adults (a hot line). While each organization has specific goals and services, housing them in one location has meant that older people do not get sent all over town to obtain services and that some costs can be shared.

> A theme that cuts across all the agencies is old people working with young people. In addition, many of the people who benefit from AGE also are volunteers at the various AGE agencies.

■ EPILOGUE

• The costs of caring for people with psychological disorders along with the loss of productivity that results from their decreased level of functioning is estimated to be in the billions of dollars per year. Many people feel that the provision of preventive services is a better investment.

■ VIDEO REVIEW QUESTIONS

1. Gloria Rodriguez says that Avance assists parents to "improve themselves emotionally, economically, and socially." In what ways does it do that?

2. Why does Avance use graduates of the program on its staff?

3. What kind of support is provided to families through the home visit program?

4. How does Mary exemplify the success of the Avance program?

5. What is meant by the statement, "Nothing is one dimensional at Avance"? What does this have to do with an overall theory of prevention?

6. What kinds of changes is Avance making in people's lives? Discuss how the program helps these changes to occur.

7. James Comer believes that young people today have more decisions to make, more models of undesirable behavior to observe, and fewer adults in their lives to support them. How does the New Haven program attempt to overcome these problems?

8. Discuss three situations in which the development of problem-solving and critical thinking skills might assist a teenager to avoid risk behaviors.

9. In what ways does the use of role-playing help participants in the Jobs Project avoid the development of psychological disorders?

10. Discuss the trade-offs between providing money for prevention and providing money for the care of people with psychological disorders. Relate your thinking to the economics of the Jobs Project.

11. What advantages emerged from placing all Austin, Texas, agencies that help the elderly in one building?

12. What is the value of combining programs that serve children with those that serve the elderly?

CASE STUDY

by Judith Rosenberger,
C.S.W., Ph.D.
Hunter College
and
Edith Gould, C.S.W.
Postgraduate Center
for Mental Health

Alan and Laura

I'm 22 years old and my husband Alan is 23. We had our first baby, Gina, three months ago. The first stage of being new parents has been an around-the-clock whirlwind. We're just beginning to get some sleep.

After the initial excitement we felt when we discovered I was pregnant, both Alan and I began to get scared. Too many things were happening at once. Alan was in the midst of making a big career change. Since high school, he'd been an auto mechanic at the local garage, but he'd been laid off and was in the process of trying to open his own auto repair business. His hours were really long. I was working as an administrative assistant for a large insurance company. Money was really tight, and Alan was worried about how he'd support our family since we had decided that once the baby was born, I would stop working, at least for a while. He also was afraid that he wouldn't be a good father. His own father had abandoned his family when Alan was very young, so being a good father was very important to Alan. I had similar kinds of fears. I knew that my family had a long history of depression and that my mother had gone into a serious postpartum depression after I was born. I was afraid that could happen to me. Also, I knew nothing about babies. I had always been afraid to even hold them, let alone take care of one. So I'd say we had an awful lot on our minds.

When I was in my first trimester I noticed a flyer at work announcing a lunchtime discussion meeting for first-time pregnant mothers. The company's Employee Assistance Program (EAP) sponsored a whole series of get-togethers on topics like that. I'd thought of going once before when they brought in a speaker on "When Your Spouse Loses A Job." But this one seemed easier to go to because it didn't mean you had a problem. The idea of talking with other women who were pregnant interested me, so I went.

A social worker led the meeting and said pregnancy was one of those important transitional stages in life where all kinds of emotional and psychological changes can take place. As the other women joined in, some of them described the kinds of fears that Alan and I had. That made me feel more normal. And I heard about how other people who had worried and had problems had seen things turn out all right. Also, just saying out loud what was bothering me made it feel less scary. It was comforting to talk to other women who were going through the same thing. The leader asked if we would be interested in continuing the group once a week and almost everyone signed up. We also decided to invite some experienced mothers. And, at our group's suggestion, the EAP started an evening group for new fathers-to-be. Alan jumped at the chance to participate.

Both of us felt that it would really help if we were prepared when Gina was born, rather than being nervous and shocked by the presence of a real live baby. Sharing our fears and hopes with other people in the same situation made us feel stronger and not alone. Also, the groups gave us information and taught us practical things like how and when to feed the baby, or what expenses to expect. I also learned all about my job benefits and options. One of the options was for the group to continue after our babies were born, even if we were on leave.

After Gina was born there were moments when we both felt unsure and scared about how we were doing, so we attended the group together, off and on, sometimes even bringing Gina. It helped me feel less alone at home, and also gave us the opportunity to ask questions about things that came up in our role as parents. The main thing for us about these group experiences was the feeling of companionship we had with the other group members and the knowledge that if we ran into trouble there was a place we could go for help. The leader was always available for information or to connect us to other services. We could see her casually before and after group meetings. Once I even made an appointment by myself to ask about family trees and depression. She gave me a very interesting booklet about the chances of depression being passed on and about the signs to look for and what to do if they occurred. She also said I could come back and discuss my situation further, but I have not done that. So far so good! It's a relief just to know I can do something about the problem if it if it ever does come up. I guess that is the main way in which the group has made a big difference. Now I see changes and problems as things that happen to everybody, and I have learned ways of coping with them so I don't get overwhelmed.

CLINICAL DISCUSSION

Alan and Laura have a combination of risk factors facing them. Some are situational — job loss for Alan, money worries, lack of experience as parents. Some are interpersonal — change in their daily roles together as Laura stays home and Alan works late trying to develop his business. Some are physiological — Laura's family history of postpartum depression and other forms of depression, as well as normal changes in pregnancy and post-delivery. While none of these factors causes a psychological disorder to occur, the amount of risk can intensify a person's vulnerability to develop a psychological disorder. In addition, stressors like the ones faced by Laura and Alan can interact with a preexisting clinical condition to affect onset, course, and remission — that is, to make the full condition start sooner, last longer, and be harder to resolve. We do not see a preexisting dysfunction in this case, but we do see Laura worrying about the possibility of becoming depressed. One of the ways in which the group leader intervenes to prevent the onset of a disorder is by providing Laura with information and leaving an open door for further consultation if Laura should develop signs of depression. While the information and access to services may not prevent Laura from becoming depressed (especially if her depression is genetically based), the damage done by such a biologically related condition as depression can be reduced substantially by early treatment. Early treatment also can salvage family relationships and job security by heading off a long and accelerating process of dysfunction.

One way to combat risk factors and reduce vulnerability is to increase the protective factors in one's life. Many were available to Laura and Alan. Besides the psychoeducation regarding depression that Laura received, the EAP group reduced her risk of psychological distress by normalizing her worries and converting them into a course of action and planning. Laura and Alan learned from others what to anticipate. They also may learn to be less self-critical about what they do not know or about common mishaps that may occur. These chances to learn by sharing reduce the self-created stress linked to anxieties about the unknown. The mutual aid of companionship in a new venture also reduces the stress of isolation itself. By setting up the groups in a way that is not problem-identified and by letting the agenda flow from the members, the social worker adds to the members' sense of being able to solve problems that do arise, rather than seeing themselves as people who have problems. The discovery of this mechanism for gaining confidence helped Laura redirect the spiral of internal stress linked to self-doubt that she was starting to feel. Involving Alan meant that problem solving and worry were not her responsibility alone and that communication about concerns and solutions could be open between them rather than protectively concealed. The relief Laura described in getting things off her chest and in feeling "normal" is an indication of the stress reduction in her psychological functioning.

Finally, Laura mentions learning about her job benefits through the EAP group. Although she doesn't indicate what her benefits are, the existence of an actual safety net is another preventive strategy. Having enough money, a job to return to, health care, and/or other benefits means ongoing avoidance of many potential psychological stressors. Additionally, access to health care and parenting support can add to a secure and healthy environment that can promote psychological as well as physical well-being. It should be added that the steps Laura and Alan have taken to reduce their own stress also is likely to contribute to a healthier environment for their child's upbringing.

CASE QUESTIONS

1. Explain the difference between preventing the cause of an abnormal psychological condition like clinical depression, and preventing its maximum impact.

2. How could being informed about the genetic transmission and signs of depression help Laura with that issue in her life?

3. Situations that are highly stressful are more likely to produce negative psychological effects than those that are less stressful, or for which one is prepared to cope. Give an example of how reducing the stressfulness of Laura's or Alan's life circumstances could relieve the stress they may feel internally.

4. Name two other important life transitions that often are stressful. How might you propose to help "normalize" the stresses they bring about? How might this help in preventing psychological disturbances?

SELF-TEST

1. Over the years most efforts toward mental health have been largely geared toward helping people only after they have already developed serious problems. Your text authors' term for this is
   a) crisis intervention.
   b) "in vivo" treatment.
   c) restorative.
   d) retrospective.

2. Which of the following types of prevention refers to efforts to emphasize prompt treatment or early detection of a mental problem that has already developed?
   a) primary
   b) secondary
   c) tertiary
   d) fourth level

3. Which of the following types of prevention refers to efforts to reduce the long-term consequences to individuals being treated for a mental disorder?
   a) primary
   b) secondary
   c) tertiary
   d) fourth level

4. Biological measures for primary prevention of mental disorders include all of the following EXCEPT
   a) drug treatment of hyperactive children.
   b) family planning.
   c) genetic counseling.
   d) "in utero" treatment of genetic defects.

5. Which of the following fields has primary prevention as its major focus?
   a) abnormal psychology
   b) clinical psychology
   c) health psychology
   d) psychotherapy

6. **All of the following are sociocultural efforts toward primary prevention of mental disorders EXCEPT**
    a) economic planning.
    b) penal systems.
    c) public education.
    d) social security.

7. **All of the following are typical of people for whom crisis intervention is appropriate EXCEPT**
    a) families confronted with unexpected stressful situations.
    b) people in a state of acute turmoil.
    c) people who feel overwhelmed by a sudden problem.
    d) people with severe personality disorders.

8. **In short-term crisis therapy the therapist usually performs all of the following functions EXCEPT**
    a) helping clarify the problem.
    b) probing for intrapsychic conflicts.
    c) providing reassurance.
    d) suggesting plans of action.

9. **All of the following therapeutic principles guide the milieu approach to treatment EXCEPT**
    a) acute and chronic patients are separated.
    b) all patients belong to social groups on the ward.
    c) patients are encouraged to become involved in all decisions concerning them.
    d) staff expectations are clearly communicated to the patient.

10. **Penk and associates found that compared to full inpatient psychiatric treatment, partial hospitalization in a day treatment setting resulted in _____ improvement.**
    a) as much
    b) less
    c) more
    d) more costly

11. **In most states, if an individual is involuntarily committed to a mental hospital for treatment, the hospital must report to the court within 60 days as to**
    a) what treatment is being administered.
    b) whether the person has been violent since being committed.
    c) whether the person needs further confinement.
    d) whether the person wishes to be released.

12. **It is relatively easy to judge a mental patient to be dangerous by**
    a) administering the MMPI.
    b) finding out after the fact that he or she has already committed a violent act.
    c) looking at EEG results.
    d) observing his or her behavior for a week before release.

13. The most difficult type of aggressive behavior to predict is the impulsive violent act of

    a) a paranoid schizophrenic.

    b) a person with a delusional disorder.

    c) a seemingly well-controlled "normal" person.

    d) an antisocial personality.

14. Under which of the following precedents are people believed to be sane unless at the time of committing the act they did not know its nature or quality?

    a) Diminished Capacity

    b) The Durham Rule

    c) The Irresistible Impulse

    d) The M'Naghten Rule

15. All of the following were unforeseen problems associated with deinstitutionalization EXCEPT

    a) board and care facilities often were substandard.

    b) community mental health centers were not prepared to provide needed services for chronic patients.

    c) it cost more than hospital care.

    d) many residents of mental institutions had no families to go home to.

16. Currently, the National Institute of Mental Health (NIMH) does all of the following except

    a) assists communities with mental health programs.

    b) conducts and supports research on aspects of mental disorders.

    c) provides grants-in-aid for students who need psychotherapy.

    d) supports the training of mental health personnel.

17. The major purpose of the World Federation for Mental Health is to

    a) promote cooperation between world governments and nongovernmental mental health agencies.

    b) promote the mental health of government officials and heads of state.

    c) upgrade the conditions influencing the mental health of the world's children.

    d) upgrade the international standards for mental health professionals.

18. Children who are neglected often show

    a) great resilience as adults.

    b) few long-term effects unless the neglect was longer than a year.

    c) impaired cognitive development, aggressive behavior, and extreme difficulty in relating to others.

    d) more understanding as parents because of what they suffered.

19. Avance seeks to

    a) provide clients with parenting and job skills training.

    b) provide financial support for low-income Mexican-American families.

    c) help Mexican-American families integrate into the mainstream American culture.

    d) provide crisis intervention.

20. In a 1991 study, Avance found that parents who were in the program were more likely than those who were not to be

    a) more punitive and better disciplinarians.

    b) more educationally oriented but less encouraging.

    c) less restrictive, less punitive, and more encouraging.

    d) different only in insignificant ways.

21. A study that looked at the Social Development Program in New Haven, Connecticut, found that compared to groups that had participated in the program for only one year, eighth graders who had learned life skills in both the sixth and seventh grades

    a) had better peer relationships and coped well with anxiety.

    b) had higher grades and less anxiety.

    c) had higher grades and participated in more extracurricular activities.

    d) did not carry these skills over into the eighth grade.

22. Research has shown that, when dealing with a problem, if you can identify potential obstacles early on and begin to plan alternative courses of action,

    a) you may increase your stress level by dwelling on the problem.

    b) you may create problems where there are none.

    c) you will be better able to cope when you actually encounter the obstacle.

    d) you may develop stress-related illnesses.

23. Research on the Jobs Project in Michigan shows that people from the experimental group showed lower levels of _____ and were more likely to be employed in higher-paying, more satisfying jobs.

    a) stress and illnesses

    b) anxiety and depression

    c) depression and alcoholism

    d) family violence and alcoholism

24. Prevention programs such as Avance, The Social Development Program, The Jobs Project, and AGE

    a) are extremely costly.

    b) cost society less in the long run than direct services to the mentally ill.

    c) are not cost effective but do reduce human suffering.

    d) have not been shown to work.

[ANSWERS: 1-c, 2-b, 3-c, 4-a, 5-c, 6-b, 7-d, 8-b, 9-a, 10-a, 11-c, 12-b, 13-c, 14-d, 15-c, 16-c, 17-a, 18-c, 19-a, 20- c, 21-a, 22-c, 23-c, 24-b]

SUGGESTED READINGS

Comer, J. P. (1988). *Maggie's American dream: The life and times of a black family.* New York: Plume/Penguin. Dr. Comer's biography tells the story of a black family in the South in the 1930s, his exit from the conditions of poverty and discrimination, and how that experience formed the basis of his work in education today.

Long, B. B. (1986). The prevention of mental-emotional disabilities: A report from a National Mental Health Association Commission. *American Psychologist, 41,* 825-829. This article summarizes an important report on preventing mental disorders.

Price, R. H., Cowen, E. L., Lorion, R. P., & Ramas-McKay, J. (1988). *Fourteen ounces of prevention: A casebook for practitioners.* Washington, DC: American Psychological Association. This book summarizes successful prevention programs that might serve as nationwide models. Each program's research evidence was critically examined to determine its success.

Schorr, L. B., & Schorr, D. (1988). *Within our reach: Breaking the cycle of disadvantage.* New York: Anchor/Doubleday. This examination of programs aimed at adolescents to change their "risk" behaviors includes chapters on teenage pregnancy, prenatal care, family life, school life, and so forth.

Smith, B. K. (1983). *Looking forward: New options for your later years.* Boston: Beacon Press. This look at the problems of aging suggests how problems can be avoided by creating positive alternatives that encourage vitality and participation.

APPENDIX: GUIDELINES FOR SEEKING PSYCHOLOGICAL AND EMOTIONAL ASSISTANCE

by Maurice J. Elias, Ph.D.
Rutgers University

It is relatively common for psychology students, like those who study medicine, to feel that they or someone they care about seems to have many of the disorders studied. In this essay, we will look at reasons one might seek counseling or therapy, the kinds of help one might seek, and how to go about finding the right kind of assistance.

It is important to note that many people use counseling services of one kind or another even though they do not have the kind of disorders described in an abnormal psychology course. It is normal to have questions, problems, doubts, and life stresses, and it is normal to want to have effective assistance. For many people, friends and family fill the bill. Studies have even shown that some people benefit from talking to hairdressers and bartenders.

■ SOME REASONS TO SEEK ASSISTANCE

College brings with it much excitement and learning, as well as a good deal of stress. When family and/or job responsibilities are added to academic demands, it is not unusual to feel somewhat overwhelmed. In such situations of heightened stress, psychological or emotional assistance could be beneficial.

Below are some indicators that you may be experiencing more stress in your life than you can manage. Think of the following as they might apply to you, a family member, or a close acquaintance, since the concerns of all of you are interrelated. Any of these indicators can be reasons for you, as well as significant others in your life, to seek out assistance:

- persistent troubled feelings with regard to managing the hassles of school, home, and/or work;
- marked changes in life circumstances, such as a change in job situation, living environment, health and well-being, relationships, or finances for oneself, a family member, or close acquaintance;
- marked decline in the quality of performance in carrying out school, work, or home responsibilities;
- prolonged strong emotional states, such as sadness, depression, hopelessness, aggressiveness, irritability, anxiety, fearfulness, denial, avoidance;
- marked changes in patterns of eating, sleeping, talking, personal hygiene, socializing; prolonged or excessive difficulties in concentrating or organizing one's thoughts.

Note the frequent use of words like "persistent," "marked," and "prolonged." This is to emphasize that many of the indicators above are experienced by just about everyone at some time. But such problems tend not to last long, not to be too severe, and not to interfere with a person's ability to function in his or her various responsibilities.

■ PLACES TO SEEK ASSISTANCE

Two of the most difficult aspects of seeking help are the diversity of approaches that people use and the diversity of helping agents available. By one estimate, there are 130 different psychotherapies. We can add to that an array of mutual aid/self-help groups covering virtually any problem that can befall someone.

Psychological and emotional support services are "any intentional application of psychological techniques by a trained individual to the end of effecting sought-after personality or behavioral changes or emotional support" (Goldstein and Krasner, 1987, p.49). With this in mind, here are the major types of places from which to seek assistance:

- university or college counseling centers;
- support groups and mutual aid/self help (MASH) groups;
- community mental health centers, community-based or private clinics, family service agencies, or mental health units in hospitals;
- employee assistance programs (EAP) at one's workplace;
- special programs for specific disorders;
- private practitioners — licensed or certified psychologists, psychiatrists, social workers, counselors, marriage and family therapists.

■ HOW TO FIND A SPECIFIC SOURCE OF HELP

Taking the first steps to get help can be hard, and persisting despite difficulty with those first steps can be harder. There are many different helpers, and you may meet some that you feel cannot help you. Remember that you would not cease to believe in medicine because you encountered a not-so-good doctor, nor would you stop eating out just because you ate at a bad restaurant. Good, competent help is out there, but it has little way of finding you. You must find it. For leads, use your most trusted sources, such as family members, friends, clergy, physicians, or college acquaintances.

University or college counseling centers are excellent sources of referral, as they often keep records of preferred places to go for different types of help. Similar assistance can be obtained by calling professional associations in your state or region. State psychological associations, associations of certified social workers, marriage and family therapists, or counselors, or the American Association for the Advancement of Behavior Therapy should be able to provide you with listings of local credentialed practitioners. The psychiatric outpatient department of a local hospital also may have the help that you are seeking.

To find out about mutual aid/self-help groups in your area, the best place to look is a self-help group clearinghouse, a computerized resource center that can help you find an appropriate group. Clearinghouses often are listed in phone books; they also should be known to university or college counseling centers (which also may run groups of this kind) or community mental health centers. Self-help groups also tend to respond quickly, and the costs are minimal, if any. These groups are most appropriate for problems relating to hassles in one's life routines or to changes in life circumstances.

■ WHAT TO LOOK FOR WHEN YOU GET THERE

Remember, the helpers are human. They may be trained and experienced, but not every helper or group is suitable for every person. Here are some things to expect and questions that you can ask yourself. Give yourself two or three sessions to get satisfactory answers.

Some Things to Expect

If you are seeking formal help or counseling from any kind of clinic or center, the first step usually is an appointment for an initial interview. This interview should be held within a few days after the time a first contact is made. In an emergency, you can usually arrange to see someone the same day. The initial interview is relatively short and is intended to assess what is troubling the person and determine what services would be of most benefit. If ongoing counseling is appropriate, regular appointments (typically one time per week for a 45-60 minute session) will begin soon after the initial interview. Private practitioners tend to be available more quickly, but the cost of their services is higher (insurance may cover some of these costs, however).

Keep in mind that difficulties you may be experiencing are interrelated to those around you. Sometimes, easing those difficulties is best accomplished when all persons involved seek some help. Family members and close acquaintances may benefit from being part of a support group, such as a group for those who live with someone who has returned to college while trying to maintain a job and/or nurture a family.

Some Questions to Ask

1. How do I know this person is qualified to assist me? Never hesitate to ask for credentials of some kind. Therapists should have some form of state or national license or certification and should be a member of at least some state, regional, or national professional organization. Clergy also should have similar appropriate credentials. Self-help group leaders should be able to share their experience with you and put you in contact with current or past group members.

2. How does the therapist or group leader believe he or she accomplishes the goals of therapy? What is it that the therapist intends to do to be helpful, and how does he or she expect it to work? It is important to ask about the basis upon which the helping experience is expected to work. In *Helping People Change*, Kanfer and Goldstein (1986) note that successful therapy is based on a positive relationship between client and therapist. An important part of that relationship is that you believe in the approaches used in treatment. Individuals with a background in psychology know several major approaches to conducting psychotherapy exist, as do many variations and spin-offs. Goldstein and Krasner (1987) identified the following major therapeutic orientations (some of the more well-known specific approaches are in parentheses):

- cognitive-behavioral (which includes social learning and rational-emotive approaches),
- psychodynamic (which includes psychoanalytic and short-term dynamic approaches),
- behavioral (which includes systematic desensitization and behavior-modification approaches),
- client-centered (which includes Rogerian and non-directive approaches),
- family therapy (which includes family systems and structural family therapy approaches), and
- social-interpersonal skills training (which includes assertiveness, communication, and problem-solving/decision-making training).

In addition, psychiatrists may utilize a more pharmacological approach to treatment, that is, they may prescribe drugs to relieve psychological symptoms. Some may focus exclusively on drug therapy, while others will combine medication with a form of psychotherapy.

Because there are so many approaches, you have every right to expect an answer to questions that will help you decide whether or not you are comfortable with the approach the therapist or group is taking.

3. Am I being listened to? Does the person seem to pick up where we left off last time? All sources agree that if this is not present, assistance is unlikely to be successful.

4. Do I get the feeling that the person is concerned about me, that he or she understands my problem, has dealt with it or similar things before, and cares that things get better for me? Through direct questions and your impressions, you should get a positive answer to this question if you expect to be helped.

5. Is the person or group doing things to try to help me? Are they trying to clarify my thinking or my feelings? Are they making suggestions that I can try? It is important to ask yourself if suggestions continue to make sense after a session is over and to expect that suggestions will be at least somewhat realistic and practical.

6. When I need clarification, explanation, or instruction in carrying out the suggestions made in the sessions, do I receive it? Is time taken to patiently explain what I should be trying to do? If I raise an objection to something, do I get a reasonable explanation about it? Getting help is really an educational process. It does not occur as a result of one or two insights or "magical" revelations. If you are going to be able to make changes in your life, you have every right to ask for and receive supportive help along the way.

As long as problems remain or situations continue to be troubling, you owe it to yourself and those who care about you to persist in obtaining effective psychological and emotional relief.

References

Goldstein, A. P., & Krasner, L. (1987). *Modern applied psychology.* New York: Pergamon.

Kanfer, F. H., & Goldstein, A. P. (1986). *Helping people change.* New York: Pergamon.